The League of Nations
Movement in Great Britain
1914—1919

RUTGERS UNIVERSITY STUDIES IN HISTORY
NUMBER SEVEN

The League of Nations
Movement in Great Britain
1914 — 1919

HENRY R. WINKLER

1952
Rutgers University Press
New Brunswick   New Jersey

Printed in the United States by
The Kingsport Press, Inc., Kingsport, Tennessee

To

ALLAN, KAREN, AND CLARE

Contents

Preface

THE CREATION OF THE League of Nations marked the cul-
mination of a drive for an association of nations to serve as the
chief mechanism in the conduct of international relations. Despite its failure, the League has served as a stepping-stone and
a warning, indicating the areas in which international cooperation is possible and necessary, and pointing up some of
the difficulties which must be overcome if such cooperation is
to develop. Hailed by many as the instrument which should
finally bring lasting peace to the world, the League had been
made possible by the emergence during the first World War of
numerous plans for the establishment of some form of world
organization. Not the least active in support of these plans were
various groups and individuals in Great Britain who looked
with horror at the destructiveness of the world conflict and
sought hopefully for some method of making war less probable
in the future. Nor was there any absence of activity in those
areas of opinion in which the idea of regularized international
cooperation was looked upon with hostility or at the least suspicion. Since Britain, followed closely in influence by France,
became from the first the most significant power in the League,
the British pattern of ideas which helped shape its characteristics is of importance for an understanding of this ill-fated
experiment.

Of even greater significance is the relevance of the story to
issues of today. The British discussion early in the century laid
down the major outlines and arguments of proposals still being

debated desperately by men and women who realize that war is no longer merely an anachronism but the most serious challenge that civilized society has ever been called upon to face. The merits and feasibility of a United Nations of sovereign states versus genuine world government, for example, were discussed and defined in a way that may throw light upon some of the problems of the present. The issues were obviously presented in the context of the World War I environment and reflected the particular character of that period. Nevertheless, they dealt with problems of universal concern, whose importance is as clear now as it was then. It is my purpose, therefore, to trace the currents of opinion in Britain which contributed to the establishment of the League of Nations, to describe the development of the concept of world organization during the war years, as well as the objections raised to it, and finally to investigate how fully the British government accepted the idea and in what manner it was molded to fit the conceived needs of British policy. I intend this to be the first of several volumes dealing with the general subject of Great Britain and the League of Nations.

There are numerous ways in which this volume might have been organized. One which suggested itself was the "problem" method, the study of a group of specific problems in international organization as they were revealed in the debate from 1914 to 1919. It might have been possible to deal with such subjects as the idea of a limited league versus a league with wider powers, with procedures for pacific settlement of international disputes, with questions such as the nature of sanctions to be employed and of the members to be admitted. But it was found that such a pattern of organization makes for repetition and encourages a mechanical and rigid handling of material, without indicating sufficiently how the ideas of various interested groups evolved. It has seemed to me that the *development* of the idea was throughout more important than an artificial lumping of "categories" of conceptions. Consequently, I have attempted to present as a whole various of the plans suggested and then to assess how those plans were accepted and handled in the more important areas of public life.

There is a certain danger that must be guarded against here. Since this is a survey of a certain group of ideas which antedated the formation of the League of Nations, the temptation is great to assume that such a body came into existence because a small group of intellectuals and politicians willed it into being. That these individuals were of utmost importance hardly needs iteration, as the following pages will attest; but it is well to keep in mind that their work grew out of a *milieu* and quite obviously expressed some of the basic aspirations and trends of the environment. The league movement was a revolution, a peaceful revolution that gained momentum during the violence of war. As has been persuasively argued, in such a situation the intellectual helps create a general awareness of dissatisfaction, contributes programs of future reforms, and may even supply spokesmen and leaders for the revolutionary movement; but all these roles assume the prior existence of a revolutionary potential. Thus the concepts here analyzed became important because many of the British people were ready to be receptive to them. The league of nations movement did not create the idea of fuller international organization; it was able to popularize the idea precisely because the world situation had evoked a general reaction—vague and ill-defined though it may have been—against traditional statecraft which had been unable to avoid plunging Europe into the organized barbarism of war. In any case, I propose to describe that movement and to analyze the various proposals for international organization made from 1914 to 1919. The result, perhaps, may help in a small way to clarify a problem that is still troubling a divided world today.

I should like to express my appreciation to the following publishers for permission to quote from books whose copyrights they hold: *The Observer* (Sir Waldorf Astor, *Cooperative Basis for a League of Nations*); Macmillan and Company, Ltd. (J. L. Garvin, *The Economic Foundations of Peace*); George Allen and Unwin, Ltd. (J. A. Hobson, *Towards International Govern-*

ment; F. N. Keen, *Towards International Justice;* H. N. Brailsford, *A League of Nations*); Oxford University Press (Sidney
Olivier, *The League of Nations and Primitive Peoples*); G. Bell
and Sons, Ltd. (H. N. Brailsford, *The War of Steel and Gold*);
A. P. Watt and Son and The Macmillan Company (H. G. Wells,
In the Fourth Year: Anticipations of a World Peace). Exact
citations to the pages quoted will be found in the footnotes of
this volume.

My other obligations in connection with the completion of
this study are great. In particular, I am indebted to the Rutgers
University Research Council for grants which not only facili-
tated my research, but also have made the publication of this
book possible.

I appreciate the permission given by the editors of the *Journal
of Modern History* and *The Historian* to use materials which
appeared, in somewhat different form, in those journals. A
grant from the American Philosophical Society enabled me to
consult certain of the materials in the Hoover Library of War,
Peace, and Revolution at Stanford University. Viscount Cecil
of Chelwood and the Right Honorable Philip Noel Baker were
good enough to furnish me with information in response to
questions which I posed, and Mrs. Woodrow Wilson's kind permission made available the papers of Woodrow Wilson in the
Manuscripts Division of the Library of Congress, where Miss
Katharine E. Brand was particularly helpful. It is a real pleasure, too, to acknowledge the advice and encouragement of Professors Reginald C. McGrane and Miriam B. Urban of the
University of Cincinnati, of Professors Louis Gottschalk and
S. William Halperin of the University of Chicago, and of Dr.
Bernadotte E. Schmitt, now the United States editor of the
"Documents on German Foreign Policy." Above all, I wish to
express my gratitude to Dr. George A. Hedger of Anaheim,
California, who, by his example, has served as a model for intellectual integrity and whose influence I hope this volume in
some small measure reflects. Finally, I should record, with more

than gratitude, my obligations to my wife Clare, whose contributions to both the spirit and the substance of this book are perhaps even greater than she herself realizes.

HENRY R. WINKLER

Rutgers University
New Brunswick, N. J.

The League of Nations
Movement in Great Britain
1914—1919

Early Plans for a Limited League

THE CONCEPTION of an organized society of nations was not something that stemmed full-blown from the conditions of the First World War. Plans for the preservation of peace by collective organization go back at least to the fourteenth century, and almost every major war in history produced some proposal to substitute such plans for armed conflict. For decades before the war of 1914 the world had been witnessing the gradual internationalization of many phases of economic life, as the advance of science in the fields of production, transportation and communications drew the nations of the earth closer together. Meanwhile, during the nineteenth and early twentieth centuries, the so-called Concert of Europe led to the calling of periodic conferences to deal with questions of world significance. Thus, to cite examples, the Congo Conference of 1885 and the Algeciras Conference of 1905–06 were important in demonstrating that problems of international importance could be settled, however unjustly or temporarily, without resort to war.

In addition, the first Hague Conference of 1899 resulted in the formation of a court of arbitration to which disputing nations might voluntarily resort. For the most part, British opinion supported this important step, and later, in 1907, the Liberal government was in part instrumental in calling the second Hague Conference. The prime minister, Campbell-Bannerman, pleaded for a halt to the armaments race, but German and

British naval plans shattered any hope for disarmament based on international guarantees. Following the second Hague Conference, the foreign policy of the British government continued to revolve about the attempt to obtain peace and security by the balance of power, working especially through agreements with France and Russia. As a result, the drive toward international agreement gave way to an undisguised power philosophy, and the hope for a world settlement grew progressively less bright.

Meanwhile, the outlook of two important sections of British political life provided a springboard for the idea of world organization. The Liberal party, despite the imperialistic aberration of an important part of its membership, thought of the British Empire as a first step toward the internationalization of the economic and commercial affairs of the nations. The doctrine of free trade and mutual exchange furnished the basis for a conception of the world according to which peace and international cooperation were essential in the interests of trade. The absence of any major world war since the days of Napoleon contributed to the optimistic hope that the desired millennium was just around the corner.

Possibly even more significant than the outlook of the Liberal party was the point of view of British labor. The election of 1906 had demonstrated the amazing growth of the Labor party. That party, as well as the Independent Labor party and other socialist societies, was affiliated with the Second International, whose interests were world-wide in scope. In 1907, the International adopted a resolution expressing labor's will to oppose any European war and to do its utmost to prevent such a conflict. The resolution was only a single example of an attitude that was prevalent. Thus, the prewar experience of British labor fostered an internationalism which, despite the fact that labor was still a relatively small minority party, was later to be of great consequence in the development of the league of nations idea.

Into this setting of growing internationalism the Great War crashed in August, 1914. Despite friction over imperialist desires, the coming of the war was a shock to most people in Great Britain. Nevertheless, they rallied to the support of the government almost en masse, relatively small exceptions being a few Liberal pacifists and the Independent Labor party led by Ramsay MacDonald. Most of the British felt that the war was being fought to save the world from Prussian militarism and the danger of future struggles. In the heat of the early war excitement they thought little of the causes of its outbreak or what might have been done to prevent it. But as the full effect of the conflict on their own lives was made apparent, many people began to turn their minds to methods of forestalling war. For to them compulsory conscription, economic sacrifice, and the loss of lives were a much stronger indictment of war than the most cogent theoretical argument. The alliance system began to be questioned, as well as the secret diplomacy it involved; "power politics" were condemned by large sections of a horror-stricken population; and Britain began to seek some stabilizing factor to ensure security and uninterrupted prosperity.

It was true that the outbreak of the war shattered all the hopes of those who had seen in the International Court of Arbitration and the Hague Conference a portent of continued peace. But at the same time, the gravity of the catastrophe gave added impetus to the drive for a world organization which should, above all else, prevent future wars. The idea of a league of nations, slow to develop in the early days of conflict, soon gained support among many individuals and organizations. For as the destructiveness of the struggle became more evident, they were impelled to agitate for the formation of some instrument to banish armed conflict from the world. The nature and the results of that agitation form a chapter in the history of international organization that merits more attention than it has hitherto received.

British plans for a league of nations inevitably developed a number of different channels of approach. That which gained most support, and which was substantially accepted by the organization especially founded to promote the league idea, envisaged a world organization whose chief—and perhaps only—

function was the provision of machinery to facilitate peaceful settlement of international disputes. Proponents of such a league assumed the continued existence of national sovereignty and attempted to mold their project to the supposed facts of international life. Underlying their arguments was a general belief that change must come slowly, that even after the war the governments of the world would not yet be ready fully to submit themselves to an international authority, and that, therefore, the scope of the future organization must be limited to specific tasks and be clearly defined so as not to challenge the position of existing governments.

The general theme of this type of plan was most clearly outlined in the early years of the war by the Fabian Society and by a study group meeting under the chairmanship of Viscount James Bryce, the former Ambassador to the United States. It is the purpose of this chapter to sketch the projects proposed by these groups. Two other schemes will be appended, because they illustrate an analysis which, while differing sharply from that of the Fabians and the Bryce Group on certain matters of detail and policy, nevertheless emphasized techniques to keep international quarrels from leading to war rather than any systematic attack upon the various causes of war itself.

The arguments of these groups, particularly those of the Fabians and of Bryce's committee, were realistic, for the governments of the world were at least willing in 1919 to attempt such a limited league, while plans of a more ambitious nature, involving serious curtailment of the dogmas of sovereignty, had little chance of acceptance. It hardly need be pointed out, however, that the realism of 1919 was not enough, for whatever reason, to prevent the hollocaust of 1939. Yet when the United Nations was established in 1945 it differed only in detail from the League of Nations. Basically it remained the limited league, firmly rooted in national sovereignty, proposed by the various groups whose ideas will here be outlined. The essential continuity of ideas should become apparent, therefore, as the various projects are unfolded.

THE FABIAN SOCIETY AND INTERNATIONAL GOVERNMENT

By 1914, the Fabian Society could look back with no little satisfaction to three decades of its existence. The policy of gradualness and peaceful social reform enunciated cogently and often brilliantly by George Bernard Shaw, H. G. Wells, the Webbs, had not yet, it is true, brought about the ultimate goal of Fabian tactics—the triumph of socialism in England. But in the thirty years, the dedicated intellectuals of the Society had made an impress on trade union development, on municipal politics, on domestic legislation far out of proportion to the numerical strength of their organization. With the coming of the war, it was quite natural that they should have proceeded, in much the same way as they had attacked domestic questions, to address themselves to the problem of future international relations. In characteristic fashion, the Fabians accepted the world as it was, then cast about for practical methods of transforming it into the kind of world they hoped it might become. They agreed that the present conflict must be fought to complete victory, but at the same time proceeded to investigate possible plans for the prevention of future wars. The result was one of the first—and one of the most detailed—projects designed to provide machinery to take the place of international conflict.

As early as January, 1915, the Fabian Research Department set up a special International Agreements Committee for the purpose of inquiring into methods of securing international peace. Leonard S. Woolf, already recognized as a competent writer on international affairs, was engaged to prepare a report embodying the results of the committee's work, and a special fund was subscribed to help defray the expenses of the investigation.[1]

Investigation by the committee and discussion among the Society's members culminated in the conference, sponsored by

[1] Fabian Society, *Thirty-Second Annual Report* (London, 1915), p. 11; *Fabian News*, February, 1915, p. 18; *ibid.*, June, 1915, p. 48.

the Research Department, which met at Barrow House in Keswick from May 22 to May 25. Among those present at the well-attended meetings were J. A. Hobson, G. Lowes Dickinson, E. Richard Cross and Raymond Unwin, all of whom were, or were later to become, prominent in the development of the league of nations idea in Great Britain. The "causes, conduct and conclusion" of the war, as well as possible territorial or financial settlements, were excluded from the discussion. Debate centered about a project for a supernational judiciary and council drawn up by the International Agreements Committee, and a number of modifications were suggested. Woolf then proceeded to draft a pair of memoranda which embodied the work of the International Agreements Committee. In June the final proofs of "On International Authority and the Prevention of War" were approved. One month later the two articles appeared as supplements to the *New Statesman,* which, under the editorship of George Bernard Shaw, served as the vehicle for Fabian ideas.[2]

After the publication of the *New Statesman* supplements, Woolf continued to investigate "all the various embryonic tissues of organized international relations . . . with a view to seeing how far these may possibly be developed into firmer structure."[3] The results of this study, together with the *New Statesman* material, were published in book form in 1916, after having been analyzed at a conference attended also by members of the Bryce group.[4]

[2] *Fabian News,* June, 1915, p. 48; *ibid.,* July, 1915, p. 54; *ibid.,* August, 1915, p. 59.

[3] Fabian Society, *Thirty-Third Annual Report* (London, 1916), p. 8.

[4] Leonard S. Woolf, *International Government: Two Reports, Prepared for the Fabian Research Department Together with a Project by a Fabian Committee for a Supernational Authority That Will Prevent War* (New York, 1916), p. xix (introduction by G. B. Shaw); Fabian Society, *Thirty-Fourth Annual Report* (London, 1917), p. 9. A recent history of the League has ranked Woolf's book with Norman Angell's prewar *The Great Illusion* as a key document in the history of the organization. See F. P. Walters, *A History of the League of Nations* (2 vols.; London and New York, 1952), I, 22.

International Government was a cogent, thorough argument
for a league of nations. Woolf's reports, which formed the first
two sections of the volume, demonstrated the conditions which
made such a body necessary and pointed to the gradual internationalization of all phases of world activity as its logical forerunner. The "Articles Suggested for Adoption by an International Conference at the Termination of the Present War"
defined the instrumentalities through which a league could
work

In his first report, Woolf's initial aim was to outline the causes
of war. These he divided into four categories: (1) "disputes
arising from legal or quasi-legal relationship," for example, conflicts over the interpretation of treaties; (2) "disputes arising
from economic relationship, trade, and finance"; (3) "disputes
arising from administrative or political relationship," including
such questions as treatment of subject races, control of territory, and the like; and (4) "disputes arising from what may be
called social relationship," that is, questions of national honor.
None of the disputes need inevitably lead to war, and the experience of the past gave ample evidence that means could be
found for their peaceful settlement. During the nineteenth century a new system of international relationships had gradually
grown up, centering about the making of international laws
and the regulation of specific international affairs at conferences of national representatives. These conferences had attacked contingent or actual disputes in three ways: by coming
to a decision binding upon the states represented, by examining the facts and expressing an opinion or issuing a report, or
by acting as a council of conciliation or mediation between disputing states. But while the usefulness of conferences in preventing war was remarkable, it was limited by the fact that the
submission of any question to a conference was itself a matter
of negotiation and thus only "a move in the diplomatic game."
Consequently, the first step toward peaceful regulation of international affairs must be to remove the question of submission
from the sphere of diplomacy and to define those cases in which
a conference could be demanded or must be called. Had such

a system existed in 1914, for example, an immediate war would have been extremely improbable.[5]

The second report elaborated the view that in "every department of life the beginnings, and more than the beginnings of International Government, already exist." A list of some thirty-three organs of international cooperation was made more impressive by a long, detailed analysis of the objectives and functioning of most of the organizations cited. The conclusion to be drawn, in Woolf's view, was that participation of states in international unions did not involve any sacrifice of national interests so long as the objects for which the unions were created were clearly defined. Similarly, therefore, it would be possible to define the questions upon which states could agree to be bound by the decision of an organ of international government. Thus an enormous step toward the abolition of war might be taken.[6]

The arguments outlined by Woolf served as an introduction to the elaborate plan for future international organization presented by the Fabian Society.[7] The proposed draft treaty was designed to be severely limited and practical, on the theory that it would be unwise to attempt anything that had little chance of acceptance by the existing governments of the world. Therefore, no merging of sovereignties, no world-state was suggested. Each state was to have the right to go to war if, in the final reckoning, it could not achieve satisfaction in the dispute in question. National disarmament was not proposed, in the hope that as international organization became stabilized disarmament would come about by itself.[8]

---

[5] *International Government,* pp. 8–9, 61–63, 132–133.

[6] *Ibid.,* pp. 149, 159–178, 361, 363–364.

[7] "Articles Suggested for Adoption by an International Conference at the Termination of the Present War," by the International Agreements Committee of the Fabian Research Department. This plan appears as pp. 369–410 of *International Government* and is also reproduced in Leonard S. Woolf, *The Framework of a Lasting Peace* (London, 1917). Subsequent page references are to the text of the plan in *International Government.*

[8] Introduction, pp. 371–372.

In tackling the problem of the machinery for international organization, the Fabian plan proposed first the establishment of an International High Court, to which the nations should agree to submit their justiciable disputes.[9] As outlined in the suggested treaty, justiciable disputes included such questions as the interpretation or application of an international treaty, the demarcation of any part of a national boundary, the amount of reparation or compensation to be paid in cases in which the principle of indemnity was admitted by all parties, and a long list of other possibilities. The court itself should be competent to decide whether a dispute brought before it was justiciable or not.[10] Decisions of this permanent judicial tribunal, made up of fifteen judges, should be reached by majority vote, and should be binding upon the nations submitting their disputes to it.[11]

An International Council was to be set up, parallel to the International High Court and without authority over it. To this council each of the eight great powers—Austria-Hungary, the British Empire, France, Germany, Italy, Japan, Russia, and the United States—was to appoint five members; other constituent states were to name two representatives. Its primary function should be to provide opportunities for the amicable settlement of non-justiciable disputes, that is, questions of national honor or imperative national interest. At the same time, the council was given the responsibility of enacting, by common agreement, such international legislation as might be practicable.[12]

A very elaborate scheme was outlined in order to prevent the council from being swamped by Central and South American representatives in cases not directly affecting them and in order to "maintain unimpaired the practical hegemony and the responsibility for preventing a serious war which have, in fact, devolved upon the eight Great Powers, whose adhesion to these Articles is essential to their full efficacy." [13] It was provided that

[9] Art. 1, p. 376.
[10] Art. 14, pp. 398–400.
[11] Art. 11, pp. 395–396; Art. 12, pp. 396–397; Art. 14, p. 400.
[12] Art. 1, p. 376; Art. 5, pp. 379–380.
[13] Note to Art. 6, pp. 382–383.

the body should sit either as a council of all the constituent states, or as a council of the eight great powers, or as a council of the states other than the great powers, or as a council for America, or as a council for Europe. In each case, such questions as seemed appropriate for any particular organ should be referred to it, so that, for example, a dispute between two South American countries would normally be considered by the council for America. In any particular case, the proceedings of any of the other councils could be referred back to that of the great powers for consideration and ratification. In addition, any of the great powers might formally claim to have a question referred to the council as a whole or to the council of eight.[14] A further guarantee of great-power control was the provision that voting power in the regional and partial councils was to be equal, but that in the council of the whole it was to be weighted to give the great powers a preponderant influence whenever any considerable number of them acted together.[15] Quite clearly, this was an arrangement which foreshadowed later developments, for if it did not appear in the League Covenant it nevertheless expressed an approach which, allowing for differences in detail, was eventually to be found in the organization of the Security Council of the United Nations. All in all, it was clearly an acceptance of the view that the major states bore the greatest responsibility in international affairs and consequently must call the turn. Like schemes of a later day, however, it did not face the converse of the problem, that the great powers were also, on any historical showing, precisely the ones most likely to involve the rest of the world in war.

In the case of non-justiciable disputes, the Fabian plan suggested a number of techniques that might be used: reference of the matter at issue to a permanent board of conciliators, the appointment of a special committee to inquire into the matter and report, the naming of a commission of inquiry to investigate the matter, or even its consideration by the council itself.[16] The

[14] Art. 6, pp. 380–382.
[15] Art. 7, pp. 383–384; note to Art. 7, pp. 384–385.
[16] Art. 9, pp. 390–393.

core of the project was that the member-states should agree (1) to accept the decision of the International High Court as final in justiciable cases, and (2) to submit all non-justiciable cases to the International Council for consideration. In the latter case, the disputants were obligated only to refrain from war for a period of one year, after which any state might take up arms if no settlement acceptable to itself had been reached.[17] Clearly, therefore, the Fabian plan was designed not to exorcise war, but merely to delay it in the hope that in the course of a year tempers would cool and reasonable counsels prevail. For the disputes which might lead to war were precisely those non-justiciable disputes over which, in the final analysis, nations were still to be permitted to resort to trial by battle.

The method of enforcing the new system of international law was outlined in great detail. If a nation failed to comply with its obligation to carry out the decision of the court or to refrain from war for a year after submitting a case to the council, it was in the power of the court to invoke any or all of a series of twelve sanctions against the recalcitrant member. The sanctions outlined gave evidence of the Fabian belief in the efficacy of economic pressure. They included such provisions as the prohibition of imports and exports to and from the state charged with a breach of treaty; the cutting-off of postal, telegraphic, telephonic, and wireless communication with it; the halting of the payment of debts to the government or citizens of the state; and, in their most extreme form, complete non-intercourse and a naval blockade of its ports. In the event that the state then resisted these economic measures by military means, the members of the world league were to be required to go to war to enforce the orders of the international authority.[18]

But the settlement of disputes by court or council was only one part—though without doubt the major part—of the Fabian proposal. The International Council was given the additional task of codifying and publicizing existing international law,

[17] Art. 4, pp. 378–379.
[18] Art. 17, pp. 406–410.

and of amending and augmenting it from time to time. Only decisions on new legislation reached unanimously would take effect. Each independent state could ratify or refuse them as it saw fit. When an enactment was ratified by a particular state, it was to become operative in all relations of that state with any other members who had similarly accepted the new law. The International Council was then to apply and enforce the legislation.[19]

An interesting feature of the plan was the provision for an International Secretariat, appointed by the council and with an office permanently open for business. The secretariat was to take charge of correspondence with member states, keep records of the proceedings of the council, conduct inquiries and investigations ordered by the council, publish an official gazette, and the like.[20]

The scheme thus evolved was a very cautious one, giving as it did the right to each individual state to prevent the application to itself of any unacceptable legislation. The Fabians reasoned that the development of a supernational legislature was of vital importance. But at the same time, they believed that the difficulties were so great that only a gradual, oblique attack upon the citadel of national sovereignty was at present possible. Consequently, like the makers of the League of Nations at Versailles in 1919, they provided a forum whose essential purpose was that of discussion and suggestion, hoping that in time the practice of legislation would also develop.[21] On paper, perhaps, the plan appeared to be a considerable advance over existing techniques of international lawmaking, for it provided a regular method of legislation. Actually, it made no real attack upon the anarchy ensured by the insistence upon complete national independence in international relations.

The views outlined in the *New Statesman* supplements and

---

[19] Art. 8, pp. 386–387.

[20] Art. 10, pp. 394–395.

[21] "The Prevention of War," *New Statesman*, V (July 10, 1915), 318.

in *International Government* were reiterated by the Fabian Society in a document published in September, 1916. At the request of the International Socialist Bureau, a report on matters to be included in the conditions of peace was prepared and printed in the *Fabian News*.[22] The report insisted that the most important task of any peace conference was to set up *machinery* for the prevention of future wars. Democratic control of foreign policy, the reduction of armaments, universal free trade, and government control of the manufacture of armaments might all be very desirable, but they were subsidiary to the main need. Only a plan for the peaceful settlement of international disputes, such as outlined in *International Government,* would offer hope for the avoidance of international conflict.[23]

By the end of 1916 the Fabian Society had determined its approach to the development of international organization. The Fabian plan laid major emphasis upon compulsory adjudication of justiciable disputes and upon delay before recourse to war in non-justiciable disputes. It provided for elaborate sanctions to enforce such a system, and even suggested a tentative approach to the problem of international legislation. After 1916, the Society was apparently content to rest upon the ideas of the "Articles for the Prevention of War." The major share of Fabian discussion of a possible league of nations was borne during 1917 and 1918 by the *New Statesman.* That periodical, in its various analyses of the problems raised by the growing debate on a league, outlined the Fabian views on a number of issues that had not been prominent in the early years of the war. It considered, for example, such questions as the role of a league in international economic organization and the control of colonial areas, but at bottom made no substantial changes in the central

[22] Fabian Society, *Third-Fourth Annual Report* (London, 1917), p. 3.

[23] *Fabian News,* September, 1916, pp. 37–39; Austin Van der Slice, *International Labor, Diplomacy, and Peace, 1914–1919* (Philadelphia, 1941), p. 125.

core of the Fabian plan. That plan, as the first widely-read project for a league of nations, was studied and referred to by private and official groups considering possible forms of future international relations.[24] It was, therefore, a major contribution to one of the main lines of thought leading to the development of the league of nations idea, despite the fact that in the later years of the war other groups were more active in propaganda for such an idea.

THE BRYCE GROUP

The classical scholar, Goldsworthy Lowes Dickinson, was perhaps the first individual in England to formulate the idea of a league of nations during the war. Very shortly after the outbreak of hostilities, he jotted down two possible schemes for such a league, and in the early autumn took the lead in setting up a committee for studying the question. Lord Bryce attended the meetings of the committee and took the position of president of the organization. Since he was the first person of public note to participate, the new "Council for the Study of International Relations" became known as the "Bryce Group." Among the members of the organization were E. Richard Cross, business manager of the *Nation,* who became secretary for the group, W. H. Dickinson, the future chairman of the executive committee of the League of Nations Society, J. A. Hobson, Arthur Ponsonby, and Graham Wallas.[25]

In the early years of the war, the Bryce Group contented itself with discussing ways and means of preserving peace, but

[24] Philip Noel Baker, "The Making of the Covenant from the British Point of View," *Les Origines et L'Oeuvre de la Société des Nations,* ed. by P. Munch (Copenhagen, 1923–1924), II, 18–19.

[25] E. M. Forster, *Goldsworthy Lowes Dickinson* (New York, 1934), pp. 163–164, 173; E. E. Reynolds, *The League Experiment* (London, 1919), p. 50. With regard to E. Richard Cross, Mary Agnes Hamilton writes that "his was the master mind in working out, in close association with J. A. Hobson, the plan for a league of nations. He did not appear in this; . . . he preferred to give credit to others." *Remembering My Good Friends* (London, 1944), p. 136.

shied clear of publishing its findings in the fear that the ideas would be branded as pacifist and thus made impossible to defend.[26] A proposed treaty was drawn up and used as the basis for discussion.[27] It was modified and rewritten as experience seemed to suggest, and finally in 1917 was ready for publication.

Meanwhile, the members of the group were in constant communication with organizations in England and America whose purposes were parallel. Bryce himself, Cross, the Dickinsons, and Hobson kept in touch with the American League to Enforce Peace which was formed in 1915.[28] In that same year, some of the members joined with other interested persons to form the League of Nations Society, the first public group dedicated to development of such an organization.

The entrance of the United States into the war convinced the Bryce Group that the time was ripe to bring their proposals before the public. On April 12, 1917, the "Proposals of a British Group" appeared in the *Manchester Guardian* with a prefatory letter in which Lord Bryce explained that it was desirable to parallel the work of the American League to Enforce Peace by the development of public opinion in England. He realized that no practical steps could be taken till the end of the war, but in the meantime the idea should be considered and plans formed for the postwar period.[29] The proposals were widely circulated

[26] Bryce to Theodore Marburg, October 1, 1915, in John H. Latané (ed.), *Development of the League of Nations Idea: Documents and Correspondence of Theodore Marburg* (New York, 1932), p. 76. Also "Notes on a conversation with Lord Bryce, July 31, 1916," in Burton J. Hendrick, *The Life and Letters of Walter H. Page* (New York, 1923), II, 165.

[27] *Proposals for the Avoidance of War* (*Private and Confidential, Not for Publication*), cited in Sylvester John Hemleben, *Plans for World Peace Through Six Centuries* (Chicago, 1943), p. 138.

[28] At the third conference of the American League to Enforce Peace the *Proposals for the Avoidance of War* were considered by the membership. Latané, *op. cit.*, I, vii. See also G. L. Dickinson to Marburg, July 5, 1915 (p. 46), Cross to Marburg, August 26, 1916 (pp. 66–67), Hobson to Marburg, March 6, 1916 (p. 94) in Latané, *op. cit.*, vol. I.

[29] *Manchester Guardian*, April 12, 1917.

in the press and were reprinted in *War and Peace,* the supplement of the Liberal periodical, the *Nation,* which was devoted to the discussion of future international relations. Finally, later in 1917, they appeared as a separate volume under the title, *Proposals for the Prevention of Future Wars.*[30]

The Bryce project, like the Fabian plan, specifically denied any intention of setting up a world-state or even a European federation. It proposed merely that existing states, retaining their sovereignty, should accept a treaty arrangement designed to preserve peace.[31] As a start, the great powers and such European powers as were willing to join should make up the membership. Other powers might then be admitted by the original members.[32]

The plan to which the member states were asked to subscribe had certain features in common with that of the Fabian Society. The signatory powers were to accept an obligation to refer all justiciable disputes to the Hague Court of Arbitration or to some other arbitral tribunal for settlement,[33] and to accept the award of the tribunal.[34] Justiciable disputes were defined as "disputes as to the interpretation of a treaty, as to any question of international law, as to the existence of any fact which, if established, would constitute a breach of any international obligation, or as to the nature and extent of the reparation to be made for any such breach."[35] The arbitral court itself should have competence to determine whether any dispute was justiciable.[36]

For the settlement of non-justiciable disputes, a permanent

[30] "A Plan for a League of Nations," *War and Peace,* V (May, 1917), 6; Viscount Bryce and others, *Proposals for the Prevention of Future Wars* (London, 1917). All subsequent citations are to this edition of the Bryce plan.

[31] "Introduction," pp. 12–13.

[32] Art. 1, p. 31.

[33] Art. 2, p. 31.

[34] Art. 3, p. 31.

[35] Art. 4, pp. 31–32.

[36] Art. 5, p. 32.

council of conciliation, appointed by the signatory powers, was to be constituted.[37] All such disputes not settled by diplomatic methods were to be submitted to the council, which would then publish recommendations for amicable settlement.[38] In the case of a dispute between a member-state and a non-signatory power, the latter might be granted temporary representation on the council if it agreed to submit its case.[39]

Having indicated the nature of the machinery for settling international disputes, the plan then proceeded to outline how that machinery would operate. Every member was to agree not to declare war or to prepare for war against another member (a) before the dispute had been submitted to an arbitral tribunal or the council; or (b) within a period of a year after such submission; or (c) if a decision or recommendation had been published within the year, for six months after publication.[40] What was suggested was a moratorium rather than a prohibition of war.

It was believed that an enforced period of delay, consideration of the dispute by an impartial body, and the publicity given to its recommendations would be likely to prevent war by rallying the public opinion of the world in favor of peace.[41] Nevertheless, the possible outbreak of war had to be faced. If any state should break its pledge not to resort to war without first making use of the arbitral court or the council, the other signatory powers were to bind themselves to take such economic or military measures as would ensure the enforcement of the treaty.[42] In the event of the need for sanctions, it was suggested that a progressively more stringent series of economic restrictions might be imposed upon the recalcitrant power with the recognition that in the final reckoning military force might

[37] Art. 6–7, p. 32.
[38] Art. 9–11, p. 33.
[39] Art. 8, p. 32.
[40] Art. 17, p. 34.
[41] "Introduction," p. 23.
[42] Art. 19, p. 35.

be required.[43] Should a state, having submitted its dispute, refuse to accept the award of the arbitral tribunal or the recommendation of the council, the other signatories were to meet in conference and decide what collective action, if any, was to be taken in order to make such decisions operative.[44]

Despite some elements of similarity, the Bryce program was even more cautious than the Fabian plan. It insisted merely upon the submission of disputes, whether of a justiciable or nonjusticiable character. No automatic sanction was provided when a state refused to accept an arbitral decision on questions of fact or on the interpretation of a treaty, for in such a case a conference was to be called to discuss what might be done. The emphasis was upon delay, upon the moratorium as a technique of allowing tempers to cool. Equally limited was the approach to the question of international legislation. The projected treaty itself contained no mention of any lawmaking function, while its introduction merely "hoped and expected" that the Hague Conference would be given a permanent organization and would address itself to the codification and development of international law. Of course, the union suggested by the Bryce plan might adopt rules of law binding upon its own members,[45] but the methods by which such law was to grow were not outlined.

Whatever the limitations of the plan, Bryce's name lent it prestige. He was a well-known public figure in America as well as England, and corresponded regularly with eminent persons interested in the idea of a league.[46] Once he had decided that the progress of the war permitted the publication of the project, he tried to promote greater cooperation between like-minded American and British groups. In a series of letters to a number of public men in America, including Elihu Root, A Lawrence

[43] "Introduction," pp. 16–17.
[44] Art. 20, pp. 27–28.
[45] "Introduction," pp. 27–28.
[46] H. A. L. Fisher, *James Bryce* (*Viscount Bryce of Dechmount, O. M.*) (New York, 1927), II, 136.

Lowell, and Theodore Marburg, he suggested that the best jurists, diplomatists and historians in the two countries should form a joint committee further to crystallize the ideas that should go into the making of a league of nations plan.[47] During the course of the war, he felt, the members of the committee should be working out, quite privately but with the knowledge of their governments, alternative plans to be placed at the disposal of those governments when the end of the war arrived. International machinery to lessen the danger of war could not be extemporized.[48] A similar suggestion was made in a memorandum forwarded to the British government on August 8, 1917, with a covering letter to the prime minister.[49] But Bryce's idea was shattered by the persistent refusal of President Wilson to see the desirability of such planning. Wilson's view was that too great concern with details might impinge upon existing international rivalries. As a consequence, he preferred to stand unqualifiedly for some kind of league of nations after the war, but refused to give his approval to a systematic consideration of what kind it should be. The work of the private groups seeking to outline plans for a league he considered to be more mischievous than useful.[50] Nevertheless, Bryce's recommendation was not entirely wasted. As General Jan Smuts wrote him on October 22, 1917, the memorandum had been circulated in the cabinet, and Smuts himself, later one of the leading advocates of the league, had been strongly impressed by it.[51]

During the remainder of the war, Bryce himself took an

[47] Bryce to Root, December 21, 1917, in Fisher, *op. cit.*, II, 178; Bryce to Marburg, undated, received May 1, 1918, in Latané, *op. cit.*, I, 437–438; Bryce to Lowell, Fisher, *op. cit.*, II, 192–193.

[48] Bryce to Marburg, undated, received May 1, 1918, in Latané, *op. cit.*, II, 437.

[49] Fisher, *op. cit.*, II, 136–137.

[50] Wilson to Marburg, March 8, May 6, 1918, in Library of Congress, Woodrow Wilson Collection, Theodore Marburg Papers (1904–1918); Wilson to Lowell, July 11, 1918, in Library of Congress, Woodrow Wilson Collection, File VI, Box 4767.

[51] Fisher, *op. cit.*, p. 137.

active part in the propaganda for a league of peace. He spoke on the subject in the House of Lords and at several meetings sponsored by the League of Nations Society.[52] Shortly after the conclusion of the war, he published a collection of essays which included a long discussion of future international relations.[53] Substantially Bryce's article was a restatement of the early *Proposals for the Prevention of War*. But in some significant areas his ideas had undergone development. In the field of international legislation, for example, he proposed the setting up of a separate conference or congress to draft rules for international behavior and to submit them to the component states. When those rules were adopted by a prescribed majority of the states, they would become binding on all the states and constitute, subject to subsequent amendment, a code of international law. Similarly he no longer felt committed to the view that the league should restrict itself merely to compelling the submission of disputes for adjudication or inquiry. Instead he now preferred to leave the matter open, allowing room for the possibility that decisions and even recommendations might be made enforceable.[54]

Despite these evidences of change in the views of Lord Bryce himself, the main efforts of the so-called Bryce Group were in support of a league of limited objectives. Major emphasis was placed upon the creation of international organs designed to provide peaceful means for settling disputes once they had arisen. With the exception of some slight mention of techniques for developing international law, no attention was focused upon any long-run plans for dealing with the possible causes of war. Delay in the face of impending conflict was in this case, as in the Fabian plan, the essence of the proposals. A later generation, instructed by the bitter lesson of Munich, was to be presented with evidence that delay, even when achieved by inter-

[52] *Infra*, Chapter III.
[53] "Concerning a Peace League," Viscount James Bryce, *Essays and Addresses in War Time* (New York, 1918).
[54] *Ibid.*, pp. 187–188, 190.

national conference, might spell out a situation more disastrous even than war. It was to have the opportunity to discover that machinery for considering disputes was no substitute for international arrangements which minimized their possibility. Whether the lesson was learned is questionable; in any event, it was not one that was grasped by Bryce and his fellows at an earlier date.

THE UNION OF DEMOCRATIC CONTROL

Of the groups whose programs included advocacy of a league of nations, one of the most interesting was the Union of Democratic Control, founded early in the war by C. P. Trevelyan, Ramsay MacDonald, Norman Angell, E. D. Morel, and Arthur Ponsonby. Condemning the secret commitments revealed by the British government upon the outbreak of war, they set themselves the task of preventing future wars by pressing for the achievement of open diplomacy and democratic control of foreign policy. In a short time this Liberal-and-Labor quintet was joined by such members of the Independent Labor party as Philip Snowden, W. C. Anderson, and H. N. Brailsford, as well as by men from the British Labor party and the trade unions. These included Arthur Henderson, Robert Smillie, and J. H. Thomas.[55] Almost from the start, the Union was handicapped by a vicious attack on the part of the ultra-conservative press, led by the *Morning Post*.[56] It was charged with being unpatriotic, pro-German, and with desiring to see the war end in a stalemate that could benefit no one but the enemy.[57] The

[55] H. M. Swanwick, *Builders of Peace* (London, 1924), pp. 39–40; Charles Trevelyan, *The Union of Democratic Control (an Organisation Created to Secure the Control over Their Foreign Policy by the British People, and for the Promotion of International Understanding), Founded in November, 1914, Its History and Its Policy* (3rd and rev. ed.; London, 1921), pp. 1–4.

[56] Swanwick, *op. cit.*, pp. 32–33.

[57] See, for example, letters of W. Faulkner to the editor, *Morning Post*, January 18, 1916, and February 2, 1916.

real reason for the attack was that the Union of Democratic Control challenged the emotional premises upon which the all-out British effort in the war was built.

The policy of the organization was based upon a four-point program. No territory was to be transferred from one government to another without the consent by plebiscite of its population. No treaty or international undertaking was to be made by Great Britain without the sanction of Parliament, and machinery for ensuring democratic control of foreign policy was to be created. British policy was to be directed to the establishment, in place of the balance of power, of an international council whose deliberations and decisions should be public. And Great Britain should take the lead in proposing a drastic reduction of armaments, the nationalization of the manufacture of armaments, and the control of the export of armaments by one country to another.[58]

The first pamphlet published by the Union agreed that the ultimate goal to aim at was the idea of a federated Europe, involving at least the substantial reduction of standing armies and navies and the submission of all disputes to a central council. But such an objective could not be achieved at once. A simple beginning might be made by setting up a league of perhaps six powers, designed to act against any recalcitrant member who might threaten the peace of the whole. Such an arrangement would be a step forward from the prevalent system of an alliance of three of the powers against the other three. But even so simple a plan was impossible so long as the world suffered from the burden of armaments and the fate of its peoples was at the mercy of the "intrigues and imbecilities" of professional diplomatists and the ambitions of military castes. Consequently, the mass of peoples must claim the right to participate in any future settlement, protected by guarantees of

[58] *The Morrow of the War* (No. 1) (London, n.d.), pp. 1–2. The number following this title and those cited below refers to the designation of the volume in the series issued as "Publications of the Union of Democratic Control."

open negotiations and democratic control of the negotiators, and aided by an all-round limitation of armaments.[59]

Subsequent pamphlets hammered away at the idea that open diplomacy and a parliamentary check upon all actions of the foreign office were the first requisites of any lasting peace.[60] If the people had a chance to consider war before they were in it —before it had become "inevitable"—they would manage to keep out.[61] Additional information about foreign peoples and about the foreign policies of their governments would be a bond of unity among nations. Only in such a case would a world league be successful, for it might then be a league of *nations*, based on mutual understanding, rather than a sterile league of governments.[62]

Once the way had been cleared for such a league of nations, the first step would be for the powers to renounce all existing exclusive alliances. Then they would erect a league of peace which should, in the event of a dispute, offer mediation or arbitration by neutrals.[63] If one power rejected such a procedure, the league should give the support of its armed force to the power conforming to its treaty obligations. If both parties refused mediation, then the league should throw its weight

[59] *Ibid.,* pp. 9–10, 14.

[60] Some of these pamphlets include Norman Angell, *Shall This War End German Militarism* (No. 2) (London, n.d.), pp. 21–22; Arthur Ponsonby, *Parliament and Foreign Policy* (No. 5) (London, n.d.), pp. 8–9; *The National Policy as Set Forth by Mr. Asquith, Sir Edward Grey, Mr. Churchill, Mr. Lloyd George, Mr. Austen Chamberlain, Mr. Law, Mr. Arthur Henderson, and Others* (No. 6) (London, n.d.), pp. 2, 6–10; R. L. Tawney, *The War to End War* (No. 21a) (London, 1918); Norman Angell, *The Prussian in Our Midst* (No. 13) (London, n.d.), pp. 5–6, *passim.*

[61] J. Ramsay MacDonald, *War and the Workers, A Plea for Democratic Control* (No. 8) (London, n.d.), p. 13.

[62] Arthur Ponsonby, *The Control of Foreign Policy* (No. 5a) (London, 1918), pp. 3–4, 6–7.

[63] Bertrand Russell, *War—the Offspring of Fear* (No. 3) (London, n.d.), pp. 11–12; H. N. Brailsford, *The Origins of War* (No. 4) (London, n.d.), pp. 21–22.

against whichever party proved to be the aggressor. In the long run, the failure of aggressive war would lead to the cessation of all war.[64]

There was no systematic attempt in the propaganda of the U.D.C. to work out the precise nature of a future league in terms of organs, detailed procedures, or membership qualifications. As has been noted, its plan, insofar as it did outline a league, was the familiar idea of a league with limited functions, designed to offer machinery for mediation and arbitration in international disputes. But unlike the Fabian Society or the Bryce Group, it did not believe that even such a limited league was possible unless a radical change in the conduct of foreign affairs came first. Publicity and parliamentary control were the central arch of the Union of Democratic Control's proposal. Upon such a foundation a strong world league might be erected; without it, any international organization was doomed to repeat the past mistakes of international relations.

THE COMMUNITY OF NATIONS

Each of the preceding schemes agreed that the use of armed force might be required to compel adherence to its system of ensuring the peace. A little pamphlet issued by Dr. Henry T. Hodgkin, a leading English pacifist, demurred. Dr. Hodgkin proposed a plan which structurally was not particularly different from those of the Fabians and the Bryce Group. He envisaged the establishment on a definite basis of three bodies: (1) a congress of national representatives "sitting regularly to promote the common interests of nations"; (2) courts of arbitration and justice to decide upon points of difference concerning the interpretation of treaties and other disputes of a juridical nature; and (3) a council of conciliation to which disputes not of a juridical character could be referred for consideration and recommendation. Any "Sovereign State" desiring to be represented at the congress, or to present a case to the court or council, should be entitled to do so. All the states should be en-

[64] Russell, *op. cit.*, p. 12.

couraged to agree to submit all their disputes to the proper body for settlement, and to abide by the decision of the court or be "guided by" the recommendation of the council when given. One contribution of some originality suggested meetings of the foreign secretaries of the constituent states, to be held at regular intervals and at times of crises for a direct interchange of views.[65]

Thus far the "Community of Nations" was not particularly unique among league ideas. But Dr. Hodgkin made the keystone of his argument the doctrine that the essential basis for the new order must be consent and not the coercion of force.[66] His argument was based upon the proposition that armed sanctions simply saddled the new experiment with the same shackles which had caused the present regime to break down. A league to *enforce* peace would give new life to militarism, and enhance the influence of the manufacture of armaments, an influence which had already hindered human progress sufficiently. The question of the actual distribution of armed forces under a plan based on coercion would, in addition, be a fertile source of underground intrigue making for conflict. Another objection was the fact that such a proposal virtually ensured that the next war, when it came, would be universal. Therefore he proposed a league based only upon common consent and with no sanction beyond world opinion.[67]

This element of pacifism injected into the league debate proved, with one exception which will appear later, something of a sport. Virtually all those most closely connected with the campaign for an international organization agreed that it must have teeth if it were to be effective. The published material of the war years gives virtually no indication that the ideas of Dr. Hodgkin were spread more widely than among the small circle of pacifists, whose primary interest was not particularly a league of nations.

[65] Woolf, *The Framework of a Lasting Peace,* pp. 124–125.

[66] *Ibid.,* p. 125.

[67] Henry T. Hodgkin, "Uncompromising Idealism," *War and Peace,* IV (1917), 67.

II

Approaches to International Government

THE SCHEMES FOR INTERNATIONAL organization thus far discussed proposed a league of limited scope and purpose. Even the Union of Democratic Control, whose program envisaged a fundamental rearrangement of the bases of international relations, thought of the league itself as a somewhat restricted body, designed to perform one particular function—the settlement of disputes by arbitration or mediation. But some plans broached during the war years were much broader in approach. They looked beyond the immediate problem of international quarrels to a league of definite, permanent functions in the everyday cooperation of the nations of the world. Clearly, any distinction between "restricted" and "broad" conceptions contains an element of the arbitrary. Many of the proponents of the limited league looked forward to growth and development in international relations; all of the supporters of a league with wider powers took as their point of departure machinery to settle international quarrels. The touchstone in each particular case is the major emphasis, the chief stress of the plan considered.

As will become evident from subsequent discussion of the league of nations movement, support for a genuine international government with substantial and independent powers was relatively weak. The generation of Vimy Ridge and the Somme, of Passchendaele and the Marne knew less of the ultimate destructive potential of war among the nations than the generation of Hiroshima and Nagasaki. If the latter failed to flock to the banner of world government as the sole avenue of escape, it is not to be wondered that the former was even less receptive to the particular solution. Before 1919, no organized group took up the idea. The Fabian plan and the Bryce proposals shied clear of it. And the various league of nations societies usually took note of it only to protest they had no such far-reaching aim in mind. Even those who advanced plans for international government usually did so hesitantly and at times obliquely. Nevertheless, it should be pointed out that in so doing they laid down a line of attack that might in the future provide an alternative to a system, proposed by others, that was tried and, in the first instance at least, that was found wanting. In any event, some four men made significant approaches toward a system of international government. Three of them, J. A. Hobson, H. N. Brailsford, and H. G. Wells, were of course well-known to that section of the public concerned with problems of international relations. The fourth, H. E. Hyde, was a young lieutenant in the Royal Air Force who made up for his lack of reputation by offering, in a series of books and pamphlets, the most thorough scheme for world government to appear during the war.

JOHN A. HOBSON

Economist J. A. Hobson had made his mark early in the century with a searching criticism of imperialism that was destined to become a minor classic. When he first outlined his views on international organization in 1915, therefore, he wrote from a background that enabled him to lay claim to significant authority in the field. *Towards International Government* was a systematic presentation of arguments for a league with wide powers. Perhaps because he was a member of the Bryce Group, Hobson began his analysis by postulating the need for the usual court and council. He proposed that the states of the world sign a treaty or agreement setting up a league of peace and binding them

1. To submit to arbitration or conciliation all disputes or differences between them not capable of settlement by ordinary processes of diplomacy, and to accept and carry out any award or terms of settlement thus attained.

2. To bring joint pressure, diplomatic, economic, or forcible, to bear upon any member refusing to submit a disputed matter to such modes of settlement, or to accept and carry out the award, or otherwise threatening or opening hostilities against any other member.

3. To take joint action in repelling any attack made by an outside Power, or group of Powers, upon any of the members of the League.

4. To take joint action in securing redress of any injury which, by the general assent of the signatory Powers, had been wrongfully inflicted upon any member of the League.[1]

After outlining the type of disputes capable of settlement by arbitration and those susceptible to conciliation, he proceeded to indicate how the bodies for dealing with the disputes should be set up. For the court of arbitration, men of wide judicial experience were needed; for the council of conciliation, men of broad personal qualifications—wisdom, integrity, fair-mindedness. Above all, no old-style diplomatists must serve. In the case of conciliation of non-justiciable disputes, the award of the council, once it had investigated the facts, must be accepted as a basis for settlement as binding as an award of the court of arbitration. In fact, there must be the closest cooperation between the two bodies, the council often serving merely to unearth the facts necessary to make a concrete case for the court. All the powers would be required to pledge themselves to bring concerted pressure, by armed force if necessary, upon any signatory power which declined to fulfill its treaty obligations.[2]

[1] John A. Hobson, *Towards International Government* (London, 1915), p. 27.
[2] Ibid., pp. 34–36, 44–48, 62–63, 65–70, 76.

So far the plan, with the exception of the enforcement of recommendations of the council of conciliation—which were to be used only as a *basis* for settlement—was not particularly different from other schemes. But Hobson moved beyond the range of the limited league when he asked the question, what international body should be invested with the necessary executive power to make the sanctions operative? He rejected the idea that the court of arbitration or even the council of conciliation could fulfill the obligation. In both cases, the members must be completely independent and free from political pressure; the duty of carrying out their own decisions would obviously interfere with their proper role. Therefore, an independent executive must be set up as a third body to give effect to the work of the court and the council. Such an executive must assuredly not be a conference of foreign ministers, for that would be to plunge the most critical issues back into the atmosphere of diplomatic intercourse so poorly adapted to pacific settlement. It should be a permanent international council, elected by the constituent nations on a principle of representation roughly proportional to the size and population of the constituent nations. The council should have the power to draw upon the economic resources and armed forces of the members of the league, in accordance with prearranged plans, for the enforcement of the decisions of the respective international organs.[3]

All this provided machinery for settling disputes, but Hobson was convinced that it was not safe for the league of nations to wait until difficulties ripened into quarrels.[4] The "humbler schemes" of safeguarding peace by arbitration and conciliation were not likely to be satisfactory so long as nothing was done to cure the underlying causes of the grievances and antagonisms of national interests. The two chief factors making for breaches in the public peace were problems of nationality and international economic problems. In order to cope with them the In-

---

[3] Hobson, *op. cit.*, pp. 97–99, 101–102, 105–106, 109, 167.
[4] *Ibid.*, p. 6.

ternational Council must have the attributes of genuine international government.[5]

In the case of nationality problems, Hobson proposed that the International Council have the power to work for the development of the concept of autonomy, effective self-government, to be guaranteed by the league. Genuine internationalism would depend more upon this substitution of autonomy for nationalism than on any other single change. The concept alone could furnish a solution to the terrible problem of the "rights of minorities," so long a thorn in the side of virtually all national movements.[6]

It was even more urgent that an international council should have sufficient power to consider and settle large questions of economic policy which brought modern nations into conflict. Such an international government, representing all the nations, would seek to remove all restrictions which impaired the freedom of economic intercourse among nations. Restrictive tariffs, exclusive use of ports leading to vast continental hinterlands, individual exploitation of colonial areas, all would have to be attacked. The council would act to enforce equality of opportunity for commerce, for investment of capital, and for participation in the development of the world's resources. Such actions would, of course, imply some supervision of the colonial policies of the nations.[7] And in the course of time, the international organization would develop many new legislative and administrative duties. "Just as within a federal State, or a federation of States, the central power continually receives new accessions, by virtue of the widening needs and interests of the members of this national society, so that actual growth of international contacts and communications will have a similar effect in feeding the organs of international government." [8]

[5] *Ibid.*, pp. 118–119.
[6] *Ibid.*, pp. 124–126.
[7] *Ibid.*, pp. 135–148. Hobson's ideas on the administration of colonial areas are discussed in greater detail in Chapter VIII of this volume.
[8] Hobson, *op. cit.*, p. 148.

Hobson warned that the admission of Germany to the league was a prime condition of its success. Only if Germany were enlisted as an equal member of the new international order would it be possible for the German people to overthrow Prussian militarism. Outside the league, Germany would be in a position to plot and intrigue for the weakening of the league or the creation of a counter-league.[9] Finally, in setting up the new organization, he felt that it would be wise to build upon the existing structure of Hague tribunals and conventions. If more continuity, larger powers, and stronger sanctions could be secured for these bodies they might easily be developed into true machinery for international government.[10]

Having started with a narrowly conceived league, designed to settle disputes among its members, Hobson had arrived at a plan for international government granting wide powers to the central organization. He had not detailed in every respect how such a league would carry out its wider functions, but even the suggestion of those functions was a bold step in 1915. *Towards International Government* went far beyond most projects current at the time, not only in its outline of the functions of the proposed league, but especially in the spirit of genuine international thinking which informed its pages.

H. N. BRAILSFORD

H. N. Brailsford, left-wing journalist, writer on world affairs, member of the Independent Labor party, was easily the most outstanding advocate of real international government during the war years. In newspapers, periodicals, and books, he preached the doctrine that it was not enough merely to make provision against aggression and sudden war. Without international legislation to remove legitimate grievances, a league of peace, if it aimed only at repressing an aggrieved or ambitious power, would be little more than a Holy Alliance. Modern wars

[9] *Ibid.*, pp. 155–156.
[10] *Ibid.*, pp. 169–170.

arose out of deep-seated economic conflicts, and those conflicts could only be solved by handling international economic problems on an international basis. Therefore, Brailsford argued:

> Either we must break down the whole fabric of Imperialism, the world over, with its tariffs, its concessions and its spheres of influence, or else we must arrange for the equitable allotment of these exclusive areas of opportunity. To achieve either of these solutions we must advance boldly to the conception of international government. Wars in the modern world are something more than squabbles and outbreaks of accidental passion. They turn on vast and permanent questions of world policy. The methods of the court of law will not solve them. We must advance to those of the Federal Council.[11]

The first detailed exposition of such a council appeared in 1915 as an appendix to the third edition of Brailsford's book, *The War of Steel and Gold.* He sketched a federal league, with membership open to any civilized sovereign state on a purely voluntary basis. Since a single world federation might be difficult to manage, it would perhaps be expedient to develop three federations, one Pan-European, one Pan-American, and one Asiatic, linked by treaty and by the reciprocal exchange of certain advantages. The chief immediate problem was the European federation. It must include Germany as well as the chief Allies, and the United States would be an extremely useful addition. Disputes among members, if justiciable, were to be referred to the Hague Tribunal. Questions of "honor" or "interest" or of a general nature were referable to the council of the league. Refusal to obey its decision was to be considered secession from the league and mobilization of one member against another was to entail immediate expulsion. Expulsion, in turn, involved the loss of vital economic privileges, for, as will be indicated, Brailsford envisaged the league as controlling a large share of the economic resources of the world.

The council of the league was to be comprised of deputies

[11] H. N. Brailsford, "On Preventing Wars," *War and Peace,* II (1915), 72.

elected by the lower house of each national parliament on the basis of population. The alternative, a council composed of nominees of the governments, would tend to throw international affairs back into the area of secret bargaining and diplomacy which had already caused such difficulties. If, however, the more ambitious council should prove immediately impossible, then a middle course would be to create a small supreme council or senate of delegates of governments, and an advisory general council of elected deputies. The latter might then in the course of time supersede the more conventional body. In any event, international parties would soon develop in the general council—a socialist party, a free trade party, a conservative party—cutting across national lines and promoting the development of a true international legislature. Permanent officials would be chosen to carry out the executive work of the council, and they in turn would be supervised by several standing committees elected by the council from among its members.

The enumeration of the functions of the council illustrated the wide range of powers Brailsford desired to give the world authority. He proposed the following list:

1. The police of the high seas in peace and war.
2. The control of trade routes, ship canals, and free ports.
3. Trade with the unfree colonies of the Member-States.
4. The control of the competition for concessions and spheres of influence.
5. The control of dealings with bankrupt or anarchical minor states.
6. The control, at least in principle, of emigration.
7. International postal, telegraphic and railway arrangements, extradition, patent and copyright law.
8. Some cautious development of the existing rudimentary arrangements for standardising national legislation as to dangerous trades, child-labour, the white slave traffic, etc.
9. The protection in grave cases of racial minorities.
10. The decision of disputes among Members on the initiative of any national group.

11. Defence against external aggression.
12. The consequent regulation of armaments.

The striking fact about this enumeration is its emphasis upon the economic functions of the league. The settlement of disputes, defense against aggression, and the regulation of armaments appeared as the last items, after a very explicit outline of broader day-to-day functions. For, as Brailsford saw it, the key to the creation and maintenance of the league was its economic policy. Here, in times of peace, was the "chief of the cruder motives for adhering to it, the chief obstacle to secession, and therefore, the principal sanction for the decisions of its Council." Consequently, he proceeded to describe that economic policy. Among its main features were a provision for mutual most-favored nation treatment among all the members of the league, the stipulation that the non-self-governing colonies of members must be open on equal terms with the trade of the mother country to the trade of other members, and an arrangement whereby the capital of member states should share in an agreed proportion in certain joint enterprises, such as Turkish, Chinese, or African railways. General free trade was desirable, but hardly likely. Such a policy, if firmly administered, would make it difficult for an aggressive outsider or a seceding member to maintain itself in opposition to the league. Military force, therefore, would not be as important as the ability to withdraw economic benefits. Economic sanctions would be the major weapon of the league in enforcing its provisions for the settlement of disputes. But more importantly, international administration of a wide field of economic matters would in itself be the greatest guarantee of an equitable distribution of trade, resources, and opportunities for investment. The result would be a lessening of those tensions, caused by exclusion and monopoly, which most frequently led to war.

There was, however, always the possibility of a challenge to the league by recourse to force. So long as that was possible the league must have certain armaments at its disposal. National armies and fleets, subject to an exchange of plans and inventions, would at first be used. Eventually, the league might create its own fleet and army, leaving its members to train and arm a militia for internal purposes.[12]

The remarkable thing about this sketch for a federal league was that it appeared so early in the war. And having developed his major thesis, Brailsford continued to return to it as the war progressed. In 1916, for example, he contributed an essay on the organization of peace to a study of the post-war settlement edited by Charles Roden Buxton. Once again, he elaborated a "minimum plan" for machinery to forestall the outbreak of hostilities. But, he asked, would such a plan offer the hope that great and necessary changes might be effected without war, that armament races and opposing alliances would be discarded? Formally, it promised no such benefits. It provided the means to settle a limited number of disputes in certain circumstances, and to that extent was a great step forward. But only as the international temper was developed, and only as it was equipped with the organs of an international government, could the root causes of war be exorcised. The scheme of conciliation must not be allowed to remain for long the sole link between rival and isolated powers. The league must evolve into a commonwealth, conferring positive benefits upon its members, and offering thereby a new motive for prompt obedience to its decisions.[13]

Brailsford had no illusions about current proposals for a limited league. As he told his readers in the *Herald*, the Labor weekly, such a body would be legal rather than democratic in its basis. It would be too much a league of states and too little a society of peoples. It might easily become a conservative alliance of all the satisfied powers. True, it would possess a mechanism to settle disputes, but its exponents paid little attention

[12] Pp. 330–337.
[13] H. N. Brailsford, "The Organisation of Peace," *Towards a Lasting Settlement,* ed. by C. R. Buxton (New York, 1916), pp. 156–160, 170–173.

to the general causes, especially economic causes, which made for strife. Nevertheless, the idea must not be rejected. "This first sketch of the League commits only its authors. Our task must be to broaden it, to humanise it, to democratise it." For without an international parliament it was doubtful if a genuine league of nations was possible. Elected by each national parliament on the basis of population and according to a system of proportional representation, such an international body might gradually evolve into a truly sovereign world parliament.[14]

Meanwhile, during 1916, Brailsford had been integrating his ideas on international organization and incorporating them in a systematic, fully-developed book. *A League of Nations* was first published in February, 1917, and soon went through several editions. It excited considerable attention, and even the League of Nations Society, which did not agree with the major emphasis of the work, issued a pamphlet as a guide to the study of its arguments.[15]

In *A League of Nations* Brailsford was concerned primarily with laying down the fundamental conditions upon which a league should be based rather than with an elaboration of specific machinery. He did, however, sketch a draft plan for a league which indicated certain changes in detail from his earlier ideas. In the matter of the prevention of war, his modified scheme provided that league members should submit non-justiciable disputes to a council of inquiry and conciliation and justiciable disputes to a court of arbitral justice. He had apparently given up the idea of using the Hague Tribunal for the latter function, perhaps as a concession to the majority of plans being outlined in England. An executive of the league, perhaps representing the governments of the great powers, should have the task of concerting effective military or economic measures to compel observance of the fundamental obligation. Failure to accept and to give effect to the recommenda-

[14] "The League of Nations," *Herald,* July 14, 1917.
[15] *A League of Nations, A Scheme of Study* ("League of Nations Society Publications," No. 20) (London, 1917).

tion of the council or the award of the court would not necessarily draw upon the power concerned the sanctions of the
league. The executive, in such a case, would immediately determine what collective action, if any, was required to meet the
situation.[16] But, as Brailsford explained, the proposal contained
an automatic means of determining an aggressor. For any nation taking up arms without referring its case to the league, or
in opposition to the verdict or recommendation of that body,
would clearly be violating its pledges. Usually the league could
enforce its system by isolating the aggressive power, depriving
it of allies, and subjecting it to a general boycott. But it would
be a fatal error to regard economic pressure as a substitute for
military preparedness. The league, then, must have force to
draw upon, though it should work to foster a general reduction of national armaments on land and sea.[17]

But, as in the case of *The War of Steel and Gold,* such a
system for checking international quarrels was only a part of
Brailsford's plan. Here too he drew up, as an integral part of the
constitution of the league, a "charter of commercial freedom."
This he formulated in the following terms:

(a) The signatory Powers shall accord to each other in the
home markets "most-favoured nation" treatment; (b) in their
non-self-governing colonies they will impose tariffs (if any)
for revenue purposes only; (c) they will concert measures to
secure "the Open Door" to all foreign enterprise in developed
regions, particularly in China; they will appoint as an organ of
the League an International Commission to ensure free access
for the trade of all the signatory Powers to raw materials and
other natural resources.[18]

The importance of this charter was fully explained in the
text of the volume. Such economic cooperation through the
instrumentality of a league would yield positive benefits for all

[16] Brailsford, *A League of Nations,* pp. 328–329. All references are
to the second edition.

[17] *Ibid.,* pp. 63, 193, 330.

[18] *Ibid.,* p. 329.

the nations participating. In certain areas of tension, international supervision would offer a solution to a problem hitherto insoluble. The Straits, for example, might come under the control of an international commission to assure their free navigation at all times by the merchant vessels of all nationalities. In Mesopotamia, a commission might be named to develop this rich source of raw materials for the good of its inhabitants and the benefit of the world. Certainly an Arab national state under British protection was not a desirable development. Other areas might, in similar fashion, come under international control. In addition, Brailsford argued, the more the league of nations could do to foster economic independence, the greater would be its power in an emergency to act through economic pressure and without the use of force.[19]

Brailsford regarded a guarantee of the rights of nationality as second in importance only to his economic charter. He proposed an article whereby the league members would agree to accord to all racial minorities in Europe full liberty for the use of their language, the development of their culture, and the exercise of their religion. Such a settlement of the nationality problem offered the only hope for keeping the peace in those mixed areas of Europe where strife was so likely to break out.[20]

Brailsford's chief concern, then, was with the causes of war, rather than with the attempt to keep those causes from resulting in hostilities. The arguments for a league with broad powers outlined here are merely illustrative of the nature of his approach. The key to that approach was the doctrine of international change. "Unless we can make our League a possible instrument of fundamental change," wrote Brailsford, "it will rally the satisfied Powers and repel the peoples which cherish an ambition or suffer from a wrong. Our inevitably static conception of the world must learn to find a place for these restless forces which are bent on change." [21] The most promising approach to the kind of a league that might guarantee changes

---

[19] *Ibid.*, pp. 151–152, 170, 277–278.
[20] *Ibid.*, pp. 112–113, 139–140, 329.
[21] *Ibid.*, p. 84.

when necessary was the gradual evolution of some kind of federal parliament. It might at first be only a consultative body, but in the long run the league's future depended on its ability to develop a "corporate personality" independent of the governments which adhered to it.[22] In other words, the goal to aim at was the actual realization of genuine world government, and Brailsford's proposals pointed in that direction.

H. G. WELLS

The outbreak of the war offered a challenge to the imagination of the eager, impatient, often contradictory H. G. Wells. An avowed internationalist before the war, he became for a time a bitter, strident nationalist, preaching a doctrine of hate and vengeance.[23] But as the emotions released by the horror of conflict were tamed, Wells returned once more to a consideration of international organization. As always, he had his fingers in a number of pies. He was active in the drive for a league of free nations, one which should presumably exclude Germany, and he also supported the idea of a league of the Allies to be formed during the war. But in several major works and in numerous articles he outlined plans for broad international cooperation which, if not always sharply defined, were always provocative and interesting.

Wells' first wartime essay at a plan of international government appeared in a book called *What Is Coming?*, published in May, 1916. In it, he announced that if there was to be permanent peace, there must obviously be permanent means of settling disputes without recourse to war. That meant that there must be a supreme power, a high court of some kind, a universally recognized executive over and above the separate governments of the world. These separate governments would not

[22] *Ibid.*, pp. 205–206.
[23] Geoffrey West, *H. G. Wells* (New York, 1930), pp. 188–189; Wells, "The Liberal Fear of Russia," *Nation*, XV (1914), 755–757; *idem.*, *The War That Will End War* (London, 1914); letter to editor, *The Times*, August 8, 1914.

have to disappear, but they would have to surrender almost as much of their sovereignty as had the American states in making the United States. If their unification was to be anything more than a formality, they would have to delegate a control of their inter-state relations far beyond what very many were prepared to accept at present. "It is really quite idle," declared Wells, "to dream of a warless world in which States are still absolutely free to annoy one another with tariffs, with the blocking and squeezing of trade routes, with the ill-treatment of immigrants and travelling strangers, and between which there is no means of settling boundaries disputes." Moreover, no settlement could be stable which did not destroy, in backward and alien areas "owned" by the European powers, the preference given the nationals of the controlling countries, and which did not prepare for the immediate or eventual accession of subject peoples to the rank of independent states.

But how was one to get such an international government with power to handle such questions? Here Wells was more cautious. He suggested as perhaps the best approach a postwar Allied conference which would build directly from existing institutions and grow "almost unawares" into a pacific organization of the world. Since such an approach would not shock princes and diplomatists, lawyers, statesmen, politicians, nationalists, and other suspicious people, and since it would give them time to adjust to the new situation, it was wiser than to hope that anything could come from Hague foundations or the obvious logic of the war. What must be borne in mind was that if peace did not come on the basis of the gradual development of a world state, then it would come, after several more great wars, as a "Roman world peace made in Germany." Everything pointed to the imperative necessity of some great council or conference, some permanent overriding body to deal with affairs more broadly than could any nationalism or patriotic imperialism.[24]

These ideas for world government were rather ill-defined,

[24] Pp. 12–14, 26–27, 252–253, 262.

somewhat "fuzzy" in outline. In a series of newspaper articles during the next two years, Wells did his thinking in public and pieced together a series of concrete proposals. He favored the signature of an identical treaty among all the great powers binding them to certain things. In 1917, he proposed that the few great industrial states capable of producing modern equipment should take over the manufacture of all munitions of war and absolutely close the supply of such material to all other states.[25] By 1918, he was willing to compromise for an agreement giving the international league effective control over every armament industry, power and freedom to investigate the military, naval and aerial establishments of all constituent powers, and of course for a positive move toward disarmament under the league.[26] And all the powers were to be bound to attack and suppress any state building or increasing its war equipment beyond the specified limits.[27]

Next, there must be an international tribunal for the discussion and settlement of international disputes,[28] and able to adjudicate upon any such disputes whatever.[29] As an unfriendly critic pointed out, Wells made no distinction between justiciable and non-justiciable cases—all were to be subject to decision and enforcement.[30] The plan did not reveal a lack of comprehension of league proposals, as the critic maintained, but rather a resolution on Wells' part to sketch a league with thoroughgoing powers.

How strong a league he envisaged appeared as he outlined its further duties. Arguing, like H. N. Brailsford, that economic conflict was at the base of international war, Wells insisted

[25] H. G. Wells, "Ideas for a World Peace. II.—The 'Last of the Conquests'—and After," *Daily News and Leader,* January 22, 1917.

[26] *Idem.,* "A League of Nations. What It Must Be Able to Do," *Daily Chronicle,* May 17, 1918.

[27] *Daily News and Leader,* January 22, 1917.

[28] *Ibid.*

[29] *Daily Chronicle,* May 17, 1918.

[30] *New Statesman,* XI (1918), 216.

that the international tribunal must be able to consider and set aside all tariffs and special privileges that seemed grossly unfair or acted as an irritant between the various states of the world. It should have the right to pass on or revise all new tariff and quarantine regulations or on legislation for the exclusion of aliens, which might affect international relations. It should control the distribution of all the staple products of the world. For without such powers, it could do nothing to prevent countries from strangling each other by commercial warfare. The tribunal should have the power to interfere in the internal affairs of any state in order to protect foreign travellers, keep disorder from spreading over the frontier, and break up aggressive military or naval preparation.[31] In one of his articles he suggested that all this might be done by authorizing a state to bring charges of unfair or dangerous practices before the tribunal. The latter could then lay down rules to be observed by the offending state.[32]

Several of these newspaper articles were gathered together and published in May, 1918, as *In the Fourth Year: Anticipations of a World Peace.* One of the articles, "A Reasonable Man's Peace," which had appeared in the *Daily News* for August 14, 1917, was twice reprinted as a pamphlet and in that form had a circulation of about a quarter of a million.[33] *In the Fourth Year* outlined two main arguments for the necessity of merging existing sovereignties into an international and, if possible, a world-wide league. The first was the "geographical impossibility" of the present European states and empires; the second, the steadily increasing disproportion between the horrors of modern warfare and any advantage that might arise from it. Proximity and science united to make imperative some form of world government. Such a government could not be a

[31] *Daily News and Leader,* January 22, 1917.
[32] *Daily Chronicle,* May 17, 1918.
[33] H. G. Wells, *Experiment in Autobiography. Discoveries and Conclusions of a Very Ordinary Brain (Since 1886)* (New York, 1934), p. 593.

diplomatists' league. It must be based on an ideal of international cooperation, fostered by sustained, deliberate explanation, and by teaching in school and church and in the press of
the world. It should develop, as the government of the United
States had developed, by delegating certain specified powers to
the league, and no others.[34]

The specified powers covered a very wide range of duties.
The league must be able to adjudicate in all international disputes. It would have a supreme court, whose decisions would
be final, and before which any power might appear as a
plaintiff against any other power or group of powers. It must
have virtual control of the army, navy, air forces, and armament
industry of every nation of the world, with full rights of investigation. Otherwise, any power could plunge the world into
an armament race at will. The league must also have the economic powers already outlined above.[35] In this connection,
Wells developed an argument for international trusteeship over
colonial areas that was a significant contribution to the growth
of the mandates idea.[36] Finally, Wells argued, the league must
be constituted through direct participation of the peoples of
the world. Specifically, representatives to the peace conference
designed to set up the league must be directly elected by the
people.[37]

Wells gave the final touches to his argument in a long letter
to the conservative *Morning Post* which appeared on September 30, 1918. In it, he presented his familiar case for world
government, but also denounced the schemes of those whom he
called "Weak Leaguers." At present current, he declared, was
a defeatist proposal which envisaged a mere rehabilitation of
the Hague Tribunal. It was a timid scheme for delay and arbitration; some sort of international conference was to meet
occasionally; there was to be a supreme court for disputes on

[34] *In the Fourth Year,* pp. 2, 4–6, 98–99.
[35] *Ibid.,* pp. 15–19.
[36] *Infra,* Chapter VIII.
[37] *In the Fourth Year,* p. 26.

points of international law, and a court of conciliation for non-justiciable cases. No interference with the political constitution or internal arrangements of any state was contemplated. No organized disarmament or control of militarism could therefore materialize. Germany "undefeated and unregenerate will, for instance, be admitted to such a League on the expression of a few pious sentiments." Such a scheme would be perfect for German imperialism, but most sensible people desired a strong league or no league at all. Already the Allies had developed a widespread system of international cooperation; they must build upon it to form a league of free nations, into which other nations might come as they gave proof of their faith in free institutions and of their will to meet the demands of international living.

Thus, during the course of the war, Wells had outlined a scheme far-reaching in its implications for world government. He was concerned mainly with the nature of the powers to be allotted such a government, and his conception of them included control of the most vital fields of international relations. He made no attempt to set down point by point what should be the precise machinery through which it should operate. Perhaps he was too impatient for the task; perhaps he felt that the details were unimportant so long as the basic pattern was accepted. Whatever the lacunae of his plan, however, it represented one of the few wartime approaches in England to the notion that without world government the prevention of war was impossible. Despite its inconsistency on the German question, it was either too imaginative or too far-reaching to have any appeal to men obsessed by the dogma of national sovereignty and the doctrine of the practical.

H. E. HYDE

It remained for a comparatively obscure lieutenant in the Royal Air Force to outline the most unreserved plan for international government to appear in England. H. E. Hyde made up in energy for his lack of reputation. He joined the service in New Zealand, but before going to the front published a pamphlet advocating the league of nations idea. During the war he wrote and published a number of books and pamphlets sketching his project for international organization.[38] After the war he took part in the campaign conducted by the League of Nations Union to popularize the league among the British people.[39]

Hyde took the position that there must be a choice in international matters between two policies. Either the nations must establish international government on practically the same lines as national government, and having the same power over nations as national government had over individuals; or they must consciously adopt militarism as a safeguard and defense. No mere league of nations, bound together by treaties alone, was likely to be satisfactory. The principal objection to it was that in most crises a nation's support of any international decision would be determined by the nation's own conception of its interest in the results of that decision. Such a league would be a movement away from international government rather than towards its achievement.[40]

As an alternative to the methods most popular, Hyde suggested a scheme based on the establishment of (1) a parliament composed of representatives of all nations; (2) a law court presided over by a small body of judges nominated and elected by the parliament; and (3) an international armament sufficiently strong to enforce the decisions of the judges of the

[38] H. E. Hyde, *The Two Roads, International Government or Militarism* (London, [1915]); *International Government* (London, [1917]); *The League of Nations and the Peace Conference* ("League of Nations Union Publications," Ser. 2, No. 27) (London, 1918). Since his argument is essentially the same in each case, all citations are from *The Two Roads*.

[39] *The League of Nations and the Peace Conference*, p. 1.

[40] *The Two Roads*, pp. v–vi.

law court. The functions of the parliament were to be legislative—it would draw up a full code of international law to govern the relations of the nations. The law court would then give decisions on all matters of law brought before it, with no appeal from those decisions. The international force would, when necessary, carry out the decisions of the court, and act in any other way required to maintain the interests of the nations forming the world organization.

Hyde detailed a long list of suggestions which would have to be implemented if international government was to be established on a satisfactory basis. By far the largest part of the list was concerned with military matters. The international armament was to be composed of levies from all the nations on the basis of their size and importance. It was to be controlled and administered by the parliament, its component parts to be in no way connected with or answerable to the individual nations. Each nation could maintain its own police force, but the size and composition of this force was to be determined by the international parliament. The parliament must take over, operate, and control all plants throughout the world that were engaged in the manufacture of armaments. It must have full powers of investigation and inspection to make sure that no individual nation was producing weapons of war. The various nations were to receive from the international government only sufficient munitions to guard against reasonable contingencies. A host of other provisions was enumerated to guarantee that the international force should be supreme and able to carry out its functions in an emergency.[41]

All war between members of the world body was to be banned. International disputes without exception were to be settled by the law court. If any nation refused to abide by its decision, the law court was to be able to call upon the military agencies of the international government to support it. The parliament, designed to be the executive and key organ of that government, was to be composed of representatives chosen

41 *Ibid.*, pp. 17–23.

from each nation on the basis of its "status and importance." [42]

Hyde thus approached the question of world government from a point of view considerably different from those of Hobson, Brailsford, or Wells. He gave to his international parliament full powers to legislate for the world on "international affairs," but did not seem to be particularly concerned with the specific nature of that legislation. His chief obsession was the creation of a system of military force to assure enforcement of the laws of parliament. Since the world legislature was to be a representative body, he apparently assumed that it would, in general, act in conformity with the will of the majority of the world. Its chief function, in any case, was to make war impossible by the use of preponderant power; the causes of war did not enter into the analysis of Hyde in any basic fashion. Whatever the nature of the plan, it gained no considerable following and had no particular impact upon the main currents of thought on international organization. [43]

[42] *Ibid.*, pp. 18, 20. Hyde included only the "white" nations in his scheme. Residence in New Zealand, apparently, had made him a believer in the "Asiatic Peril."

[43] The plans outlined in this chapter and the one preceding it represented the major currents of thought on the question of an international organization. One other line of approach, though not significant enough for extended analysis, merits mention. A few writers took the view that the way to prevent war was simply to eliminate it entirely as an instrument of aggressive national policy. The idea cropped up occasionally in various projects whose major emphasis was on other matters, but two writers in particular made it the core of their proposals for the future. Differing on matters of detail, A. J. Jacobs and O. O. Maclagen both considered that war might be prevented by a worldwide defensive treaty designed to go immediately into operation in the event of aggression. Both believed that the security provided by such an arrangement would automatically lead to the reduction of armaments. Neither gave much attention to the development of international legislation to cope with the causes of war. Neither, so far as the evidence shows, attracted many supporters in Great Britain for this particular scheme. Cf. A. J. Jacobs, *Neutrality versus Justice* (London, 1917) and O. O. Maclagen, *Mutual Defense of Nations* (London, 1915).

III

Propaganda for a League
of Nations

THE FABIAN SOCIETY was concerned with many more problems than those connected with a league of nations; the Bryce
Group was essentially a study circle; while the Union of Democratic Control directed most of its efforts to the advocacy of a
parliamentary check on the conduct of foreign affairs. The first
organization devoted exclusively to the public promotion of the
league concept in Great Britain was the League of Nations
Society. Late in the war another group, called the League of
Free Nations Association, was set up, and in November, 1918,
the two were finally merged as the League of Nations Union.

THE LEAGUE OF NATIONS SOCIETY

In the early part of the war a small group of people, including Sir Willoughby H. Dickinson, G. Lowes Dickinson, Raymond Unwin, J. A. Hobson, Mrs. E. Claremont, and Aneurin
Williams, met at the home of Mr. Walter Rea to discuss plans
for promoting the idea of a league of nations. From this nucleus
a membership of several thousand was built up, and on May 3,
1915, the League of Nations Society was formally constituted.
Lord Shaw of Dunfermline was secured as president, and W. H.
Dickinson and Aneurin Williams, both members of parliament,
were chosen to act as chairman and treasurer respectively.[1]

[1] H. G. Wells, *Experiment in Autobiography*, p. 593; E. M. Forster,
op. cit., p. 166; Gilbert Murray, "The British People and the League of

The new organization adopted a program which involved a general acceptance of the following objects:

1. That a Treaty shall be made as soon as possible whereby as many States as are willing shall form a League binding themselves to use peaceful methods for dealing with all disputes arising among them.
2. That such methods shall be as follows:
   (a) All disputes arising out of questions of international law or the Interpretation of Treaties shall be referred to the Hague Court of Arbitration, or some other Judicial Tribunal, whose decisions shall be final and shall be carried into effect by the parties concerned.
   (b) All other disputes shall be referred to and investigated and reported upon by a Council of Inquiry and Conciliation: the Council to be representative of the States which form the League.
3. That the States which are members of the League shall unite in any action necessary for insuring that every member shall abide by the terms of the Treaty.
4. That the States which are members of the League shall make provision for Mutual Defense, diplomatic, economic, or military, in the event of any of them being attacked by a State, not a member of the League, which refuses to submit the case to an appropriate Tribunal or Council.
5. That any civilized State desiring to join the League shall be admitted to membership.[2]

Nations," in Munch, *op. cit.*, I, 194. There are brief accounts of the propaganda for a League in two French studies of the League, J. Tchernoff, *Les Nations et la S.D.N. dans la politique moderne* (Paris, 1919), pp. 62–65, and J. F. Charvet, *L'Influence britannique dans la S.D.N., des origines de la S.D.N. jusqu'à nos jours* (Paris, 1938), pp. 13–30. The latter volume repeats rather haphazardly some of the fairly vague generalities of the former.

[2] *The League of Nations Society. Explanation of the Objects of the Society* ("League of Nations Society Publications," No. 2. "Printed for Private Circulation") (London, 1916), p. 4. Hereafter publications of the League of Nations Society will be cited by the symbol LNS; those of the League of Free Nations Association by LFNA; and those of the League of Nations Union by LNU.

These proposals differed from those of the Bryce Group in several significant ways, despite the fact that a number of founders of the society were connected with that group. They more nearly resembled the Fabian plan in providing for the application of sanctions against a member refusing to accept an award in justiciable disputes. The operation of the league in compelling an outside power to use league machinery was much more clearly outlined. In general, however, the proposal was purposely vague. The definition of a "civilized" state, for example, was not attempted. Actual constitution of the council of inquiry and conciliation was not detailed. The precise nature of the sanctions to be applied in any particular case was left to the future. The Society was interested in spreading the idea of a league, and thereby promoting discussion from which detailed plans might stem. In addition, it was hoped that such a general plan might be found acceptable to the existing governments. For, as a privately-circulated explanation of the objects of the Society pointed out, any scheme, however perfect it might be in itself, was of no immediate value unless those governments were willing to accept and apply it.[3]

The League of Nations Society moved slowly during the first two years of the war. Popular attitudes in that period were not conducive to any widespread acceptance of its cause. There was little outright opposition to the idea of a league as yet, but there was just as little general interest. The "quiet but not ineffective" propaganda of the Society found its chief success among a number of members of Parliament, publicists, writers, clergymen, social workers, and the like.[4] Officials of the group kept in constant touch with the American League to Enforce Peace,[5] spoke before small groups interested in the idea,[6] and

[3] *Ibid.*, p. 25.

[4] Murray, "The British People and the League of Nations," in Munch, *op. cit.*, I, 194; Theodore Marburg, to W. H. Short, September 11, 1916, in Latané, *op. cit.*, I, 157.

[5] See Latané, *op. cit.* I., pp. 59, 83–85, 98, 158, 294–295.

[6] Forster, *op. cit.*, p. 168.

occasionally addressed letters to the press outlining the purposes in mind.[7]

The executive committee of the Society carried on its propaganda chiefly by means of the distribution of literature until well past the end of 1916.[8] The provisions of arbitration treaties drawn up by certain states were outlined as an indication of the foundations upon which a general treaty for all the nations might be built. Addresses delivered before the Society itself were published, along with pamphlets reiterating the major aims of the group and pointing out how a league could be brought into being.[9]

Not until early in 1917, however, when the entrance of the United States into the war seemed only a matter of time, were conditions thought to be good for a really vigorous campaign to gain popular backing. The active propaganda of the Society was directed into a few main channels. Mass meetings were sponsored at which prominent public men outlined the desirability and discussed the organization of a league. Conferences were held at which such groups as church leaders or members of the legal profession were encouraged to consider the idea from their own particular points of view. The Society continued to publish a large number of pamphlets, some of which demonstrated the growing acceptance of the league idea in all sectors of the population, while others offered specific proposals for

[7] *E.g.*, letter of W. H. Dickinson and Aneurin Williams to the editor, *The Times*, November 3, 1918; statement of the society, *Westminster Gazette*, February 2, 1917.

[8] *Proceedings of the First Annual Meeting Held at the Caxton Hall, July 20th, 1917* (LNS, No. 16) (London, 1917), p. 8.

[9] *Treaty between the United Kingdom and the United States of America with regard to the Establishment of a Peace Commission* (LNS, No. 4); *The Treaty between the Argentine Republic, the United States of Brazil, and Chile* (LNS, No. 5); *An Address Delivered by the Right Honourable Lord Shaw of Dunfermline at a General Meeting of the Society, 15th December, 1916* (LNS, No. 7); Aneurin Williams, *A League of Nations: How to Begin It* (LNS, No. 8); *How to Prevent War* (LNS, No. 10) (all published in London, 1917).

international organization devised by individual members. At the same time, it attempted to digest and collate the various plans suggested, finally arriving at an official scheme of organization which was published in September, 1918.

American participation in the war actually did open the way for a tremendous expansion in the activities of the League of Nations Society. It was possible to stimulate interest in the organization by pointing out that the parallel American League to Enforce Peace was not only patriotic beyond reproach, but that it had even been addressed by President Wilson, who had come to the support of the idea of a society of states after the war. Partly for this reason, when the Society sponsored its first mass meeting on May 14, 1917, it was a huge success.[10] Central Hall, Westminster, was crowded, and the speakers represented an impressive section of influential opinion. Lord Bryce was in the chair, and the principal speakers were the Archbishop of Canterbury and General Jan Smuts. Lord Buckmaster and Lord Hugh Cecil also spoke.

The meeting was called not to discuss the various plans for a league, but only to consider its general aims, in order that the British people might understand and come to support them. In introducing the speakers, Lord Bryce indicated that those aims were two in number. First, the recasting of a body of rules to define international rights and to create some means of enforcing them. And second, the creation of a combination of peace-loving states which would seek to substitute for war methods of arbitration and conciliation. Whether the prospects for the success of such a scheme were good or bad, it must be tried. The alternative was a period like that prior to 1914, a period of suspicion, anxiety, or alarm.

General Smuts followed Bryce on the platform and moved the following resolution:

> That it is expedient in the interests of mankind that some machinery should be set up after the present war for the purpose

[10] Carolina E. Playne, *Britain Holds On, 1917, 1918* (London, 1933), p. 80.

of maintaining international rights and general peace, and this meeting welcomes the suggestions put forward for this purpose by the President of the United States and other influential statesmen in America and commends to the sympathetic consideration of the British peoples the idea of forming a union of the free nations for the preservation of permanent peace.

In presenting the resolution, Smuts took up a number of the problems connected with the league idea. Cautioning against attempting too much, he declared that none of the schemes thus far elaborated appeared very practicable. But whatever the international organization devised, it must have certain elements if it were to succeed. It must be a union with force behind it and which was bound to use force when the occasion arose. In addition to a court of law and a police force, it must have a periodic conference or other institution to provide legal means of changing the *status quo*. It must be accompanied by disarmament, for there would be no use trying to prevent war when the nations were armed to the teeth. Finally, provisions for such an organization must be included in the peace treaty drawn up after the war.

Other speakers touched upon still other aspects of the problem. Lord Buckmaster in particular brought up a touchy subject when he argued that without the inclusion of Germany in the league it would merely be another form of the old, discredited alliance system. The argument required considerable courage, for many of the advocates of a league apparently considered it merely as a guarantee against future German aggression. In any event, at the close of the session the resolution proposed by General Smuts and seconded by the Archbishop of Canterbury was carried unanimously.[11]

[11] *Report of Meeting, May 14, 1917. Speeches Delivered by Viscount Bryce, O. M., General Smuts, the Archbishop of Canterbury, Lord Buckmaster, Lord Hugh Cecil, M.P., and Others* (LNS, No. 2) (London, 1917), pp. 3–13, 16–17; *The Times*, May 15, 1917. General Smuts' speech is also reproduced as "A League of Nations" in his *War-Time Speeches: a Compilation of Public Utterances in Great Britain* (New York, 1917).

The meeting fulfilled all the hopes of the League of Nations Society. It was widely reported in the press,[12] and in some areas elicited very favorable comment.[13] The fact that men of such prominence had supported the idea almost inevitably helped gain a hearing for the project. The various speeches were printed by the Society and circulated as part of its pamphlet series.[14]

The May 14 gathering pointed the way to a number of other meetings in the subsequent months. None of them was quite so huge an affair, but many were attended by men in public life. Among the speakers at various meetings, for example, were C. A. McCurdy and Major David Davies, both Members of Parliament, and the economists, Sir George Paish and Hartley Withers. Meanwhile, a series of conferences on the subject of a league was arranged. In July, 1917, two such important gatherings were held, one a meeting of clergymen, the other a conference of lawyers. In the first two months of 1918, other panel discussions were arranged, including one for various associations of educators held at University College, and another for women in industry.

The interdenominational conference of religious leaders which met on July 17, 1917, was mainly concerned with the moral basis of a future league. The Bishop of Oxford, who presided, pointed to the tremendous strides democratic feeling was making in the world as a sure foundation for success. Most of those present at the meeting, among whom were Dean Inge, the Reverend William Temple, and the Reverend J. E. Roberts, agreed that Germany must not be kept out of the league. A resolution was passed in favor of appointing a small committee

[12] *The Times, Manchester Guardian, Westminster Gazette,* all of May 15, 1917.

[13] *Westminster Gazette,* May 15, 1917; *Daily News and Leader,* May 17, 1917.

[14] *Report of Meeting, May 14, 1917.* Also in *A Handbook for Speakers on a League of Nations* ("Compiled by the League of Nations Society") (London, 1918).

to work as an auxiliary to the League of Nations Society in promoting the league principle in the churches. Subsequently the committee was formed and took the lead in directing the thought of religious leaders to the achievement of peace through international organization.[15]

The meeting of the representatives of the legal profession was presided over by Lord Parmoor, later to be one of the few Labor Lords in Parliament. Among those in attendance were Lord Shaw of Dunfermline, president of the Society, Lord Buckmaster, who had spoken at the May 14 meeting, Sir Frederick Pollock, who had already published his views in support of a league,[16] and Sir Walter Phillimore, chairman of an unpublicized governmental committee studying the various projects for a league.

The lawyers were in substantial agreement as to the type of league that would be necessary to keep the peace. Lords Pollock, Parmoor, and Shaw all pointed out that for the settlement of justiciable disputes a real court, with full legal power, was required, not merely a board of arbitration. Lords Parmoor and Shaw also held that without disarmament a viable league was impossible. The only dissent from this view came from Sir Walter Phillimore who argued that the line between justiciable and non-justiciable disputes was so thin that it would be more practicable merely to compel submission of disputes for mediation, conciliation, or judgment, with sanctions to be applied only in the case of failure to submit the question. This idea, closely resembling the published plan of the Bryce Group, presaged the approach that was later to be taken by Phillimore's committee in its report to the British cabinet.

Some disagreement was evident in the discussion of member-

[15] *Second Annual Report, March 1917–March 1918, As Approved at the Annual Meeting, June 14, 1918* (LNS, No. 38) (London, 1918), pp. 6–7; *The Times,* July 18, 1917.

[16] Sir Frederick Pollock, "What of the League of Nations?" *Fortnightly Review,* C (1916), 895–904; *idem,* "The Difficulties of the League of Peace," *The New Europe,* II (1917), 112–114.

ship in a league. Lord Parmoor insisted that unless all countries could join if they so desired, the world would inevitably
be divided into two hostile camps. In refutation, Sir Frederick
Pollock remarked that he would never trust a Germany that remained under its present system of government. Regardless of
such differences of opinion, there was enough agreement on the
general desirability of a league to prompt an all but unanimous
acceptance of a resolution proposed by Lord Buckmaster to the
effect that "this meeting desires to assist in formulating a practicable scheme in accordance with the principles of the League
of Nations to maintain international peace and justice after the
war." The League of Nations Society then reproduced the discussion at the conference in a pamphlet which was circulated as
a contribution to the development of a practical plan of organization.[17]

During 1917 and 1918 a wide range of pamphlet material appeared under the sponsorship of the Society. The society itself
did not take responsibility for the views expressed in articles
signed by their authors. These individual contributions considered the league of nations project from various standpoints,
and all were designed to help clarify popular thinking on the
proposals. For example, Sir Francis Younghusband, of Tibet
renown, and Leonard S. Woolf pointed to the breakdown of international suspicion as perhaps the greatest gain to be expected from a league. Younghusband emphasized that no
league would succeed, unless it could gradually develop a sense
of the "community of nations." Woolf approached the question
from a slightly different angle by arguing that the league itself,
in providing for a guarantee against aggressive war, would also
lay the foundations of an organization of states based on permanent international cooperation rather than on hostility and
competition. H. N. Spalding agreed that the most important

[17] *Report of a Conference of the Legal Profession (Convened by the
League of Nations Special Conference Committee) to Discuss: "The
Possibility of a Durable Settlement by means of a League of Nations"*
(LNS, No. 17) (London, 1917), pp. 2–3, 5, 8–9, 11–12, 14, 19.

guarantee of the effectiveness of the league was the good faith of its members, but nevertheless wanted to prepare for a possible breach of faith by the provision of adequate sanctions.[18]

Other pamphlets took such divergent approaches to the league question as a discussion of its economic background and a study of the relation of disarmament to a society of nations. The editor of *The Statist,* Sir George Paish, who had been interested in the league idea throughout the war, argued that the whole world had now become one economic family. In economic matters, one now thought not nationally, but internationally. Such economic interdependence was a trailblazer for the political cooperation represented in the creation of a league of nations. Sir Willoughby Dickinson related the problem of disarmament to the league of nations. Pointing out that without it the world would be no further forward than it was in 1914, he took the position that mutual disarmament depended on mutual security, upon the guarantee that a nation disarming in good faith would not be subject to aggression. Hence the first step toward disarmament would be to institute a league of nations standing together to restrain forcible aggression by one party against another. Such a league would also be of great value in helping determine the methods by which disarmament might be accomplished.[19]

Perhaps the most impressive of the booklets intended to encourage interest in a league was a compendium of articles gathered together in the summer of 1917 as *The Project of a League of Nations.* In this fair-sized volume an introductory

---

[18] Sir Francis Younghusband, *The Sense of a Community of Nations, an Address by Sir Francis Younghusband* (LNS, No. 13) (London, 1917), p. 5; Leonard S. Woolf, *A Durable Settlement after the War by Means of a League of Nations* (LNS, No. 21), p. 4; H. N. Spalding, *What a League of Nations Means* (LNS, No. 22) (London, 1918), pp. 4–5.

[19] Sir George Paish, *The Economic Interdependence of Nations* (LNS, No. 27) (London, 1918), p. 20; Sir W. H. Dickinson, *Disarmament and a League of Nations* (LNS, No. 28) (London, 1918), pp. 2, 4–8.

explanation of the objects of the League of Nations Society was followed by articles by G. P. Gooch and T. J. Lawrence, historian and international lawyer respectively. Gooch traced the growth of the concepts of the concert of Europe and the balance of power while Lawrence discussed the development of the use of international arbitration. Aneurin Williams then discussed the use of force by a league of nations in terms of a comparison of the views of the American League to Enforce Peace and the English League of Nations Society. With an obvious preference for the English plan he pointed out that it postulated the application of sanctions against a nation failing to accept a judicial decision and against an outside nation not willing to refer its disputes with a member to a peaceful hearing. Such a plan, of course, went far beyond the American proposal, which simply involved compulsory submission of quarrels for judgment or conciliation, but did not provide that any decision, even in justiciable cases, need be accepted. In a section on disarmament and the league, Sir Willoughby Dickinson took up his favorite theme that the security offered by a league of nations was the prerequisite of any effective disarmament. Still another chapter presented Leonard S. Woolf's argument for periodic conferences of the league as a means of developing international law and changing the *status quo* as the progress of the world required. The final sections of the volume sketched the plan of the American League to Enforce Peace and the league movement in neutral countries, traced the position of women in relation to the project, and discussed the connection of America with such a league. The collection was a relatively thorough study of many facets of the league idea, representing as it did the composite work of a number of competent students of the subject.[20]

[20] The articles were G. P. Gooch, "The Concert of Europe and the Balance of Power," pp. 5–7; T. J. Lawrence, "The Development of International Arbitration," pp. 7–10; Aneurin Williams, "The Use of Force by the League," pp. 11–12; W. H. Dickinson, "Reduction of Armaments and the League," pp. 12–13; L. S. Woolf, "Progress Without War," pp. 14–15;

These discussions of the various aspects of the league idea were paralleled by a series of pamphlets outlining a number of possible constitutions for the proposed organization. Particularly interesting were plans by two of the original founders of the Society, published in July and October of 1917 under the title *Schemes of International Organization.* In the first, Aneurin Williams sketched a league that contained the barest skeleton of machinery designed to provide means of helping maintain the peace. The second, by Raymond Unwin, was an elaborate outline of a league which provided for almost every conceivable detail of organization.

Williams based his argument for a "minimum of machinery" on the assumption that it would be difficult at first to get the nations to agree to any very elaborate organization. Especially unlikely was the acceptance of a permanent conference with power to call upon the members to make war. Such a body would be regarded as a super-state, impairing the sovereignty of the existing national states. As a consequence, he proposed a constitution in the following terms:

(A) A Tribunal in permanent session to hear all complaints, give judgment in justiciable disputes and communicate to all the Member States any breach of the Treaty.

(B) A Council of Conciliation to be summoned as required, but having its Bureau in permanent session as a watching body ready to offer its good offices.

(C) The Ambassadors accredited by the Member States to The Hague to act as:

　(1) The representatives of their countries in their dealings with the Council and Tribunal; and

　(2) When the Tribunal or Council has become seized of a dispute, or a breach of the Treaty has been declared by the Tribunal, to act as a Council of Ambassadors,

---

Noel Buxton, "America and the League," pp. 15–17; Theodore Marburg, "The American League to Enforce Peace," pp. 17–21; Dr. DeJong Van Beek En Donk, "The Movement in Neutral Countries," pp. 21–25; Mrs. Creighton, "The Women's Movement and the League," pp. 25–26.

constituting a centre of communication between the Member States.

(D) A Conference, or Parliament, of the League called to-gether from time to time to suggest amendments in, and to codify International Law; and to consider and report upon International Questions of general character, *i.e.*, affecting or likely to affect all or many of the members.[21]

This brief outline actually contained almost all the elements of more elaborate plans. Its chief note of caution was to make of the conference a temporary body, called together from time to time to take up questions of international relations, but not designed to serve as a central organ of the permanent league machinery.

The plan presented by Unwin was considerably more de-tailed and complex. He defined the four main functions that must be provided for as (1) the consultative or quasi-legisla-tive, (2) the administrative, (3) the judicial, and (4) the con-ciliatory. To perform the first function, Unwin proposed a con-ference, in accordance with the suggestions in the "Objects of the League of Nations Society." But he warned that such a conference must come to final decisions and agreements, not merely act as a debating body. Once agreements had been reached they should be embodied in a law or treaty. But for the time being each state must have the right to veto any such law or treaty—hence the term, "quasi-legislative." In keeping with the realities of the international situation, representation in the conference should be weighted in favor of the major powers.

Administratively, it was necessary to provide for carrying on of the affairs of the league, arranging for intercourse, common action, and for the execution of any of its decrees. Since the legislative conference seemed to be the best body for handling such tasks, Unwin suggested that it control the administrative functions of the league, and that when the conference was not

[21] Aneurin Williams, *The Minimum of Machinery. Schemes of Inter-national Organization No. I* (LNS, No. 18) (London, 1917), pp. 1, 6.

in session such functions should be handled by an administrative committee appointed by the conference and responsible to it.

A judicial court, elected from among themselves by a group of candidates named by the member states, was to be set up to deal with interpretation of international treaties or laws, and to administer justice based upon them. But such a court of judges trained to decide questions strictly on the basis of law or agreement might not be suitable to handle non-justiciable disputes. Therefore, a council of conciliation was to attempt to compose such difficulties and in the event of failure to issue a report stating the settlement it would recommend as most expedient and fair. Detailed provisions were made for cooperation between conference, court, and council.[22] These provisions were an addition to the shorter plan outlined by Aneurin Williams, and the idea of an administrative committee, however limited in scope, went beyond the use of the ambassadors at The Hague for carrying out certain permanent duties of the league. But the main elements of the project still remained three bodies to settle justiciable disputes, offer mediation or conciliation in non-justiciable disputes, and occasionally to meet to consider questions of international law. Unwin's court, council, and conference were merely Williams' tribunal, council, and conference "writ large."

Other projects were publicized by the Society from time to time. In April, 1918, for example, a reprint appeared of the draft convention prepared by a private group in America under Theodore Marburg, based on the program of the American League to Enforce Peace.[23] A month later a scheme devised by Major David Davies was published. The Davies plan provided for a league in the conventional terms, but in addition made

[22] Raymond Unwin, *Functions of a League of Nations. Schemes of International Organization No. II* (LNS, No. 19) (London, 1917), pp. 2–10.

[23] *Tentative Draft Convention by an American Committee, Schemes of International Organization No. III* (LNS, No. 30) (London, 1918).

certain suggestions for an immediate start in its constitution. The author proposed the calling together of a convention or standing advisory council of the Allied governments to prepare a practical and workable scheme for postwar international relations. In this way the league would grow out of the cooperation of Allied—and neutral—nations during the war. In order to be successful it must be based upon a just settlement at the end of the war, and must have the necessary powers, economic, diplomatic, and military, to enforce its decisions.[24] The project of Major Davies was one of the first guns in the campaign for a "league now" which was soon to grow to considerable proportions in England.

Still another group of League of Nations Society pamphlets, published for the most part in 1918, pressed home the idea that public support for an association of nations was rapidly increasing. In February, 1918, for example, a collection of extracts from the resolutions of labor organizations and the speeches of labor leaders was compiled. The extracts, an introduction by the Society pointed out, demonstrated a strong and wide labor demand in all countries for a league. It warned that the Second International, though important to labor, could not take its place as some of the more extreme working-class organizations were of course rightly suspected of believing.[25]

A similar booklet was prepared to show church support. It indicated that by June, 1918, an impressive list of church organizations had passed resolutions in favor of a league. Included were the upper and lower houses of the Convocation of Canterbury, the National Council of the Evangelical Free Churches, the Baptist Union of Great Britain and Ireland, the Congregational Union of England and Wales, the Wesleyan Conference, the Chief Rabbi's Committee of London Ministers, and the British and Foreign Unitarian Association. Particularly

[24] Major David Davies, *Some Problems of International Reconstruction and a League of Nations* (LNS, No. 31) (London, 1918), pp. 2, 4.

[25] *The Demand of Labour for a League of Nations* (LNS, No. 25), pp. 1–2.

striking sermons on the league were occasionally reproduced as
well.[26] Nor was the backing of men in public life permitted to
go unnoticed. *World-Wide Support for a League of Nations*
listed a large number of statesmen in England, Allied, enemy,
and neutral countries who had expressed themselves in sym-
pathy with the league idea. In addition, it reiterated the position of the various religious and labor groups whose views had
been outlined in special pamphlets.[27]

While carrying on so extensive a propaganda for a league
during 1917 and 1918, the Society at the same time endeavored
to arrive at an official scheme for international organization. At
the time of the first great public gathering in May, 1917, the
only meeting of minds among the Society's members was on
general objectives. There was as yet no real agreement with
reference to the detailed machinery necessary to carry those
objectives into effect.[28]

The difficulty of reaching such agreement is revealed by a
partial list of the members who attended the first annual meeting of the Society on July 20, 1917. Among those present were
Sir Willoughby Dickinson, Lord Parmoor, Aneurin Williams,
Sir Francis Younghusband, Noel Buxton, G. Lowes Dickinson,
F. N. Keen, Raymond Unwin, Leonard S. Woolf, Delisle Burns,
A. E. Zimmern, and J. A. Hobson. Each of these men had published—or would indicate later in the war—his views as to the
constitution of a league of nations. In almost every case, the
author had a favored idea or a particular emphasis which he
considered imperative, but which the others looked upon with
indifference. J. A. Hobson thought in terms of full-blown international government; Aneurin Williams, of a league of very

[26] *The Demand of the Churches for a League of Nations* (LNS,
No. 33) (London, 1918), pp. 6–9; Father Paul B. Bull, *Sermon on "The
League of Nations" Preached at Holy Trinity, Sloane Street, on July 7th,
1918* (LNS, No. 41) (London, 1918).

[27] *World-Wide Support for a League of Nations* (LNS, No. 34)
(London, 1918), pp. 2–6.

[28] W. H. Dickinson to Theodore Marburg, May 17, 1917, in Latané,
op. cit., I, 302.

limited liability. Sir Willoughby Dickinson wanted a system that should delay the outbreak of war; Alfred Zimmern preferred a treaty that made war a crime in any circumstances.

Despite such fundamental divergences, the members at the July meeting found it possible to make certain changes in the "Objects of the Society." There was general agreement on the proposition that the projected league must use force—whether economic or military—to compel resort to league machinery. Clause 3 had merely read: "That the States which are members of the League shall unite in any action necessary for insuring that every member shall abide by the terms of the Treaty." It was now made more concrete by the addition of the words ". . . and in particular shall jointly use forthwith their economic and military forces against any one of their number that goes to war, or commits acts of hostility against another, before any question arising shall be submitted as provided in the foregoing articles." In addition it was felt that the new international body should be used for the purpose of developing international legislation, though of course there was no complete understanding as to the extent of such legislative functions. The result was a new clause advocating conferences to take up the problem, but not supporting a permanent conference to deal with international law on a day-to-day basis. The clause provided

> That Conferences between members of the League shall be held from time to time to consider international matters of a general character, and to formulate and codify rules of international law, which, unless some member shall signify its dissent within a stated period, shall thereafter govern in the decisions of the Judicial Tribunal mentioned in Article 2(a).[29]

During the next year a "Basis Sub-Committee" was appointed to draft a scheme of league organization. Its members were Raymond Unwin, F. N. Keen, G. Lowes Dickinson, A. W.

---

[29] *Proceedings of the First Annual Meeting,* pp. 5, 11–13.

Claremont, and Lord Parmoor.[30] The sub-committee studied a number of independent projects, some of them published by the Society, and at last prepared a very detailed plan for a league of nations. This scheme of organization was published by the Society in September, 1918, with an introduction by Sir Willoughby Dickinson that was careful to point out that the project "does not profess to be more than the result of the labour of a few individuals and is not put forward as an authorised or even a considered scheme by the League of Nations Society." [31] Nevertheless, since a formal sub-committee had drafted the plan, it was the nearest approximation to a set of official proposals to be offered by the Society during the course of the war.

Like some projects discussed in previous sections of this volume, the *Scheme of Organisation* kept its eyes firmly on a continuance of national sovereignty. It merely aimed at correlating with such a system a "system of united international effort" for certain limited purposes. At the same time, it attempted to provide machinery so elastic that it might develop as nations became accustomed to its operations and gained confidence in its efficacy.

The proposals called for a league made up of four organs: a supreme court, a council of conciliation, a conference, and an administrative committee. The supreme court was to be composed of fifteen judges, selected by the conference from candidates proposed by the states for a term of nine years. The functions of the court were similar to those provided for in plans such as those of the Bryce Group or of Raymond Unwin. One representative from each state was to be appointed to the council of conciliation, whose functions, in addition to investi-

[30] *Second Annual Report,* p. 13.
[31] *League of Nations: Scheme of Organisation Prepared by a Sub-Committee of the League of Nations Society, 1918, with a Foreword by the Rt. Hon. Sir W. H. Dickinson, M.P.* (LNS, No. 42) (London, 1918), p. 1.

gation and conciliation of disputes referred to it by the parties concerned, were also to include dealing with questions handed over to it by the supreme court.

Membership in the proposed conference was to be allotted by a weighted scheme which gave greater representation to the more populous states. The conference was to meet once in three years, unless a special meeting was called at the request of five members. The conference was to be given the task of appointing judges to the supreme court, examining treaties for possible alteration or development, and preparing and submitting international laws for acceptance by the states. It should also appoint an administrative committee, consisting of the two leading officials of the conference and nineteen other members.

The administrative committee was charged with the actual day-to-day work of the league. Its functions included the management of the funds of the league and the collection and preservation of all information, statistics, documents that might assist the league to discharge its duties, to keep in touch with the member states and set in motion the machinery provided for dealing with war or the threat of war.[32]

Such machinery was based upon an elaboration of the original objects of the League of Nations Society, which had in turn been heavily influenced by the work of the Bryce Group. The members of the league were asked to undertake the following obligations:

(a) To refer to the Supreme Court of the League for final decision, all disputes among them arising out of questions of international law or the interpretation of treaties or otherwise of a justiciable character, and to carry into effect the decisions of the Court.

(b) To refer to the Council of Conciliation of the League for investigation and report, all disputes among members of the League other than those that are referable to the Supreme Court as aforesaid.

[32] *Ibid.*, pp. 3–4, 10, 16–18, 20–24.

(c) To unite in any action necessary for ensuring that every member shall abide by the terms of the Treaty.

(d) To support the League in enforcing the decision of the Supreme Court against any member of the League failing to carry it into effect.

(e) To jointly use forthwith both their economic and their military forces against any member that goes to war or commits acts of hostility against another member either (i) before any dispute arising shall have been referred to and decided by the Supreme Court, or in defiance of any decision or order of the Court, or (ii), in the case of a dispute referable to the Council of Conciliation, until the expiration of six calendar months after the publication of the final report of the Council.

(f) To co-operate in making provision for mutual defence, diplomatic, economic, and military, in the event of any member being attacked by a State not a member of the League, which refuses to submit its case to an appropriate Court or Council.

(g) To register with the League all Treaties to which they are parties.[33]

This latest scheme presented by the League of Nations Society was, then, in most respects simply a restatement of the conventional plan for a limited league. In two areas, however, it did reveal a considerable advance in thought. A permanent conference, meeting regularly every three years, was probably more likely to develop effective functions than a body called together "from time to time." And the administrative committee, like the international secretariat of the Fabian Society, was now conceived as a permanent body with important duties instead of as a mere temporary committee serving when other organs of the league had adjourned.

On the whole, however, the plans of the League of Nations Society were probably less important than its propaganda. In the meetings which it sponsored, and particularly in the material it published, the Society kept the idea of a league before

[33] *Ibid.*, pp. 13–14.

the public. How effective its work was is virtually impossible to determine, but it is clear, as later discussion will indicate, that by the middle of 1918 the idea of a league had achieved support in almost all circles of British life. Meanwhile, another organization, also concerned with a league of nations, but somewhat impatient with the methods of approach favored by the League of Nations Society, was developing. This group, the League of Free Nations Association, was to unite with the Society at the very end of the war. The two formed the League of Nations Union whose activity continued down to the demise of the league itself.

FROM THE LEAGUE OF FREE NATIONS ASSOCIATION TO
THE LEAGUE OF NATIONS UNION

Early in 1918 a movement was launched to establish another society for the propagation of league of nations ideas. The leaders in this drive were two members of Parliament, Charles A. McCurdy, Liberal Coalitionist supporter of the Lloyd George government, and Major David Davies, a Liberal of the Asquith school. These men felt that the League of Nations Society tended to be viewed as a fad of liberal and religious idealists.[34] They hoped to put the league idea on a strictly practicable plane. They took the position that a militarist, autocratic Germany could have no part in any international organization. Only a defeated and democratized Germany would be acceptable. Therefore, they proceeded to advocate the immediate setting up of a "League of Nations" by the Allies, as a nucleus for a future more inclusive body.

In a series of letters to the press, McCurdy developed the thesis that the first step must be taken by the Allied states. The formation of a league would strengthen the morale of the Allied peoples and would help divide opinion in Germany. If it should prove impossible to make such a beginning among friends and

[34] Murray, "The British People and the League of Nations," in Munch, *op. cit.*, I, 194.

allies, then it would be better to dismiss the idea completely, for certainly the Hohenzollerns were not going to support a real league of nations to limit armaments and prevent war.[35] Major Davies outlined similar views in a pamphlet published by the League of Nations Society, and others joined in making the same argument.[36]

In short order a committee was organized, which included not only Liberal and Labor party members like Major Davies, J. A. Spender, Gilbert Murray, H. G. Wells, and J. H. Thomas, but Liberal Coalitionists like McCurdy and Sir Mark Sykes, and even more conservative journalists like Wickham Steed and J. L. Garvin. Finally, in July, a new society came into being called the League of Free Nations Association. Preparations had already been made for the setting up of a research committee, and the new group undertook to study the possibilities of achieving a league while the war was still in progress.[37] Many members of the League of Nations Society objected to the new scheme on the ground that it would defeat the whole object of a league by making it practically certain that the Central Powers would never join after the war. Others simply feared to risk dividing the league movement on the question of present political tactics, whatever their own views on the subject.[38]

In any event, the League of Free Nations Association made its public debut at a conference held at Northampton on Sep-

[35] *Daily News and Leader*, January 25, 1918; *Daily Chronicle*, March 16, 1918; *Morning Post*, March 20, 1918.

[36] See, for example, Davies, *Some Problems of International Reconstruction and a League of Nations* and letter of John Galsworthy to editor, *Daily News and Leader*, March 1, 1918.

[37] Murray, "The British People and the League of Nations," in Munch, *op. cit.*, I, 194–195; Geoffrey Wells, *H. G. Wells* (New York, 1930), p. 204; League of Nations Society, *Monthly Report of Members. No. 10* (October, 1918), pp. 4–5; letter of H. G. Wells to editor, *Daily Chronicle*, June 22, 1918.

[38] *New Statesman*, XI (1918), 283; League of Nations Society, *Monthly Report* (October, 1918), p. 5.

tember 13. McCurdy and Davies both spoke, and in the evening Lord Bryce addressed the conference. He stated that the settlement of disputes by arbitration and conciliation was possible only if a sufficient number of strong powers were willing to use their united strength against any disturber of the peace, warning that the league must not be used merely as a weapon against Germany. For example, the economic boycott, which was imperative for the success of the league, must be reserved for the purpose of checking aggression. The threat of economic war could be used to ensure a just peace, argued Bryce. Why then throw away that weapon by announcing that the boycott would be applied against Germany in any case? Such an attitude would again provoke rather than prevent conflict. Whether or not the founders of the Association took the warning of Lord Bryce to heart, they addressed a memorandum to the press, describing the inaugural meeting and pointing out the aims of the group.[39]

In September, too, an official pamphlet was issued outlining in considerable detail the new plan for a league of nations. According to the pamphlet, the Association realized that the league of free nations must be a world league, but wanted the present Allies to set up the provisional framework with a view to the eventual inclusion of states at present neutral or hostile. Germany could not be admitted, since the plan was based on the thesis that only free, democratic nations could be trusted to discharge the obligations. "To such a League," the pamphlet stated, "a liberalised and democratised Germany, no longer war-proud and war greedy, will be welcomed as a member; of such a League a militarist, autocratic Germany can form no part."

The objects of the Association went considerably beyond

[39] *The Times,* September 14, 1918; *Morning Post,* September 19, 1918. Bryce's speech was later reproduced by the League of Nations Union as *War after War. The Inaugural Meeting of the League of Free Nations Association Held in the Town Hall, at Northampton on September 13th, 1918. Speech by Viscount Bryce* (LNU, Ser. 2, No. 13) (London, 1918).

those of the League of Nations Society. It proposed a league of free peoples determined to end war forever and willing to agree to the following program:

1. To submit all disputes arising between themselves to methods of peaceful settlement.
2. To suppress jointly, by the use of all means at their disposal, any attempts by any State to disturb the peace of the world by acts of war.
3. To create a Supreme Court, and to respect and enforce its decisions.
4. To establish a permanent Council to supervise and control armaments, to act as mediator in matters of difference not suitable for submission to the Supreme Court, to concert measures for joint action in matters political and economic affecting the rights and interests of members of the League.
5. To admit to the League on terms of equality all peoples able and willing to give effective guarantees of their loyal intentions to observe its covenants.[40]

Stripped of all excess verbiage, what this plan seemed to an advocate was an out-and-out ban on war, except for defense. The inclusion of point 2, providing for joint suppression of any attempts to disturb the peace of the world by acts of war, apparently meant that a recommendation of the council in cases of mediation was to be as enforceable as an award of the supreme court. Such an interpretation coincided with the views of the original advocate of a league of free nations. In an article for the *Daily News*, C. A. McCurdy wrote that a league must be based on the idea that "all aggressive war is a crime not to be tolerated by civilised peoples as an instrument for enforcing claims, however just." And again, in *War and Peace* he urged: "Let the Allies declare that for their part there shall never be

[40] "A British Organization to Promote an Active Propaganda for the Formation of a World League of Free Nations as the Necessary Basis of a Permanent Peace" (excerpt from "Official Pamphlet," September, 1918) in Latané, *op. cit.*, II, 818–819.

war between them any more, let them make that declaration in plain words incapable of misunderstanding." [41]

In respect to the council, also, the Association's project was more ambitious than that of its predecessor. A permanent council, supervising and controlling the military and naval forces and the armaments industries of the world, dealing with questions of transit, tariffs, access to raw materials, migration, health and international welfare generally,[42] went far beyond proposals for the discussion of possible changes in international law. Thus, while the membership of the league was to be limited—at the beginning at least—its functions were to be very wide in scope.

Despite the marked differences of approach between the Society and the Association, there were many members of both groups who felt that the league propaganda would be served by an amalgamation. As early as August, Gilbert Murray of the Association and G. Lowes Dickinson of the Society had inquired of Viscount Grey whether he would serve as President of a joint group. Grey acceded and negotiations were begun to attempt to find a common meeting ground. Representatives were appointed to meet at dinner at the National Liberal Club. Present for the Society were the two Dickinsons, J. A. Hobson, and Leonard Woolf. The Association sent C. A. McCurdy, Gilbert Murray, Wickham Steed, and H. G. Wells.[43] An exchange of views resulted in the preparation of a formal statement indicating the areas of agreement. The Association, perhaps because the war's end seemed imminent, consented to accept the view that a league of nations, in the full sense of the term, could not be formed until the close of hostilities. On the other hand, the Society agreed that the present Allies could formulate and accept the terms of a scheme under which such

[41] *Daily News and Leader,* May 2, 1918; C. A. McCurdy, "A League of Nations Now," *War and Peace,* V (1918), 289.

[42] "A British Organization," in Latané, *op. cit.,* II, 818.

[43] G. M. Trevelyan, *Grey of Fallodon* (London, 1937), p. 348; Forster, *op. cit.,* p. 169.

a league should be formed. "The most practical method," the statement declared, "would be for the Allies to form at once among themselves some organisation for the prevention of future wars." Such an organization might then expand into a league of nations after the war.[44]

The scheme arrived at retained the substance of the League of Nations Association plan, while offering a sop to the susceptibilities of the Society. Such at least was the view of some of the members of the latter organization, notably J. A. Hobson and Lord Parmoor.[45] But the plans for union went ahead, and a joint meeting was arranged for October 10.

On that day, Viscount Grey addressed a packed gathering at Central Hall, Westminster. Perhaps the greatest crowd at any public meeting during the war assembled to hear him break a silence of almost two years. He noted that he had never felt that a league of nations could be created during the war. The governments were too busy with immediate war problems to give the idea proper attention. But such a league must be instituted immediately after the peace. Delay beyond that would probably prejudice any chance of formation. Therefore it was imperative to work out plans for a league now, in order that they might be ready when the war ended. The former foreign minister then went on to treat some aspects of the question which had excited discussion. The league, as he saw it, must not be used as a weapon to isolate Germany. Neither the League of Nations Society nor the League of Free Nations Association wanted a league of Allied nations to coerce the vanquished foe. Germany must come in, but it must be a purified and democratized Germany. Disarmament could not be effected until Germany, the "great armer," had disarmed. The league might use its power of economic boycott against a nation advancing too far in armament building. But above all, the

[44] "Agreed Statement to a Common Policy in Regard to the Societies' Advocacy of the Creation of a League of Nations Amongst the Allies during the War, October, 1918," in Latané, *op. cit.*, II, 819–820.

[45] Forster, *op. cit.*, p. 170.

sense of security offered by the league would itself be an incentive to disarmament. Grey outlined a number of functions which the league might perform, and emphasized that such an organization was practicable because the world had now learned what its alternative meant.[46] All in all, the speech was a very successful step in the popularization of the idea of a league. Grey's comments were widely circulated in the press[47] and were favorably received, particularly, it goes without saying, among Liberal newspapers.[48] Pamphlet reprints were soon ready to take advantage of the interest aroused by such influential backing for the project, and the National War Aims Committee took cognizance of that interest by printing one million copies of the speech for free distribution.[49]

The October meeting signalized the virtual amalgamation of the two groups. The final details were ironed out at a conference held in November at Caxton Hall. In addition to Viscount Grey, Herbert Asquith, Arthur Balfour, and finally the prime minister agreed to be honorary presidents.[50] A formal statement was issued, explaining the basis upon which the new League of Nations Union had come into being. Its terms marked a virtually complete surrender on the part of the League of Nations Society. The agreement is worth quoting as illustrative of its close parallelism with the official program of the League of Free Nations Association. It provided

[46] *Daily Chronicle, The Times,* October 11, 1918.

[47] See, for example, *The Times, Manchester Guardian, Daily News and Leader, Daily Chronicle,* all of October 11, 1918.

[48] *Daily Chronicle, Daily News and Leader, Manchester Guardian,* October 11, 1918.

[49] *Viscount Grey on a League of Nations at a Meeting Held at Central Hall, Westminster, October 10, 1918* (LNS, No. 44) (London, 1918); *Viscount Grey Explains Why a League Is Necessary and What It Will Do* (LNU, Ser. 2, No. 19) (London, 1918); W. H. Dickinson and Gilbert Murray to editor, *Westminster Gazette,* November 2, 1918; *Grey's Message. The League of Nations* ("National War Aims Committee") (London, [1918]).

[50] *Westminster Gazette,* November 18, 1918; *The Times,* November 8, 1918; Murray, "The British People and the League of Nations," in Munch, *op. cit.,* I, 195.

I. That the name of the amalgamated society shall be the League of Nations Union.

A British organization founded to promote the formation of a World League of Free Peoples for the securing of international justice, mutual defence, and permanent peace.

Constituted by the union of the League of National Society and the League of Free Nations Association.

Associated with the American "League to Enforce Peace" and other kindred societies in the United Kingdom and abroad.

II. That the following be the general object of the union:

The establishment as soon as possible of a League of Free Peoples desirous of ending war forever and willing to agree:

1. To submit all disputes arising between themselves to methods of peaceful settlement.

2. To suppress jointly, by the use of all the means at their disposal, any attempt by any State to disturb the peace of the world by acts of war.

3. To create a Supreme Court, and to respect and enforce its decisions.

4. To establish a permanent Council, which shall provide for the development of international law, for the settlement of differences not suitable for submission to the Supreme Court, for the supervision and control of armament, and for joint action in matters of common concern.

5. To admit to the League all peoples able and willing to give effective guarantees of their loyal intention to observe its covenants, and thus to bring about such a world organisation as will guarantee the freedom of nations; act as trustee and guardian of uncivilised races and undeveloped territories; and maintain international order; and thus finally liberate mankind from the curse of war.[51]

The membership of the League of Nations Union was fairly small. At the time of its formation it comprised fewer than four thousand persons.[52] Like its constituent societies, the Union

[51] *Westminster Gazette,* November 18, 1918. The plan was also reproduced in *The League of Nations Union* (LNU, Ser. 2, No. 10) (London, 1918).

[52] Murray, "The British People and the League of Nations," in Munch, *op. cit.,* I, 195.

carried on its propaganda by means of a series of pamphlets. From about October until the peace conference met at Versailles a very large number of such leaflets appeared. They were small, concise, and simple. Few made any pretense of literary quality. And few compared with the pamphlets of the League of Nations Society for careful preparation and impressive format. Some of the Union's publications were outdated before they appeared. These included a number of pamphlets already in preparation by the League of Free Nations Association, advocating the formation of a "league now." [53] For with the end of the war, there could be genuine agreement that the time was ripe for a league. As a result, it was possible for the Union to concentrate upon explaining the nature of the proposed organization and gaining additional support for it.

Like the League of Nations Society, the Union adopted a number of approaches in its literature. One group of pamphlets, for example, traced the development of the idea of international cooperation and argued that such an idea was in harmony with the most passionate desires of the people of the world. [54] More concretely, it was pointed out that unless a league were set up, the expenses of armament would compel a drastic reduction of world standards of living. [55] Another group demonstrated that various ecclesiastical leaders were fully in accord with the movement for a league and called upon the church to

[53] Major David Davies, *Why Not Form the League Now?* (LFNA, Ser. 2, No. 2); *idem, Why an Association Is Necessary* (LFNA, Ser. 2, No. 6); Sir Henry Jones, *Form the League of Peace Now: an Appeal to My Fellow-Citizens* (LFNA, Ser. 2, No. 5); *A Great French Statesman Explains Why We Must Form the League of Nations Now* (LFNA, Ser. 2, No. 9); Arnold Bennett, *The Embargo v. the Gun* (LFNA, Ser. 2, No. 1) (all London, 1918).

[54] William Menzies Alexander, *League of Nations in History* (LNU, Ser. 2, No. 14) (London, [1918]); Silas K. Hocking, *The Moral Aspects of the League of Nations* (LFNA, Ser. 2, No. 8) (London, [1918]).

[55] Hartley Withers, *The Financial Aspect of a League of Nations* (LNU, Ser. 2, No. 11) (London, [1918]); H. E. Hyde, *The League of Nations and the Peace Conference,* pp. 4–5.

take up the cause and launch a crusade in its behalf.[56] A few
pamphlets looked to still other specific sections of the population—labor and women, for example—for support.[57]

Conventional explanations of the main features of the proposed league were of course included among the Union's publications.[58] Perhaps of the greatest significance was the fact that
a number of pamphlets came out squarely for an international
police force that should be able to carry out the decisions of
the new organization.[59] In general, supporters of such a police
force considered that it might be made up of contingents from
the member states, but that it must have unity of command, under the central world council, to be effective. "The need would
not be met by contingents summoned, however hastily, from
the several Powers *after* action was seen to be necessary." [60]
If munitions of war continued to be produced in national
arsenals, they must be under strict international supervision;
preferably, they should be manufactured in international factories. Nationally controlled armies and navies must be reduced
to a size sufficient to enable them to cope with internal police
problems only; the league "must have the only forces capable

[56] Rev. Edward S. Kiek, *Brotherhood and World Peace* (LNU. Ser.
2, No. 22); Rev. Daniel Lamont, *The Church and International Peace.
Substance of Presidential Address Delivered to the Glasgow College
Union by the Rev. Daniel Lamont, B.D., of Hillhead United Free Church,
Glasgow* (LNU, Ser. 2, No. 25); Archbishop of York, *The Need for a
League of Nations* (LNU, Ser. 2, No. 28); David Davies, *The Church and
the League of Nations* (LNU, Ser. 2, No. 17) (all London, [1918]).

[57] James Gribble, *Your Case, Mr. Workman. An Appeal to Labour*
(LNU, Ser. 2, No. 20) (London, [1918]); Irene McArthur, *Women and
the League of Nations* (LFNA, Ser. 2, No. 4) (London, [1918]).

[58] *The League of Nations Union;* John Clifford, *The League of Free
Nations: Facing the Facts* (LNU, Ser. 2, No. 18) (London, 1918);
Sir Harry R. Reichel, *"Why a League of Free Nations?"* (LNU, Ser. 2,
No. 21) (London, [1918]); Joseph Knight, *Leaguing the Nations. How?
What For?* (LNU, Ser. 2, No. 30) (London, [1918]).

[59] Hyde, *op. cit.;* Knight, *op. cit.;* F. Herbert Stead, *The Case for an
International Police Force* (LNU, Ser. 2, No. 17) (London, [1918]).

[60] Stead, *op. cit.,* p. 10.

of war as it is now understood." [61] Such proposals meant a
league armed with real power. In the hands of a body representative of most nations of the world, an international force
might be a real instrument of peace in security; controlled by
the exclusive league envisaged by many backers of the Union,
it could be used as a means of coercing a defeated and outlawed enemy of the powers originally making up that league.
In any case, it was clear that some of the leaders of the League
of Nations Union had discarded the fetish of integral national
sovereignty that hampered any attempt to think in truly international terms.

While carrying on its propaganda, the League of Nations
Union also addressed itself to a further study of the various
aspects of a league. A research committee, which had already
been projected by the League of Free Nations Association, was
accordingly set up. Its members constituted an impressive list
of men interested in international organization: Ernest Barker,
Lionel Curtis, G. Lowes Dickinson, Viscount Grey, John
Hilton, Gilbert Murray, H. Wickham Steed, J. A. Spender,
Leonard Woolf, William Archer, A. E. Zimmern, and H. G.
Wells. Many of the members, however, apparently did little or
no work while serving on the committee, [62] and it produced
only two studies before the Versailles conference was convened.

The first of these studies, *The Idea of a League of Nations,* [63]
pointed out that the choice before the world was simply that of
organization or destruction. Without a league, there would inevitably occur a race in armaments that would ultimately destroy civilization. As for the nature of world organization, the

[61] *Ibid.,* p. 4; Hyde, *op. cit.,* p. 10.
[62] Wells, *Experiment in Autobiography,* pp. 603–604.
[63] Research Committee of the League of Nations Union, *The Idea of
a League of Nations: Prologomena to the Study of World-Organization*
(London, [1918]). This study, with a few minor changes, was published
in the United States in the *Atlantic Monthly,* CXXIII (1919), 106–115,
and then by H. G. Wells and others, *The Idea of a League of Nations*
(Boston, 1919). Reference is to the Research Committee edition.

research committee tended to believe that a group of the most powerful states, "including perhaps a chastened Germany" and agreeing among themselves to organize and enforce peace, was the most probable of all immediate possibilities. In a section answering objections to the League, the warning was given that "Geneval Conventions and such palliative ordinances" made ultimately for the persistence of war as an institution. Only a real league of nations to prevent war could serve the needs of mankind.[64]

The second study was a detailed plan for the setting up of the league and a series of suggestions for its functions. The committee advocated that the peace conference itself should remain in existence as the new world organization instead of dissolving when its work was done. In the settlement of future disputes it could build upon the system adopted in existing arbitration treaties, especially the American treaties of 1914. Such a plan, of course, was the nucleus of the projects already outlined by the Fabians, the Bryce Group, and the league of nations societies themselves. As for guarantees, the committee moved more slowly than some of the other members of the Union. It reached no decision on the question of whether sanctions should be applied by an international force or simply by the deputized armies of the member states. Such a decision, it held, would eventually grow out of the experience of the future. What was important was that for the present there would be no difficulty in making the will of the conference respected. The nations there represented had an irresistible force at their disposal, thanks to efficient wartime organization.[65]

The pamphlet then went on to discuss a series of functions the league might assume in addition to settling the disputes of its members. It was recommended that the league should undertake supervision of all prewar international unions, ad-

[64] *Ibid.*, pp. 11, 17–18, 30.
[65] Research Committee of the League of Nations Union, *The Way to the League of Nations: a Brief Sketch of the Practical Steps Needed for the Formation of a League* (London, 1919), pp. 5–13.

minister some of the inter-Allied war organizations, and set up certain new administrative commissions. The latter were to include agencies for the supervision of undeveloped countries and for overseeing national administration of areas such as Equatorial Africa.[66] All in all, the committee envisaged an international body that would engage in widespread activities and exercise broad powers. Provisions for control of backward territories, for example, illustrated how far the ideas of the league of nations groups had developed since the formation of the original League of Nations Society in 1915.

The idea of a league of nations was kept before the public in various ways. Thus in December, 1918, during the general election, the press reported that the League of Nations Union had sent out a questionnaire to some 1,500 candidates for Parliament. By December 14, 538 candidates had expressed complete agreement with the league idea, one had dissented, and one was non-committal.[67] Again, when President Wilson arrived in England, a deputation from the Union waited upon him to offer their support in his fight for an international organization. The deputation included Viscount Grey, Herbert Asquith, Lord Bryce, Sir Willoughby Dickinson, and Gilbert Murray.[68]

By the end of 1918, the idea of a league of nations had "caught on." Perhaps the horrors of the war just ended, or perhaps the influence of Woodrow Wilson, had stimulated British interest. But in any case the league societies had contributed something to the result. The small League of Nations Society which had first met in 1915 had developed slowly, and until the last years of the war its activities were limited. Specific proposals, of the League of Free Nations Association as well as the League of Nations Society, had not stood the test of discussion and had been dropped or modified. But as the war went

[66] *Ibid.*, pp. 15–20.
[67] *The Times*, December 14, 1918.
[68] *Ibid.*, December 30, 1918.

on propaganda for the league as an idea had been expanded. By the time the League of Nations Union was formed some of the most important men in public life were associated with it. The idea had been "sold." What remained to be seen was how it would be implemented.

Individual Contributions to
the League Debate

THE VARIOUS SCHEMES outlined in the first chapters of this
study were not, of course, the only ones to appear in Great Britain. Nor was the work of the organized league of nations groups
carried on merely through their official meetings and propaganda. A great many individuals—some of them connected with
one or another of the groups, some of them acting entirely in-
dependently—also published plans and pleas for international
organization. Those plans and pleas appeared in the press, in
various periodicals, and in books separately issued during
the war years. Postponing a consideration of the first two for the
time being, the present chapter aims at a description of the
more important of the individual volumes dealing exclusively,
or at least significantly, with the league project. Most of them
followed substantially the lines laid down by the Bryce Group,
the Fabians, and the league of nations societies. Some dealt
with certain aspects of the question in somewhat greater detail.
And a few supported a severely limited league, but in half-
hearted fashion and with considerable reservation.

Probably the most active British individual in the drive for a
league of nations was the well-known classicist and political sci-
entist, Goldsworthy Lowes Dickinson. Not only was he a moving figure in the Bryce Group, the League of Nations Society,
and later the League of Nations Union, but throughout the war
he tried to reach the public with arguments and explanations to

strengthen his campaign. Those arguments and explanations varied, for Dickinson moved slowly toward his conception of what a league should be. Very early in the war, he published *The War and the Way Out,* in which he attacked the view that wars were inevitable and the states natural enemies. If Europe could be rearranged on the basis of nationality, he argued, the way would be open for a permanent league. To secure peace, the peoples of Europe must hand over their armaments, and the use of them for any purpose except the maintenance of order within their own frontiers, to an international authority. Such a league must then apportion armaments among the different nations according to their wealth, population, and resources, giving special consideration to geographical position. All disputes that might arise between members of the league must be settled by judicial process.[1]

In short order, Dickinson came to believe that he had perhaps gone too far in his first suggestion. The world was apparently not ready for control of armaments by an international body, nor for judicial settlement of all disputes. In 1915, therefore, he issued a little pamphlet which clearly showed the trend toward ideas later elaborated by the Bryce Group and the League of Nations Society. This time a court of arbitration was proposed for justiciable disputes, and a council of conciliation for all other cases. Military force and economic pressure were to be used to ensure submission of disputes, but no provision was made for the enforcement of an award of the court or of a recommendation of the council. If even a delay of a year could be gained, Dickinson felt, public opinion would in most instances not tolerate a war. Although limitation of armaments was desirable, it would most naturally grow out of the sense of security offered by a league, rather than precede its formation. But the success of the league would depend upon the number of peoples entering it. A league of Great Britain, Russia, and France would be a mere repetition of the present Entente; one

[1] G. Lowes Dickinson, *The War and the Way Out* (London, n.d.), pp. 34–37, 39–41.

joined by Italy and the United States would be better. Most to be desired, however, was the inclusion of the Germanic powers [2]—not a popular idea in 1915.

About a year later, *The European Anarchy* appeared. In this work, which was to go through numerous editions, Dickinson approached the problem of international organization from still another angle. By far the largest portion of the book was devoted to a long historical analysis of the diplomatic events leading to the outbreak of the war of 1914. The account hammered home the idea that war had become inevitable because no machinery was readily available for the peaceful settlement of disputes. The lesson to be learned was simple. Nations must agree to submit to law and to right for the settlement of their disputes. But the will to do so was not enough. As the separate colonies of America could not effectively unite until they had formed a constitution, so the nations of Europe and the world would be unable to maintain peace, even if all the world desired it, unless they constructed some kind of machinery to settle their disputes and backed that machinery by force.[3] *The European Anarchy* made no attempt to outline a detailed plan for a league, but it was a cogent and effective plea for its necessity.

The Choice Before Us filled in the details which had been omitted in *The European Anarchy.* This volume contained by far Dickinson's most fully worked out explanation of the nature of his league of nations. The problem, as he saw it, was to find the greatest measure of organization that the postwar world would tolerate, which meant that a world-state or even a European state was as yet inconceivable. What then was possible? He proposed the usual tribunal for justiciable and council for non-justiciable disputes, with an obligation only to give effect to the awards of the tribunal. Such an arrangement would provide the basic requisites for a peaceful world, and perhaps might be built up as time went by. For the prevention of war,

[2] *Idem, After the War* (London, 1915), pp. 26, 30–34, 36.
[3] *Idem, The European Anarchy* (London, 1916), pp. 141–144.

important though it was, was a negative act. The states must develop machinery for joint action in matters of common concern. They must learn to legislate and administer in common. Thus, for example, the new league would set up administrative committees to supervise the execution of existing international treaties in relation to undeveloped territories. It might prepare legislation looking towards a general world system of free trade, or at least enforce the principle of the "open door" in the dependencies of the member states. But whether such functions were immediately possible, machinery for the keeping of the peace, backed by force, was plainly the first essential.

Dickinson's plan also took up the question of membership. He admitted that it was probably desirable that all states should join, but it was imperative that at least all the great powers be included. If Germany were excluded, for example, the league would become an alliance against her. Within the league, Germany could be controlled. Since the admission of the smaller states might complicate the working of the league, it was probable that an effective start would have to be made with a limited organization. In such a case, the members should make for themselves rules of international law, to be adopted by other states as they came in.

Another question discussed by Dickinson was the nature of the sanctions to be employed. He concluded that economic pressure of various kinds should, in the first instance, be the instrument of coercion. But in the final analysis, force might be necessary to deal with a recalcitrant power. Some kind of international body would have to be developed to summon the states to apply those sanctions, but it would grow out of the logic of the league arrangement. An international force might be desirable, but there was at least some question as to its possibility. As for armaments, since the league would guarantee its members against sudden aggressive attack, the main motive for piling them up would tend to disappear. Still other elements of the plan designed to check the forces making for war were a provision for the democratic control of the foreign policies of member states and an absolute prohibition of all secret treaties.[4] This very full outline was in some respects a curious piece of work. Dickinson's own inclinations seemed to take him along the road that led to a fully worked out scheme of international government. He considered, and clearly did not reject, such things as the control of large areas of the world by a league of nations, the development of an international police force, and the drafting of international legislation. But as if fearing that he might elaborate suggestions unacceptable to the existing governments, he constantly reiterated that his plan need start only in a very limited fashion. Machinery to prevent war agreed upon by the great powers was the primary requisite. All else, he apparently hoped, would develop in time.

Nevertheless, by 1918 Dickinson felt compelled to take a more positive stand on some of the issues he had raised. In that year, he contributed a lengthy introduction to a series of articles taken from the *Recueil de rapports* published by the Central Organization for a Durable Peace (an international association founded for the study and support of plans leading to a permanent peace after the war). In this introduction he made no change in the basic structure of his league plan, but did alter his emphasis on certain questions. For example, he had now come to believe that the establishment of a league must be accompanied by an all-round limitation of armaments. For while the league enhanced the possibility of limiting them, it was precisely the existence of armaments which created and maintained universal suspicion and fear. Thus the two projects must be carried out together. Similarly, the conception of a league dominated by the great powers was no longer stressed. Instead emphasis was placed upon the entrance, not only of the enemy states, but of the smaller states as well.[5] By 1918, then, Dickin-

----

[4] *Idem, The Choice Before Us* (London, 1917), pp. 168–170, 179, 189, 193–200, 211–213, 216–222, 245, 259.

[5] *Problems of the International Settlement* (London, 1918), pp. xii–xiv, xvii.

son had completed the circle leading back to ideas he had espoused in the earliest days of the war.

Dickinson's wartime essays made up a formidable arsenal of arguments for a league of nations. They helped keep the idea alive and before a certain portion of the public. In sum, they represented a volume of material that on any showing made their author the one man in England most closely identified with the drive for a league of nations.

Like G. L. Dickinson, Frank Noel Keen was active from the very beginning in the organized league of nations movement. He produced a number of works whose basic pattern was the same, but in which certain developments of detail could be traced as time went on. Keen's first essay into the analysis of postwar organization was a little book of some sixty pages, called *The World in Alliance*. In introducing his plan, he remarked that most international arrangements made so far were mainly calculated to deal with disputes which would usually have a good chance of being settled without recourse to war.[6] In their place, he proposed the constitution of a permanent international council with power to alter state boundaries, to adjust all relations and settle all differences between states and even between subjects of one state and the government or subjects of another. The council was to be composed of representatives appointed in proportion to population by the member states. It should be able to deal with both justiciable and nonjusticiable disputes, appointing, if it seemed convenient, a small judicial committee from among its own members to handle the first type of cases. In addition, it would be necessary for the council to prepare and promulgate a complete written code of international law, and to amend and add to it from time to time. Such a code would be binding upon all the states signatory to the international agreement. In order to carry out the decisions of the council, a second committee of the council would be required to act as a kind of international executive. It must have

[6] F. N. Keen, *The World in Alliance. A Plea for Preventing Future Wars* (London, 1915), p. 13.

the power to requisition agreed contingents from the component states to apply compulsion in enforcing the council's decisions, as well as to protect any member against attack from
outside. While member states might keep national forces in addition to those which they could be called upon to contribute
to the international council, the growth of a feeling of security
could be expected in the course of time to lead to a reduction
of such forces.[7]

This early plan thus envisaged a very simple but very strong
scheme of organization. Only one international organ was to be
responsible for all types of decisions, as well as for the development of international law. Little attention was given to the
precise techniques by which such international law might be
evolved. In 1917, Keen took up a number of those matters in
a work appropriately entitled *Hammering Out the Details*. He
now thought of a judicial court and council of conciliation as
distinct bodies, set up as a permanent part of the international
organization, but still selected by the members of the central
international body. That body, now called an international conference, remained the core of Keen's league. Most schemes,
Keen felt, underrated the importance of such a legislative conference, which would be attended by the greatest statesmen of
the constituent states and entrusted with the task of formulating a code of international law and supervising the work of the
court and council. Though he spoke in general terms of international law, Keen insisted that the original instrument creating
the league of nations must not seek to lay down general principles for regulating the economic, commercial, political, or
other action of the members. Such principles, even if it seemed
possible to embody them immediately in general international
laws, ought to be dealt with by the conference, after long and
careful consideration. He also insisted that the league must be
open to all states, particularly those considered to be likely dis-
turbers of the peace. For if the league was to prevent war, it
must not be representative merely of a limited group of powers,

[7] *Ibid.*, pp. 32–33, 41–47, 54, 57–59.

having interests that might conflict with those of other states.[8]
In other respects, his plan followed the lines laid down in *The
World in Alliance*.

At the very end of the war Keen published an essay called "A
League of Nations with Large Powers." Together with his earlier works this was issued after the war as a single volume entitled *Towards International Justice*. Judicial, "semi-judicial,"
legislative, and administrative functions were again outlined in
very much the same terms as before. But this time Keen emphasized a point that had not been pressed home so strongly in
his earlier work. He proposed that the new organization be
built upon the structure of the existing international institutions
at The Hague, for in such a case it was more likely to command
support than if it took on a wholly novel and unprecedented
character. The Hague Conference, however, would have to be
endowed with larger powers from the start. These Keen listed
as follows:

> The first is the substitution of a majority vote of the Inter-
> national Council in place of unanimous confirmation by the
> member-States as the condition for giving binding force to
> International Laws.
> The second is the imposition of an obligation upon the mem-
> ber-States to submit non-judiciable disputes to final decision
> instead of merely to consideration and recommendation.
> The third is the introduction of an obligation for the member-
> States to enforce by joint action the decisions of the organiza-
> tion and to restrain aggression by one member-State against
> another.
> The fourth is the introduction of some provision for control
> over the national armaments of the member-States.
> The fifth is the extension of the sphere of authority of the
> organisation beyond the limits of the member-States into regions
> where it will affect the action of outside nations.[9]

[8] F. N. Keen, *Hammering Out the Details* (London, 1917), pp. 13,
23–26, 31–32.
[9] *Idem, Towards International Justice* (London, 1923), pp. 106–
110.

Keen's view of the league of nations, as developed in these three discussions, was the conventional one of a league whose main duty was to prevent war when it threatened, but with additional emphasis upon its role in the development of international law. In that respect it went beyond many other plans whose only mention of international law was an incidental reference or two. But even Keen's project could not be classed among those insisting upon genuine international government. It was vague about the nature of the legislation to be drafted by the league and equally vague about the causes of war, an attack upon which was usually the sure sign of a desire to push toward such international government. It served perhaps as a bridge, or at least a possible link, between ideas for a limited league and those for a league with broad and general international power.

Other men connected with the league of nations societies also supplied plans or arguments for the campaign. Late in 1918, for example, the Oxford University Press began the publication of a series of pamphlets on the nature of the league. Among the most important were the essays contributed by a number of outstanding Liberal and Angelican Church members of the societies. Gilbert Murray, like Dickinson a classical scholar and also a close friend of Sir Edward Grey, and like Dickinson one of the real leaders in the league movement, prepared an article called *The League of Nations and the Democratic Idea.* The plan of organization which he sketched was the conventional scheme for adjudication and conciliation, though in place of a tribunal for justiciable disputes he preferred arbitration courts chosen by the disputing powers from a permanent panel supplied by the league of nations.[10]

Ernest Barker, another Liberal contributor to the Oxford series, suggested that in addition to councils of conciliation and arbitration, the league should have a third organ, a congress. He proposed that the congress be a permanent body which would legislate, deliberate and also undertake the essential ad-

[10] Gilbert Murray, *The League of Nations and the Democratic Idea* (London, 1918), pp. 21–23.

ministration of league affairs. But then, as if realizing how bold this idea was, he qualified it by the recommendation that in matters involving such serious decisions as the taking of military action the votes of representatives be subject to ratification by their governments. A further qualification was the usual provision for representation weighted in favor of the larger powers. Another conception advanced by Barker, that of regional confederations within the league, was faintly reminiscent of the Fabian scheme. But Barker intended that the smaller nations should combine to act as units within the main body, and not, as the Fabian plan hinted, be shunted aside to an inferior council where they would not interfere with the work of the major powers. He also broached an idea that was actually to be incorporated in the League of Nations when it was formed, the idea that world-wide empires like the British might follow a reverse procedure, so that such units as Australia and Canada would enter the league as separate entities.[11] These proposals made Baker's design for a league a very stimulating and useful one; nevertheless, they did not significantly alter the basic plan of an organization limited in functions and controlled by the national governments of its chief members.

Probably the most significant book in the league of nations series of the Oxford Press appeared in June, 1918. In it, Viscount Grey presented his case for an international organization. The destructiveness of war, he urged, taught that no peace terms would be of value unless the future relations of the nations outlawed the return of militarism anywhere. Just as law was the only regulator of the social lives of private individuals, so must international law backed by international force be the regulator of the interrelations of nations. If that lesson was disregarded, warned Grey, the whole of modern civilization might perish, because conflicting militarisms could only lead to more terrible wars.[12] Grey's outline for the structure of a league fol-

[11] Ernest Barker, *A Confederation of Nations: Its Powers and Constitution* (London, 1918), pp. 20, 46–50.

[12] Viscount Edward Grey, *The League of Nations* (London, 1918), pp. 4, 12–15.

lowed substantially the pattern of Dickinson and Barker and Murray, and resembled very closely the proposals of the League of Nations Society. The pamphlet attracted press attention and the ministry of education gave it wide circulation in neutral and enemy countries during the month of June.[13] Interestingly enough, no similar attempt was made to familiarize the British people with the idea.

Church leaders associated with the league of nations groups also contributed to the Oxford series. The Bishop of Winchester developed the theme that a league represented the only moral and Christian approach to international relations.[14] The Bishop of Oxford, who had been one of the main figures in the church auxiliary to the League of Nations Society, made the same argument for a league, but then proceeded to detail precisely how such a body would operate. He outlined provisions for handling justiciable and non-justiciable disputes and placed emphasis on the value of the league in enforcing delay. He stressed the necessity of a reduction in armaments and insisted that Germany, democratized and purged of her militaristic leadership, must become a member of the new body.[15]

A much more thoroughgoing approach from a nominally Liberal source was exemplified by the work of Norman Angell. Early in the war Angell was of course active in the Union of Democratic Control, but he found time to argue, in *America and the New World State* published in 1915, for a world society based upon cooperation rather than nationalistic "Prussianism." A few years later, *War Aims: the Need for a Parliament of the Allies* offered a fully-developed scheme for a league as the key to a proposal for a negotiated peace.

[13] *The Times,* June 20, 1918; *Manchester Guardian,* June 21, 1918; Bonar Law in House of Commons, June 27, 1918. *Parliamentary Debates,* Commons, CVII (1918), 1123.

[14] Bishop of Winchester, *The Spiritual Sanctions of a League of Nations* (London, 1919), pp. 7–9.

[15] Bishop of Oxford, *The League of Nations. The Opportunity of the Church* (London, 1919), pp. 43–44, 52–58.

Angell's plan resembled those of H. G. Wells and H. N. Brailsford much more than it did the schemes of the leaders of the league of nations societies. He proposed the immediate formation of a parliament of the Allies, not to formulate peace terms in the sense of delimiting frontiers and adjusting territorial claims, but to outline peace-preserving arrangements for the postwar period. This body would frame the international arrangements by which the nations of the world, including the Central Powers, were to be assured due protection of nationality, equality of commercial opportunity, economic rights of way, access to markets and raw materials, without being obliged to resort to competitive armaments.

Such an arrangement, Angell held, would not only benefit the nations of the world, but would give to the league a sanction far more effective than mere military coercion. Though military force was necessary, it was not enough. The League of Nations of the future, he insisted, "must be so organised that, apart from any question of repression, or obligation to repress others, it is more advantageous from every point of view for a nation to become a member, even though membership should involve reduction of armaments, than to remain outside." A real league of nations would be in a position to determine the conditions upon which those outside it might have access to raw materials, markets, and areas of exploitation in undeveloped countries. Its members would give each other favored nation treatment in tariffs, harbor dues, railway rates, and a host of other things so necessary for the conduct of modern international life. Such a proposal, warned Angell, outlined the only basis upon which a league could operate. Vaguely and generally to approve the idea as an ideal for the future was one thing; really to accept the changes and conditions which alone could make it workable was quite another.[16]

Angell's view of the league, however, was not a popular one, not even in circles otherwise very close to him. Early in the war,

[16] *Idem, War Aims: The Need for a Parliament of the Allies* (London, [1917]), pp. 12, 18–19, 31–32, 116.

and again at its end, C. E. Fayle prepared two reports for the Garton Foundation, an organization devoted to the study of international relations and especially of the approach outlined by Angell in *The Great Illusion,* his important antiwar tract of the prewar period. In both his books, *The Great Settlement* and *The Fourteenth Point,* Fayle attacked the idea of a "United States of Europe" with a permanent council having legislative powers. For the question, as he saw it, was not what was ultimately desirable, but what was immediately attainable and necessary. To attempt too much was to run the risk of setting the whole idea back a century, for nothing was so fatal to the healthy development of political institutions as prematurity.

Fayle's own plan was the conventional one, and need not be described in detail. He placed his major emphasis on the value of a period of delay, perhaps a year, before recourse to hostilities. Nevertheless, he apparently believed that it would be possible to enforce the recommendations of a conciliation council as well as the awards of an arbitration court. Consequently, he outlined an elaborate series of sanctions, ranging progressively from diplomatic breaks through economic boycotts to the eventual application of military force. In the case of decisions requiring military action, he provided that not only must they be acceptable to a majority of the representatives of all the member states, but also to a majority of the delegates of the great powers, upon whom the chief burden of such action would fall. And at the same time, he shared the widespread belief that the presence of machinery to settle disputes would encourage the sense of security prerequisite to a reduction of the burden of armaments. Finally, in the field of organization, he was willing to go so far as to suggest a consultative council to discuss matters of common international interest. He hoped that this council might, in the course of time, develop into a body capable of codifying international law and handling a large variety of economic matters world-wide in scope.[17]

[17] C. E. Fayle, *The Great Settlement* (New York, 1915), pp. 268, 274–276, 283; *idem, The Fourteenth Point: A Study of the League of Nations* (London, 1919), pp. 23, 91–97, 121–123, 135–136.

A number of lawyers and international lawyers also published works on the league idea. Some of them were active in
the organized league movement, others pursued an entirely independent course. All of them tended to be narrow and conservative in their approach. Of the books published by this
group, the first to appear was Sir Walter Phillimore's *Three
Centuries of Treaties of Peace and Their Teaching*. The future
chairman of the British Cabinet Committee on a League drew
very cautious conclusions from his study of previous treaties.
Most of his recommendations had to do with matters of territorial settlement. He did, however, suggest that the peace
treaty should contain an agreement to submit every dispute to
arbitration or mediation before going to war. He felt that there
were some rights no state would part with except under the
compulsion of defeat in war. Consequently, compulsory acceptance of a mediation award was inconceivable. He placed his
hopes for peace in the period of delay called for under the
agreement which he suggested. Other proposals, including the
limitation of armaments, he found impractical and impossible.[18]

An even more rigidly conservative approach was that of the
Recorder of Ipswich. Heber L. Hart, a Doctor of Laws from the
University of London, started from the proposition that any attempt to create a world state, or even a supreme executive
power to enforce international law, was not only doomed to
failure, but would jeopardize less ambitious schemes by weakening the influence of the great powers, who alone could keep
the peace. *The Bulwarks of Peace* took the frank position that
if the great powers would refrain from fighting among themselves and would act collectively to prevent strife outside their
own borders the peace of the world could be secured. This
rather obvious conclusion was accompanied by the suggestion
of an international council controlled by the great powers,
whose members were to agree that they would not, without the
council's authorization, engage in hostilities against any other
state except to preserve the *status quo*. At times, Hart seemed

[18] Sir Walter Phillimore, *Three Centuries of Treaties of Peace and
Their Teaching* (London, 1917), pp. 172–177.

rather confused. For while he gave the council power to "take cognizance of any interstatal relations by which the peace may be threatened" and to "undertake the function in the last resort of settling disputed claims," he also specified that the "separate sovereignty of each of the Allied Powers must remain substantially unimpaired by the constitution and operations of the League." [19] Thus the league was not to employ force against any Power except when it had commenced hostilities. Apparently Hart was willing to waive the "settling of disputed claims" so long as war did not result. His plan was a blueprint for the entrenchment of those powers who were reluctant to see any change in international conditions. It might have prevented war, but, in the final analysis, a system of domination by one autocratic power would have achieved the same result.

Three very prominent international lawyers, Sir Frederick Pollock, Lassa Oppenheim, and T. J. Lawrence, presented essentially similar schemes for a league well towards the end of the war. All three thought in terms of courts to settle judicial cases and councils for the handling of non-justiciable disputes. All three agreed that the league must have the backing of military force in order to carry out its decisions and protect its members from outside aggression. And all three made it clear that their plans did not involve any serious interference with national sovereignty. [20] Each plan, of course, stressed those par-

[19] Heber L. Hart, *The Bulwarks of Peace* (London, 1918), pp. 40–41, 171, 176, 179, 182.

[20] Sir Frederick Pollock, *The League of Nations and the Coming Rule of Law* (London, 1919), pp. 6–11; T. J. Lawrence, *The Society of Nations, Its Past, Present, and Possible Future* (London, 1919), pp. 167, 177–178, 181–182; Lassa Oppenheim, *The League of Nations and Its Problems: Three Lectures* (London, 1919), pp. 18–19, 22–24, 39–41. Pollock, interestingly enough, recently has been virtually credited with the paternity of the League idea, the "actual impetus that gave effect to the notion" being traced to a conversation between him and Lord Phillimore early in the war. While he was active in the League movement, the contribution of many others seems clearly to have been more significant (and undertaken earlier) than that of Pollock. See Sir John Pollock, *The Everlasting Bonfire* (London, 1940), pp. 131–132.

ticular aspects of the league proposal most interesting to its author.

Sir Frederick Pollock, for example, wanted it clearly understood that in matters involving economic or military coercion the great powers must have a preponderant voice. And he was equally clear that the great powers, at least at the start, must not include Germany. Like H. G. Wells and many members of the League of Free Nations Association he saw the wartime alliance against the Central Powers as the foundation for a league of peace. Needless to say, he did not share Wells' other views on the league. He showed no particular interest in attacking the causes of war, but merely urged that the league apply itself to the "restoration and better definition" of international law. With favorable conditions such a job might be done in ten years.[21]

T. J. Lawrence, in the published and expanded version of a series of lectures given at the University of Bristol,[22] argued like Pollock for a court of justice and council of conciliation backed by power to compel their use, and for a gradual "improvement and extension" of the international law the courts would have to administer. In addition, he devoted considerable effort to the argument that the courts and councils should be developed by "carrying a little further" the plans formulated and inaugurated at The Hague in 1899 and 1907, and by broadening existing international alignments.[23] In general, his approach was even more strictly legal than that of Pollock, and evidenced little consideration of the forces underlying international tensions.

The same may be said of the work of Lassa Oppenheim. Professor Oppenheim was particularly vehement in his strictures against the advocates of an international parliament. "A Federal State comprising all the single States of the whole civilised world is a Utopia," he wrote; "and an international Army and

---

[21] Sir Frederick Pollock, *The League of Nations and the Coming Rule of Law,* pp. 4–5, 11–15.

[22] Lawrence, *The Society of Nations,* p. v.

[23] *Ibid.,* pp. 177–178, 186–187.

Navy would be a danger to the peace of the world." Instead, within the league, as formerly outside it, some kind of balance of power alone could guarantee independence and equality for the smaller states.[24] Having demonstrated that world government was "impossible," Oppenheim then turned to a program of his own. His conception of a league as an instrument for arbitration and conciliation was no different from most legal schemes, except that it was considerably more complicated and detailed. It gave the impression of obscuring the forest of international cooperation by too-great attention to the trees of international machinery. Boiled down to its essentials, Oppenheim's scheme rested on the view that judicial settlement of questions of law, along with conciliation of non-justiciable problems, would be sufficient work for any league of nations.[25]

One lawyer, W. F. S. Stallybrass, attempted to blast the myth of integral national sovereignty in the course of his defense of the league idea. He contended that any treaties entered into by a nation were as much an abnegation of sovereignty as any possible demand placed upon it by an international organization. The Telegraph Union, the Postal Union, and many other such organizations, while having no legal authority to enforce their decisions, likewise operated to curb sovereignty because public opinion tended to support their decisions. No recognized scheme for a league of nations made any such demand. The most extreme suggestion was that conferences should from time to time formulate rules of international law, to be employed by the league unless some signatory indicated its dissent within a stated period. Such a conception, he argued, contained no threat to the susceptibilities of any sovereign state.[26] With such a point of view, Stallybrass could have been expected to outline a plan similar to those worked out by the other lawyers already

[24] Oppenheim, *The League of Nations and Its Problems,* pp. 18–19, 21.

[25] *Ibid.,* pp. 23–24, 39–41, 65–67, 72–73.

[26] W. F. S. Stallybrass, *A Society of States* (London, 1918), pp. 17–23, 55–57, 70–71, 74.

noted, and such a project was duly proposed in the rest of his book.

At least as cautious as the lawyers were the majority of the historians who contributed books on the idea. The historian most closely associated with the organized league movement was A. F. Pollard, student of Tudor England and of English constitutional development. In a pair of volumes, Pollard noted that the inevitable progress of mankind was directed toward the unity of the world. Just as the establishment of the state met a human need without abolishing the individual, so would the institution of a league be a step forward without endangering the nation state. The gist of Pollard's argument was that questions of sanctions or tribunals were of little importance when compared with the growth of international cooperation through a league whose functions should at first be restricted to the sole task of preventing war. In such a gradual extension of the scope of the league Pollard saw the greatest hope for success. He proposed a treaty binding its members to resist with all their forces any recourse to arms without first trying methods of peaceful settlement. The specific method by which disputants settled their quarrels, he said, could be safely left to them. The league need not even provide a court for their use, since the very act of seeking peaceful means to end a controversy would ensure a delay sufficient to avoid a precipitous leap into war.[27]

Ramsay Muir was more historically-minded but less league-minded than Pollard. Most of Muir's work on a league appeared in the *Edinburgh Review* and the *New Europe*, but in a book called *Nationalism and Internationalism* he developed the thesis that the growth of nationalism was leading to international cooperation, and that the present war was the last struggle before the birth of the new world order. The working out of the national principle had made possible the substitution of the idea of the cooperation of free nations for the impracticable

[27] A. F. Pollard, *The League of Nations in History* (London, 1918), *passim; idem, The League of Nations. An Historical Argument* (London, 1918), pp. 50–51, 55–56, *passim.*

idea of a single world dominion. Any international system was impossible until there was a reasonable assurance that the boundaries of states could be regarded as fairly permanent. The impact of the nationalist movements of the nineteenth century made international organization eventually possible. Internationalism was dependent upon nationalism.[28]

Muir treated the idea of an immediate league virtually as a pious hope, and Bernard Pares followed in his footsteps. Pares declared that it might be possible to work out some kind of inter-state machinery for the prevention of wars, but the real basis must be the individual nations themselves. "This is the substance," he insisted, "and the League of Nations is a hope which can be founded on it and on no other foundation."[29] Whereupon he proceeded to sketch the problems of nationality in Poland, Czechoslovakia, the Turkish Empire, and so on, apparently well content to wash his hands of the disturbing league idea.

J. A. R. Marriott considered the league plan in greater detail, but with little real enthusiasm. In *The European Commonwealth* he analyzed the plans of the League of Nations Society and the American League to Enforce Peace, largely in order to point out the difficulties such plans entailed. He doubted, for example, that international law was so well developed as to permit application of the league idea. "International Law is itself in an inchoate condition at present," he wrote; "until it is more amply developed it would not be easy for a judicial tribunal to interpret its rules, nor would it be easy to secure obedience to its decrees." To imagine that a league of nations could be formed without some curtailment of national sovereignty, he warned, was not only to be mistaken about present conditions but to set the stage for inevitable disappointment in the future.

[28] Ramsay Muir, *Nationalism and Internationalism* (London, 1916), pp. 222–223.
[29] Sir Bernard Pares, *The League of Nations and Other Questions of Peace* (London, 1919), p. 13.

What then could be done? Marriott proposed to start with the two "leagues of nations" which existed, the British Empire and the wartime alliance. The next and most obvious step towards a league of free nations was a closer union between the British Empire and the United States. Other steps might follow in due course, but haste would merely result in reaction and disappointment. The alliance which had come into being in defense against German aggression might gradually be transformed into a commonwealth but it would be unwise to include nations of different stages of political growth. Membership in the league, in the first instance, must be confined to states "reasonably equal in power, not disparate in government, inheriting similar traditions, and inspired by common ideals." To attempt more would be to risk all.[30]

Least cautious of the historians was William Harbutt Dawson, already well-known for his studies on Germany. He suggested the creation of tribunals for arbitration and of councils for mediation, but went even further and insisted that in the event of failure of mediation states must agree to submit to compulsory arbitration. But his *Problems of the Peace* did more than outline machinery to settle disputes. It also sketched a plan for a permanent legislative conference, with delegates elected by proportional representation in the various member states, but responsible to their respective parliaments—not their governments—for ratification of their acts. Such a conference might work out plans for a progressive reduction of armaments and for the adoption of the principle of the open door in various parts of the world. It must emphasize the right and duty of national parliaments to control the foreign policies of the various member states which they represented.[31] Certainly this was no full-fledged plan for world government, but international su-

[30] J. A. R. Marriott, *The European Commonwealth* (Oxford, 1918), pp. 362–370.

[31] W. H. Dawson, *Problems of the Peace* (London, 1918), pp. 305–308, 320–324.

pervision of the "open door policy" and parliamentary control
of foreign affairs went far beyond the schemes of the other historians who considered the league idea.

A few authors who helped publicize the idea wrote from a labor point of view. Arthur Henderson, for a time a member of
the war cabinet and chairman of the Labor Party executive,
contributed a volume to the Oxford Press series. *The League of
Nations and Labour* saw a world federation as a guarantee of
security for all workers, relieving them of the economic burden
of militarism and putting an end to conscription and trade wars.
More important, in the opinion of Henderson, was the fact that
labor favored the creation of a league because it would promote
among nations the same spirit of international goodwill and understanding that labor organizations had for many years been
attempting to develop among the workers of the world.[32]

George Bernard Shaw can hardly be called a spokesman for
labor, but since he was editor of the *New Statesman* and active
in the postwar planning of the Fabian Society, his views may
best be considered here. After the war had ended, Shaw graci-
ously and gratuitously offered his advice to the statesmen who
were to attempt to make the peace. *Peace Conference Hints*
was typically Shavian in opposing many of the main currents
of thought on the league, but was also typical of the shrewd-
ness of the author, however irritating his point of view. Shaw
took issue with men like Lord Robert Cecil who argued that
there could be no league of nations unless all the nations of the
world were included. The obvious truth was that the league
would prove practicable and successful only if it were limited
to a carefully selected group of politically and psychologically
homogeneous constituents. Each member must have a responsible government, for "an autocracy cannot deliver the goods."
Only responsible governments could give pledges that com-
manded absolute confidence. But there must be more than
mere pledges between the constituent states of a league, said

[32] Arthur Henderson, *The League of Nations and Labour* (London,
1918), pp. 5–8.

Shaw. They must have a supernational legislature and tribunal, in the same way that the United States had developed such institutions. But people could not have a common legislature and common courts of justice unless they were agreed on their ideas of right and wrong, law and justice. "The difficulty then in forming a League of Nations," said Shaw, "is not to get every nation into it, but to keep the incompatible nations out of it." [33]

According to Shaw, any league must include the United States, Great Britain, France, and Germany to be successful. And once it was formed and believed to be genuine, Belgium, Holland, Denmark, Norway, and Sweden would join automatically. Italy, Spain, and Greece might come in, but on the score of heterogeneity of temperament, the combination might be more workable without them. This league must not only act to limit war by providing tribunals for the settlement of disputes; it would have to consider legislation defining the extent to which any nation could be permitted to limit the "general human right of way" or to monopolize any natural product. It would have to prohibit the production of high explosives and artillery in threatening quantities and the equipment of submarines with torpedo tubes, but any absolute prohibition of armaments was as yet impracticable. The league could not make war physically impossible and should not attempt to do so. Finally, all talk about economic sanctions was thoughtless and mischievous. Economic boycott was a weapon that injured the nation applying it as well as the victim. The only effective sanctions were force and conscience. Force was necessary until the view that war was a crime against humanity became firmly fixed in the consciousness of mankind. [34]

The comparative originality of Shaw's approach was equalled though not paralleled by that of Sir Waldorf Astor's *Co-operative Basis for a League of Nations*. In this work Astor, a Labor member of Parliament, presented many of the ideas outlined in

[33] George Bernard Shaw, *Peace Conference Hints* (London, 1919), pp. 67–69.

[34] *Ibid.*, pp. 71, 84–85, 93.

November, 1918, at the Plymouth conference of the Devon and Cornwall Association for Industrial and Commercial Reconstruction.[35] The gist of his argument was that the stress hitherto laid on the juridical element in a league of nations had led to the neglect of other factors. A court with power to enforce international agreements and prevent aggression was of course essential, but if the league was to endure it must be based on common interests and on the habit of cooperation in many fields. Many dangers—famine, disease, a general loosening of the bonds of law and order—might lead to another European or even world-wide conflagration. Consequently, it would be wise to build upon the institutions developed by the Allies during the war and provide for international control of cereal supplies, prices, and trusts. For economically, the aim of the league must be the elimination of selfish commercial competition. Obviously, the league could not immediately develop a full-fledged economic organization for the world—that must come gradually. But even at the earliest stage it would have to deal with some international economic problems, above all, those concerned with the revictualling of Europe. Therefore, Astor suggested, the league would have to be equipped on the administrative side with permanent machinery to deal with the following matters:

(a) The purchase and distribution for a short period of any one or more of the essential foods and raw materials required by all the nations alike, and the regulation of international trusts.

(b) The regulation of international communications, whether by sea, river, canal, railway, or air.

(c) The consideration of industrial conditions in each country, with a view to providing a standard (in so far as this is possible) for the well-being of the working classes and the prevention of undercutting due to the employment of cheap labour.

[35] Sir Waldorf Astor, *Co-operative Basis for a League of Nations* (*Some Problems of Reconstruction*) (London, [1919]), p. 3.

(d) The securing of free and equal conditions for the trade and commerce of all countries by the prevention of secret rebates or other means of frustrating international commercial agreements.

(e) The prevention, through systematic action of the spread of disease, and the promotion of scientific research.[36]

Here was a charter of action which attacked some of the basic causes of international conflict. Astor, like Brailsford and Wells, realized that the prevention of war was more than a matter of providing courts and councils and outlining a procedure for arbitration or mediation. By emphasizing the economic functions of a league, he brought to the fore matters of extreme importance which, except for the labor parties, as we shall see, were relatively neglected during the war years.

To be sure, a few writers not connected with labor also took up certain economic aspects of international organization. Hartley Withers, editor of *The Economist,* considered the subject in one of the Oxford volumes on the league. Withers, however, was not concerned with elaborating the economic functions of the league, but rather with demonstrating what would be the economic effects of its constitution. Without a league, he argued, the productive activity of the nations would be diverted to the invention and manufacture of destructive weapons. Enormous taxation would reduce the buying power of the individual citizen and divert it to the state for the purposes mentioned. Every people would strive for self-sufficiency, in fear of the next war, and international commerce and investment would tend to dry up. And when that war came, it would be so hideous as to wipe out what economic gains had already been achieved by civilization. A league, on the other hand, would establish an international police force, for which each nation's quota would cost infinitely less than the unregulated armaments of an anarchical world. Taxation for armaments would be incalculably lighter, and the energy of nations, set free from

[36] *Ibid.,* pp. 6–24, 30–31.

the competition in the arts of destruction, would be applied to the purposes of peace and production. International rivalry would become a race to increase the standards of living and well-being of the citizens of the various nations.[37] A similar analysis was made by the editor of *The Statist*, Sir George Paish, who pointed out that in the absence of a league each country would not only demand concessions of territory but also would seek to control as much as possible of the world's supply of food and raw material, whatever might be the consequences to other countries. In that direction, warned Paish, lay the way to a world in arms after the war.[38]

Men of conservative temper in general were not particularly enthusiastic about a league, but J. L. Garvin, editor of *The Observer*, published a long detailed statement on its economic functions well after the end of the war. Like most other writers, Garvin prefaced his analysis with a conventional scheme for the central machinery of the league.[39] But most important in his scheme was the role he assigned to the economic agencies. He favored the constitution of a supreme economic council, divided into a number of sections, to supervise the economic life of the world. Of these sections one of the most necessary was the council of food and raw materials, whose task it would be to develop and make available the resources of the world, so that no nation need go to war to satisfy its vital needs. Next was a council of communications and supply to supervise the use of commercial airplanes, railways, inland waterways, and the like. Then there was to be a labor commission to deal with international labor problems in order to ensure decent living standards and fair competition among the nations of the world. Finally, Garvin's plan called for the creation of a customs commission to work for freer trade, and of a financial commission

[37] Hartley Withers, *The League of Nations. Its Economic Aspects* (London, 1918), pp. 6–7, 13–16.

[38] Sir George Paish, *A League of Nations* (London, 1918), pp. 34–35.

[39] J. L. Garvin, *The Economic Foundations of Peace* (London, 1919), pp. 219–228.

to handle such problems as war debts and international exchange. In Garvin's opinion, the league was to serve the purpose of guaranteeing the economic independence and security of all member nations and so eliminate the necessity for war. He also emphasized the necessity for American participation in the postwar league. Since he saw the league as primarily an economic instrument, Garvin recognized that without full American cooperation it could not succeed in organizing the international services and the economic strength of the world in a spirit of collaboration rather than hostility.[40]

Garvin's league, however, was to have at least one function not too closely allied with the spirit of world collaboration. He bluntly advocated an attack upon the new regime in Russia. He pointed to the excesses of the Russian Bolsheviks and concluded that "intervention in the decisive sense, which we have seen to be the only likely means of restoring Russia in the manner necessary for the world's peace and security, would be the best way in which the League of Nations could begin, and would do more than anything to confirm belief in its real efficiency and prospects of successful development."[41] Despite its economic functions, the league was apparently to act the part of policeman for the world, putting down revolution and preserving the conservative *status quo*.

The foregoing description of the most important individual works on a league of nations does not, of course, exhaust the list. Other books, of varying quality, appeared during the war.[42] But it is sufficient to indicate the considerable volume of sup-

[40] *Ibid.*, pp. 137, 157–160, 253, 270–317, 411–412, 413.

[41] *Ibid.*, pp. 400–402.

[42] See, for example, the following: C. R. Ashbee, *The American League to Enforce Peace. An English Interpretation* (London, 1917); Lieut. Trevor T. Berry, *The Hope of the World. An Appreciation of the League of Nations Scheme* (London, 1919); Walter Walsh, *The World Rebuilt* (London, 1917); Sir Charles Walston, *Patriotism, National and International* (London, 1917); *idem, The Next War, Wilsonism and Anti-Wilsonism, with an Open Letter to Col. Theodore Roosevelt* (Cambridge, 1918); *idem, The English Speaking Brotherhood and the League of Nations* (Cambridge, 1919).

port and discussion which had developed by the time the Paris conference met. Virtually every possible argument in favor of a league had been adduced, most of its potential functions had been described, and numerous specific schemes of organization had been worked out. How these arguments appealed to, or were rejected or developed by, the political parties forms the material for the next sections of this study.

Conservatives and the League Idea

THE PROPOSALS AND ORGANIZATIONAL efforts thus far described were of prime importance in the development of the
league of nations idea in Great Britain. But if the idea were to
have any possibility of being turned into effective reality it was
necessary for it to gain support in some of the areas of political
control, that is, among the political parties. The extent, therefore, to which that support was given or denied by the Liberals,
Conservatives, and Labor requires consideration in the following chapters.

Even the most cursory examination of the Great War period
reveals that at the very least the bulk of the Conservative party
and its various media of public opinion were not enthusiastic
about the league project. It is true, as Chapter IX will point out,
that in 1917 and 1918 Conservative members of the Coalition
government, whether because they felt it politically expedient
to follow the lead set by President Wilson or because they were
genuinely convinced of the need for international organization,
were willing to make various public statements, however vague,
favoring some form of league after the war. Equally true is the
fact that a Conservative member of the cabinet, Lord Robert
Cecil, became in 1918 the leading official advocate of the
league. But apart from members of the government and a few
Conservative publicists who appeared late on the scene, few
prominent Conservative figures felt it necessary to speak or
work for the idea. The prevailing temper was either indifference

or a flat rejection of the whole scheme as utopian or worse. There were, of course, exceptions, but they served only to make more apparent the fact that most Conservatives had little use for anything so revolutionary in conception.

A survey of the first three years of the war fails to reveal that individual Conservative party members were paying any attention to plans for future world organization. The league idea had not as yet come into prominence, so that a policy of dignified unconcern seemed perhaps the best way to deal with an unimportant suggestion of a few misguided individuals. By the last months of 1917, however, the situation had changed. In the first place, agitation for a league began to be developed on an organized basis, and the propaganda appeared to be catching on in various politically important quarters. Even more significantly, the United States had entered the war, so that the position of President Wilson had changed from that of a meddling neutral, advising Europe how best to conduct its affairs, to the role of an associated leader of tremendous prestige and power. The British government, certainly, realized the changed situation and during 1917 became considerably more forceful in its formal adherence to the league idea. Inevitably, therefore, the Conservative approach to the question could no longer remain one of complete neglect. International organization required attention, whether for the purpose of damning it as a chimera or to make certain that its proponents were kept within what the Conservatives considered moderate and reasonable bounds.

The sensational letter written by Lord Lansdowne and published in the *Daily Telegraph* on November 29, 1917, provided the signal for Conservatives, and others, to stand up and be counted. The Lansdowne letter was essentially a plea that the Allied powers investigate every possibility of achieving a negotiated peace with Germany. The gist of his argument was that the peace party in Germany would be immensely stimulated if the Allies made it clear that they had no intention of annihilating Germany as a great power and did not desire to impose upon Germany any form of government other than that of her own choice. With regard to the league, Lansdowne argued similarly that peace would be more likely if the Allies indicated that they were prepared to enter into an international pact under which ample opportunities would be afforded for the settlement of international disputes by peaceful means.

Such sentiments, when expressed by Liberal pacifists or Socialists, might safely be dismissed as the usual mouthings of visionaries or pro-Germans. But coming from the former Conservative foreign minister, they acquired an added importance and weight. The result was a flurry of comment in Conservative circles. The *Telegraph,* which had printed the letter, did not even mention Lord Lansdowne's reference to a league of nations in its discussion of it. Editorially it professed to believe that the letter called merely for "co-ordination" of Allied war aims, and hence for greater unity. Its main objection was to Lansdowne's statement on freedom of the seas. Even the implication that Britain's unchecked use of naval power should be modified by international control was anathema to the *Telegraph.* The British fleet had been for centuries the chief guarantor of European civilization and must remain so. On the matter of British sea rights, which, said an editorial of November 30, 1917, had nothing to do with war aims, there could be no compromise. "They constitute the sheet-anchor of civilisation, and we must not cut the cable or permit it to be weakened, either to-day or in the future."

Newspapers of the Northcliffe chain were even more outspoken. The powerful *Times* had already indicated its position by refusing to print the Lansdowne letter.[1] Its more strident fellow, the *Daily Mail,* rushed into print with the accusation that Lord Lansdowne was raising the white flag of surrender. As for a league, such a body already existed. "Eighteen States are now engaged in defending freedom. . . . If this League of Liberty cannot now enforce its will against the central autocracies then all leagues are foredoomed to impotence." Even President Wilson, who, on May 28, 1916, spoke of a peace as-

[1] *Lord Riddell's War Diary.* 1914–1918 (London, 1933), p. 297.

sured by a "universal association of nations," had come to realize by April 2, 1917, that he could only get it by fighting for it.[2]

It remained for the rock-ribbed reactionary *Morning Post* to attack the Lansdowne proposals without equivocation or qualification. The league of nations, it proclaimed, was a proposal from which it had never derived comfort or satisfaction. For how was such a league to keep the peace? If by an international police, then British nationality would disappear, for nations would have to abandon their sovereignty to a majority of other powers. But if armies and navies were retained under the sovereignty of the various powers in the league, nothing could prevent one of them, or a combination of several, from breaking away and fighting the rest. Lord Lansdowne had shown that "Mr. Norman Angell is . . . his intellectual guide and Mr. Ramsay MacDonald his spiritual counsellor. The Union of Democratic Control and the League of Nations to Enforce Peace may henceforth meet under the shadow of Lansdowne House." In effect, charged the *Post*, Lansdowne was asking the nation to abandon the principle of national sovereignty and entrust its existence to an international body of which the Central Powers would also be members. "He asks us to build no longer upon the rock of our island nationality—but upon the rotten detritus of international courts of arbitration." To the *Post* no indictment could be more damaging.[3]

These samples of Conservative press reaction do not reveal the full scope of the opposition to the Lansdowne proposals. On November 30 a special conference of the National Unionist Association was called for the purpose of considering the letter. Among those present were such Conservative stalwarts as Bonar Law, Lord Robert Cecil, and Sir Edward Carson. Resolutions were passed deploring the publication of the letter and declaring the Association's firm adherence to the war aims of

[2] *Daily Mail*, November 30, 1917.
[3] *Morning Post*, November 30, December 1, 1917.

the Allies as defined by Lloyd George, Bonar Law, and Herbert Asquith. In his speech to the Conference, Bonar Law attacked Lord Lansdowne's suggestions bluntly. No purpose was served, as he saw it, by thinking in terms of a league of nations until the Germans were defeated and had learned their lesson. No one would pretend that because they said they were ready for a pact of nations they would be bound by any treaty they signed. The whole world was now organized against the Germans, and if it was unable to insist upon its rights now, any hope for the future was exceedingly dim.[4] Thus Lansdowne's letter and its league of nations trial balloon were rejected by the most powerful organization of the party to which he belonged, as well as by the Conservative leader in Commons and cabinet.

Once the gates had been opened, Conservative opponents of the league idea apparently felt it possible to make their views public. Sir Edward Carson, already famous—or notorious—for his Irish policy, and at present a member of the War Cabinet, lost no time in denouncing the scheme in terms that seemed to admit no qualification. On December 7, in the course of a speech on Rumania's part in the war, he erupted: "Talk to me of treaties! Talk to me of the League of Nations! Every Great Power in Europe was pledged by treaty to preserve Belgium. That was a League of Nations, but it failed." And a few days later, on a different note but with little change in intent: "Talk of a League of Nations! Let us at all events begin with a League of British Nations."[5] Curiously enough, when Arthur Henderson called attention in a letter to *The Times* to Carson's statements, the latter denied that he had ever attacked the idea of a league of nations. He insisted that he merely felt Germany must be completely defeated first, and then a league might have a reasonable chance of success.[6] On the other hand, he was

[4] *Daily Telegraph,* December 1, 1917.
[5] *Liberal Magazine,* XXV (1917), 604, 606.
[6] *The Times,* December 31, 1917.

careful not to point out that the Carthaginian peace he desired for Germany would have made any real league utterly impossible except as a union of the wartime Allies.

In the early spring of 1918 a pair of Conservative peers joined the chorus of attack. Lord Denbigh, the bulk of whose experience had been along military lines, sent a letter to *The Times* in which he somewhat gratuitously announced that he declined to have anything to do with the "underground agitation" for discussing the question of a league of nations. The main job was to defeat Germany; instead, "intriguing, chicken-hearted" politicians and supporters of conscientious objectors were calling for consideration of a league. There was no use, at the present time, to distract people's minds with such nonsense. A few days later, Lord Denbigh filled out his argument against the league. Such an organization could never succeed until "human nature" changed and man was no longer a fighting animal.[7] The obvious implication was that such a change was hardly to be expected in the appreciable future.

Lord Sydenham, also in a letter to *The Times*, was slightly less blunt. His line of approach was the tactic of delay. The only hope for a valid league of peace, he wrote, was such a settlement after the war as would remove causes which must inevitably lead to future conflicts. For that reason, he argued that talk of a league was a waste of words at a time when all national effort must be concentrated on defeating Germany.[8] Discussion of a league was evidently to be postponed until the Greek kalends.

Still another variation on the same theme was made somewhat later by Donald Macmaster in a speech to the National Unionist Association at Chertsey. How was it possible, he asked, to contemplate a league in which Germany would be a partner? The true league of nations was the league now fighting against her brutal tyranny and rapacious greed. The main job of the

[7] *Ibid.*, March 29, April 5, 1918.
[8] *Ibid.*, April 5, 1918.

British nations was to stand together and maintain their common interests.[9]

These few public comments on the question represented a large part of individual Conservative contributions to the discussion. And with the exception of those Conservative members who spoke as representatives of the government, the record in parliament was quite similar. In the main, Conservative legislators merely ignored the league idea, while the few who undertook to consider it did so only to criticize. Thus, as early as December 21, 1916, Mr. N. P. Billing expressed the opinion that a league of nations would not be possible after the war, basing his view upon the broad ground of the present imperfection of the peoples of the world. Several months later another Conservative member of the House of Commons, a Commander C. W. Bellairs, concluded that advocates of a league were those who desired that Germany should escape punishment for her crimes. Any league founded on such ideas would surely fail. A successful league must be based upon punishing the transgressor during the war, and after it was over as well. The tenor of this speech pointed to the standard thesis that the group of nations engaged in war against Germany was a league of nations already. Still another twist to the argument was developed by Brigadier General Croft. In May, 1917, he argued that only a knockout blow against the Central Powers would tend towards universal peace. For in a league of nations composed of police forces from the member states there was always the danger that Germany, Austria, Turkey, and Bulgaria would unite their police armies for aggression.[10] Such Conservative thinking obviously could not see beyond the immediate slogans and myths of the war, so that its contribution to the league discussion was inevitably thin and unenthusiastic.

[9] *Ibid.*, August 15, 1918.
[10] *Parliamentary Debates*, Commons, LXXXVIII (December 21, 1916), 1750, XC (February 12, 1917), 356, XCIII (May 16, 1917), 1723–1724.

Perhaps the only single Conservative figure of any prominence actually to support the league idea in parliament, always
excepting the members of the Coalition government, was Lord
Lansdowne. And, as has already been noted, he was in the very
bad graces of the official Conservative organization for his
views on war aims and international cooperation. On March 19,
1918, the first full-dress debate on a league of nations was
launched in the House of Lords. The discussion of the question
was almost exclusively carried on by a few Liberal peers, but in
the course of the sitting Lansdowne added his backing to the
proposal and noted a few requirements if the league were to
succeed. He argued that it must have within it all the more important powers, including Germany, who could then be held in
check, if necessary by league sanctions. Those sanctions must
include a moral pressure for resort to conciliation, but in addition economic and physical coercion might be necessary. Lansdowne tended to agree with the prime minister, who had declared some time previously that the league could not be set up
until the war was over and must come from the work of the
postwar peace conference.[11] Certainly this was no startling doctrine—it did no more than go a little way along the road with
the "moderate" advocates of a league. But it gains importance
as being a virtually unique pro-league statement on the part
of an individual Conservative not motivated by the rather
peculiar influences of official position.

Neither the antagonism nor the even more striking indifference of most Conservative party members gives the complete
picture of the Conservative reaction to the league. It is necessary to enquire what were the positions of some of the leading
Conservative media of opinion, to see how the idea was received by some of the important Conservative newspapers and
periodicals. In the case of the periodicals, an attempt has been
made to investigate the major Conservative weeklies and
monthlies, but in that of the newspapers, a much more restricted sample has had to be used. Consequently, the discus-

[11] *Ibid.*, Lords XXIX (March 19, 1918), 492, 495, 497–498.

sion of the Conservative press is based upon a study of four newspapers: the ponderous, influential *Times;* its less dignified and more violent Northcliffe fellow, the *Daily Mail;* the temperate, if conservative, *Daily Telegraph;* and the super-nationalistic, unrestrained *Morning Post*. It is felt that a reasonably accurate estimate of Conservative tendencies in the league discussion may be gleaned from these sources.

The majority of the Conservative papers listed above kept hands off the league question for the first few years of the war. The idea had not gained sufficient prominence to merit attention, and certainly these were not sources in which to expect any lead in a drive for international organization. Only the *Morning Post* took up the league idea in the early years, as a kind of added attraction to its campaign against such organizations as the Independent Labor party and the Union of Democratic Control. The *Post* professed to believe that the idea of an international council of Europe, supported by the I.L.P. and U.D.C., was the work of foreign intriguers intent upon the destruction of Great Britain. Its attitude was epitomized in the sneer, "Venezuela and Colombia, Costa Rica, Bolivia, and Peru, would no doubt have a seat at the round table and a vote in the foreign policy of Great Britain." The *Post's* own alternative was a policy of single-minded concentration on the war, and a postwar alliance of Britain, Russia, France, and Italy to enforce the peace of Europe. In enforcing the peace, the Allies would also find it possible to wage trade war upon Germany for the benefit of all concerned.

Again and again throughout 1916, the *Post* reiterated the charge that the league proposal derived its central idea from German propaganda and was being used as a cloak to conceal the designs of the enemy. Other whipping-boys were discovered as well. "To the International Jew a League of Nations is a most convenient idea; but it should not be quite so pleasing to those of us who have countries of our own and have some reason to value them." Sir Edward Grey and Lord Bryce were bitterly denounced for their support of the league movement, which would result in pulling the claws of the British navy. Should a league be formed, "England, as a lonely maritime Power, would be in a minority of one at least upon all naval questions, and her diplomacy, it is safe to say, would stand no chance against the wiles and brutalities of the Teuton." [12]

While the *Post* was making its position clear, President Wilson had lifted the league idea to the level of governmental consideration by his support at a meeting of the American League to Enforce Peace on May 28, 1916.[13] Their methods of handling the President's speech revealed that the *Telegraph, Times,* and *Mail* all agreed substantially with the *Post* at this time. The *Telegraph* merely carried its correspondent's account of the speech with no editorial comment at all.[14] The *Times,* in an editorial, did not even mention Wilson's support of the league idea, but instead politely warned him not to offer proposals of peace to an England that was bent on victory.[15] And the *Daily Mail,* rather less politely, reminded its readers that 1916 was an election year in the United States and candidates for the presidency should be expected to use any tactics to promote their personal and party interests.[16]

As has been noted several times, 1917 witnessed a tremendous growth in the propaganda for a league, part of the impetus being supplied by the entrance of the United States into the war. The development of the idea served only to make the *Morning Post's* antagonism more adamant. In editorial after editorial the *Post* hammered away at a few simple ideas. The league, at best, could not prevent war, it merely concealed the fact that it was designed for war by calling its united armies an international police; it was a plan to hand over control of Brit-

[12] *Morning Post,* February 5, March 30, April 7, 22, October 30, November 18, 1915, April 23, October 25, 30, November 28, December 27, 1916.

[13] Ruhl J. Bartlett, *The League to Enforce Peace* (Chapel Hill, 1944), pp. 54–56.

[14] *Daily Telegraph,* May 29, 1916.

[15] *The Times,* May 29, 1916.

[16] *Daily Mail,* May 30, 1916.

ish affairs to foreigners, a plan acquiesced in by the leaders of British labor and the pacifists; it would tend to lull the public into a sense of false security and, as reliance upon Britain's own force relaxed, would bring ruin, disaster and defeat to the country. In damning the league, the *Post* slashed indiscriminately at its various supporters, the League of Nations Society, former Prime Minister Asquith, Arthur Henderson, Norman Angell, H. G. Wells, the Labor party, to say nothing of Germany and the ubiquitous, if ill-defined, foreign devils of other species.[17] If the *Post* were to have its way, Great Britain would reject any idea of cooperation—except a possible alliance—and, with its armor girded on, take its stand upon the rock of national power.

None of the other newspapers under consideration was so consistently outspoken as the *Morning Post*. The *Times,* in fact, hardly deigned to notice the league agitation in 1917, leaving the Northcliffe reaction to be sought in papers like the *Daily Mail.* The *Mail,* in its turn, occasionally had something to say about the league, and echoed the *Post*'s denunciation with some variation. Its first major appraisal of the league idea appeared on Empire Day, May 24, 1917. An editorial argued that those who would secure peace by a league of nations need look no further than the British Commonwealth for the "image and adumbration" of such a league. Once they looked, they would no longer need dream of any more far-reaching organizations. A few months later, the *Mail* took up the plan of H. G. Wells for a world league in order to oppose it by the argument that the "Grand Alliance" against Germany already approximated the league of his dreams. But this type of approach did not reveal the full extent of the paper's opposition. In December, the *Mail* felt compelled to strike out against the comprehensive "Memorandum on War Aims" drawn up by the British Labor party. A leading article claimed that the impossible schemes of labor's leadership did not represent the views of the British

[17] *Morning Post,* May 15, August 16, 23, December 21, 23, 26, 29, 31, 1917.

worker. "We do not for an instant believe," wrote the editorialist, "that the average British workingman, here at home or at the war in France, wants any such visionary nonsense. He is out to win the war, not to set up Super-National or Super-Natural Authorities for trying and probably letting off the enemy." [18] Such a point of view obviously showed little difference from that of the jingo *Post*.

The *Telegraph*, alone of these Conservative papers, revealed some slight change in attitude during 1917. In January, it greeted President Wilson's "peace without victory" speech by the usual argument that the league of peace he desired was already shaping up in the Allied coalition against the Central Powers. It was willing to accept Wilson's league idea, but always with the knowledge that no covenant was possible until predatory militarism had been beaten. By December, the *Telegraph* was emphasizing its support of the league as being in agreement with the views of leaders such as the prime minister and Herbert Asquith, as well as following the pattern laid down in the Allied statement on war aims circulated early in 1917. But the *Telegraph*'s acceptance of the idea was as general as that of the British government. Such an organization, it agreed, was the "right policy after victory," but the main task was first to win the war. The problems of a league were extremely difficult from a practical standpoint, a fact which enthusiasts seemed to neglect. [19]

The tendency of the *Telegraph* to move towards a contingent and limited acquiescence in the league scheme anticipated by only a short time similar tendencies in other newspapers. In January, 1918, President Wilson made his famous "fourteen points" speech and Lloyd George outlined Allied war aims, including a league of nations, before a special trade union conference. The two statements impressed more definitely the stamp of official support on the idea of a league and gave it a re-

[18] *Daily Mail*, May 24, August 23, December 27, 1917. For the Labor party memorandum see Chap. IX.

[19] *Daily Telegraph*, January 24, December 12, 15, 29, 1917.

spectability that may have made it more palatable to some Conservative editors.

It is true that in commenting upon Lloyd George's speech the *Daily Mail* overlooked completely his mention of the league of nations, that it printed Wilson's speech with no editorial comment,[20] and that for months thereafter it refrained from any serious discussion of the subject. But to offset this, the powerful *Times* began to give grudging approval to the league.[21] In February, for example, it tacitly accepted the league idea by discussing the conditions essential for its success. The league, as seen by the *Times,* was to be a limited body, formed without German participation, and prepared to compel German compliance with its arrangements by force of arms. In any case, only a democratic Germany could be permitted to join. In June, after Lord Curzon, speaking for the Government, had given guarded support to the league in the House of Lords, the *Times* agreed with his arguments, emphasizing that such an organization must come gradually, not hastily, for the problems involved were formidable. By August, the *Times*—or perhaps it was the Government—had been so won over to the idea of a limited league that it was arguing that "devotion to country, determination to make the best of land and race, measures to secure their independence of aggression and penetration—these things are no more incompatible with the League of Nations project than village or country pride is incompatible with love of England, or the patriotism of New Zealand and Canada with allegiance to the British Commonwealth."

In subsequent editorials, however, the *Times* made it clear that it took the position that until a dictated peace had been imposed upon Germany such a league of nations was impossible. Nevertheless, as the war drew to an end, the influential daily had come over completely to the view that a league was

[20] *Daily Mail,* January 7, 9, 1918.
[21] See comments of Ray Stannard Baker in his report to the United States Department of State. Ray Stannard Baker, *Woodrow Wilson and World Settlement* (New York, 1922), I, 216.

possible and desirable. In commenting upon the surrender of Bulgaria, it pointed out that this development had stimulated practical preparation for the future league "which, in spite of doubters and scoffers, is coming more and more into the domain of practical politics." A few days later, it commended Viscount Grey for his warning that preparation for a league must begin immediately. And once committed to the project, the *Times* used the interval between the end of the war and the meeting of the peace conference to support it with some enthusiasm. It discovered that "the very idea is as English as it can be" and applauded the appointment of Lord Robert Cecil to the British League Commission to the conference.[22] Thus, even though the *Times* never outlined a fullfledged plan for a league and in fact seemed to think in terms of only the most limited functions, by the end of 1918 it had come to support the general idea and, in so doing, to give it added importance.

With the *Times* in the league of nations camp, it is reasonable to look for a similar conversion in the editorial pages of the *Daily Mail*. And indeed such a change did appear, though not so systematically or gradually as in the *Times*. In October, the *Mail* took the occasion of Viscount Grey's League of Nations Union speech to signalize its new attitude. Instead of denouncing Grey bitterly, as had been the custom, the *Mail* accepted his projected league and praised him for pointing out that its constitution was impossible until Germany was defeated. At the same time, the editorial stressed that the present alliance was the germ of a league of free nations with an opportunity to "devise machinery for using their immense power against future malefactors among the nations." [23]

The most striking evidence of the new point of view was a long article entitled "From War to Peace," written by Lord Northcliffe himself. In discussing the league, Northcliffe advised caution, but made it clear that he committed himself to

[22] The *Times*, February 25, June 28, August 1, 24, 26, October 5, 11, December 6, 14, 1918.
[23] *Daily Mail*, October 11, 1918.

the idea. He declared that to accomplish a change so great as the adjusting of national organizations to fit into new supernational machinery must be difficult and slow. But "the very steps necessary to make it possible are steps that will slowly make it actual." That is, the cessation of hostilities would leave the world short of food, of transport, of raw materials. The machinery that had regulated those matters during the war would have to continue in operation after the war. There would be international commissions at work for a long time, on these and other problems. And the very act of meeting the various problems so as to make a league possible would furnish the lesson and habit of cooperation to help get rid of the passions and fears of war.[24]

Thus, by the end of the war, both the *Daily Mail* and the *Times* had climbed aboard the league bandwagon. The *Telegraph*, too, espoused the cause during 1918, emphasizing the difficulties, calling for a decisive victory first, advising caution, and in general supporting the official government position. In January, for example, the *Telegraph* welcomed speeches by Lloyd George and his foreign minister, Arthur Balfour, as ensuring the fact that the plan of a working league of nations presupposed the attainment of British war aims, that is, complete victory over Germany. It also approved the important statement made in the House of Lords by Lord Curzon on June 26. An excerpt from the *Telegraph*'s comments will illustrate the terms upon which moderate Conservatives seemed willing to accept the league:

> Some are prepared to go farther than others. There are enthusiasts who desire to set up at once a complete juridical system for the future goverance of the world. There are others who want a League of Nations to be started without delay, so as to give the world an object-lesson of what is meant. All these are likely to be disappointed with Lord Curzon's speech, and he will probably be accused of throwing cold water on the whole project. But if it is carefully studied it will be the better

[24] *Ibid.*, November 4, 1918.

realized that if any agreement is to be reached, the preliminary steps must be taken very cautiously. Moreover, as he pointed out, there are two Leagues of Nations already in existence. One is the British League of Nations, whose Imperial War Cabinet is now in session in London; the other is the League of Allies.

The *Telegraph* reacted in the same guarded fashion [25] to pro-league statements by public figures like Herbert Asquith and Viscount Grey. In general, the *Telegraph's* position by the end of the war can best be summarized by its reaction to a speech delivered at the University of Birmingham by Lord Robert Cecil.[26] If the nations of the world would pledge themselves to wage war on any one of their number which drew the sword before first submitting its case to a conference appointed for the purpose, a great step would have been taken towards international peace. Such a limited objective was all that was at present feasible. Like Lord Robert, the *Telegraph* could find no plan for disarmament that seemed safe and practicable. It would be much better, therefore, "to take one step at the Peace Conference and stand firm than to take two and stumble." [27]

Only the *Morning Post* remained inflexible. In 1918 it reiterated its arguments of the previous year. Thus in response to the "fourteen points," the *Post* declared that England could only approach the league with serious reservations. In any case, it was not a matter with which any country had time to deal at the moment. Such cautious and polite comments were required for statements of President Wilson; British labor, on the other hand, might be flayed unmercifully for holding views similar to his. The *Post's* editorial reaction to the Labor party's memorandum on war aims and to speeches by labor leaders such as Arthur Henderson was typical. They proposed, claimed the Conservative organ, to hand over Britain's national independence to an international body. "We should be delivering

[25] *Daily Telegraph,* January 7, 12, June 27, September 28, October 11, 1918.
[26] See Chap. IX.
[27] *Daily Telegraph,* November 12, 1918.

ourselves over, bound hand and foot, to a body of foreigners. And not only so, but Mr. Henderson and his friends propose to work for the creation of an International Parliament, to which apparently our national affairs would be subject. The British working man does not love the foreigner so much as to be willing to deliver over to foreigners the vital interests of his country." Similar reactions greeted speeches in the House of Lords by Lords Lansdowne and Parmoor, as well as the little volume on a league published by Viscount Grey.

Consistency was not one of the virtues of the *Post* in its attack upon the league project. At times, enthusiasm for a league of nations was portrayed as primarily a "Free Trade stunt," designed to serve the ends of muddle-headed theorists at home. At others, it was a scheme devised by the Psychological Bureau at Berlin with the object of affording Germany a line of retreat or re-entry if she lost the war.[28]

But if consistency was lacking, there was nevertheless no absence of discussion of the league idea. In addition to its various leading articles, the *Post* featured in October a long and controversial correspondence on the subject between H. G. Wells and Ian Colvin. In essence, Wells stressed the need for a new internationalism in the face of the destructiveness of modern war; while Colvin tended to minimize the horrors of war and hold firmly to an uncompromising nationalism and patriotism.[29] In its article noting the end of the debate, the *Post* gave its accolade to Colvin. "Mr. Wells," it stated, "speaks of the renunciation of patriotism as though it could be achieved by an effort of will. In deference to Mr. Wells, we would say that he is asking the biologically impossible. Men and women inherit the attachment to their nation; inherit, if Mr. Wells prefers the expression, racial prejudice; it is bred in their bones, and is not so much the product of education as a fact of Nature." The conclusion, as far as the league was concerned, was that so

[28] *Morning Post,* January 10, March 6, 21, June 20, July 31, August 2, September 9, 1918.

[29] *Ibid.,* October 1, 3, 4, 9, 10, 1918.

artificial a structure, which ignored the claims of nationality, would collapse at the first shock.[30] All in all, the *Post* had little use for the project of an international organization to guarantee peace, and overlooked few opportunities to make its position clear.

The four leading Conservative newspapers gave evidence of certain differences of approach to the league idea. All of them had greeted it with skepticism and no real enthusiasm. The most intransigeant continued to reject it down to the very end of the war. The rest gradually came to adopt the project, but with reservations and with repeated warnings of the difficulties to be encountered in bringing it to fruition. The attitude was apparently fairly representative of Conservative opinion, for the outstanding Conservative journals showed essentially the same pattern in their treatment of the idea. The curve from outright denunciation to something like lukewarm acceptance may be traced in the pages of *Blackwood's Magazine*, the *Nineteenth Century and After*, the *Quarterly Review*, and the *Spectator*.

Of the Conservative periodicals opposed to the league, *Blackwood's* was the most outspoken. Its handling of the subject certainly did nothing to jeopardize its century-old reputation as a bulwark of Tory opinion. During the entire war, the magazine printed not a single signed article on the league. And for the first three and a half years of that period it made no comment of any sort. Then, in the early months of 1918, the editor evidently discovered that such an idea existed and proceeded to attempt to demolish it. The result was a series of violent attacks in the editorial "Musings without Method," a monthly feature of the periodical. *Blackwood's* minced no words about its attitude. The very first discussion of a league included the following:

> It has not a pleasant sound—a League of Nations. It suggests a worst thing still—that Palace of Cant at the Hague, whose

[30] *Ibid.*, October 10, 1918.

benediction was the proper prelude to the greatest war the world has ever seen. To attempt to bind savage and warlike nations by treaties, scraps of paper which can be torn up at will, is like attempting to stem a torrent with a matchbox.[31]

A few months later *Blackwood's* returned to the attack. Commenting on Viscount Grey's pamphlet, it revealed its conviction that the "sad and fatuous experiment" was impossible. Even if it were possible, it would be undesirable. The task for the future was not to chatter about leagues of nations, but by controlling the raw materials of the world to see to it that the Germans would never again be able to spring upon an unprepared world. Similarly, in November and December, the editorial musings coined new phrases of opprobrium for the league. It was not a policy, it was a superstition; and like other superstitions, it had little meaning and should have no influence upon agreements of peace. Fortunately, thought *Blackwood's,* the league would probably remain a pious aspiration. When peace came the Allies would feel so strong a confidence in themselves that they would not ask for mischievous safeguards. "To put the Sermon on the Mount upon the statute-books would be an admirable enterprise, if all governments were honest and virtuous. But Governments, as we have them, are seldom virtuous and never honest, and, if England accepted the League of Nations, she would expose her throat to the assassin's knife." [32]

The conservatism of the *Nineteenth Century and After* was more dignified, if no less emphatic, than that of the strident *Blackwood's.* Its opposition found expression not in editorial comments, but in a series of articles accepted for publication during the war. The articles took various lines of approach in order to prove the inadvisability of a league. John Hall, for example, in an article entitled "The Failure of the Holy Alliance," pointed to that experiment as a possible key to what

[31] "Musings without Method," *Blackwood's Magazine,* CCIII (1918), 413–414.

[32] *Ibid.,* CCIV (1918), 267–273, 692–695, 837.

might be expected of a league of nations. Any league, like the Holy Alliance, must, to a large extent, be based upon the maintenance of the *status quo*. In such a situation, would it not be discovered that "healthy national development may be stifled as effectually by a democratic league as by the sinister alliance which the craft of Metternich cemented?"[33] A companion article, by F. G. Stone, compared the league to the Hague Tribunal, and warned that just as Germany had used that body to cloak her aggressive designs, so might the new international body serve to further the ends of the enemies of England.[34] In somewhat similar vein, the historian, J. A. R. Marriott, pointed out that there had been holy alliances and leagues of peace before; "the difficulty has been to find the sanctions, and to find them without such an interference with the domestic concerns of individual and independent States as will sooner or later bring ruin to the best-laid schemes of philanthropic statesmen." Marriott emphasized that the projected league might easily come into conflict with the principle of nationality, upon which the future settlement must rest if it were to be durable.[35]

The general tone set by the *Nineteenth Century* in 1917 continued through 1918 and into 1919. Lord Sydenham, former governor of Bombay and an official of the Royal Colonial League, brought up difficulty after difficulty to demonstrate that a league of nations was unworkable. "The only League conceivable at the present moment," he insisted, "is a Holy Alliance to secure the rights of nations great and small against Prussian domination. Happily such a League already exists and is painfully but surely marching to victory."[36] A like analysis

[33] John Hall, "Leagues to Enforce Peace. (I) The Failure of the Holy Alliance," *Nineteenth Century and After*, LXXXI (1917), 690, 698–699.
[34] F. G. Stone, "Leagues to Enforce Peace. (II) An Illusion of To-day," *ibid.*, pp. 704, 708.
[35] J. A. R. Marriott, "The Supreme Issue," *ibid.*, pp. 721–723.
[36] Lord Sydenham, "The Greatest 'League of Nations,'" *ibid.*, LXXXIV (1918), 256.

was made by W. S. Lilly. After justifying vengeance on Christian grounds, he pleaded for a continuation of the postwar alliance to humble Germany for many years.[37] Herbert Stephen, who had already attacked the league in an article in April, 1917,[38] returned to the attack after the war had ended. He, too, outlined all the difficulties surrounding the league project, emphasizing the view that if such a body were constructed, Britain would rely on it, rather than on its own resources, to keep out of war. When it failed, the nation might be caught at a horrible disadvantage. In order to have the league, Britain must share control of her navy with foreign nations. All in all, the British people "are asked to sacrifice the best things we have in order to obtain a remote and exceedingly improbable advantage," and, Stephen continued, "our only wise course is to recognise the truth at once, and destroy an insane project by plainly and openly refusing to have anything to do with it." [39]

The only *Nineteenth Century* articles that might be interpreted as supporting some kind of league came from the pen of Dr. Arthur Shadwell. In July, 1918, he rejected all plans for a supernational authority or a federation of states, but agreed that a limited league, based upon the present allies, was quite practicable. The alliance might well become a permanent union, and the more states that joined it the greater would be its influence for peace. If all the great powers belonged to it such an organization might be a notable advance in international relations. But Germany could not be included without complete recantation.[40] Several months later, Shadwell, with evident approval, reported on a scheme for league sanctions devised by the Swiss international lawyer Professor Nippold. Again he wrote in terms of a future league, but from which Germany was

[37] W. S. Lilly, "Vengeance," *ibid.*, pp. 401–409, 413–414.

[38] Herbert Stephen, "The American Dream of Peace," *ibid.*, LXXXI (1917), 799–810.

[39] *Idem*, "The League of Dreams," *ibid.*, LXXXV (1919), 19, 24.

[40] Arthur Shadwell, "Is Peace Possible?" *ibid.*, LXXXIV (1918), 19–20.

to be barred.[41] Despite the limited approval of Shadwell, however, the overall picture in the *Nineteenth Century* revealed an obvious suspicion and rejection of any idea tending towards a league of nations with wide and effective powers.

In contrast to the *Nineteenth Century*, the important *Quarterly Review* remained completely aloof from the league controversy throughout the course of the war. Only in January, 1919, did it publish an article by Lord Phillimore, who had headed the official British committee to study the league project. The article contributed nothing new to the discussion. It advocated a league to provide machinery for settling international disputes, but hesitated to compel acceptance of any decisions handed down by league organs. The emphasis was on a compulsory period of delay, nothing more.[42] Since such a suggestion could be found in the most cautious of all the league plans that had been proposed during the war, it can hardly be felt that the *Qaurterly Review* displayed any vital interest in a league of nations.

One Conservative journal, while not accepting the usual league of nations plans, did offer in their place a project of its own. The "Liberal Unionist" *Spectator*, edited by J. St. Loe Strachey, looked with considerable suspicion upon plans such as those of the League to Enforce Peace and its British counterparts.[43] Their objectives were excellent, but their methods of achievement positively dangerous. To the *Spectator* the conventional league idea was to be rejected because it interfered with principles of humanity and justice by petrifying the *status quo*. Nations must have the opportunity to go to war if intolerable conditions should happen to arise.[44]

[41] *Idem*, "A Swiss Jurist on the League of Nations," *ibid.*, pp. 486, 501–504.

[42] Lord Phillimore, "A League of Nations," *Quarterly Review*, CCXXXI (1919), 206–207.

[43] *The Spectator* can be considered Conservative from 1909. See *A Newspaper History 1789–1935* (Reprinted from the 150th Anniversary Number of *The Times*, January 1, 1935) (London, 1935), p. 116.

[44] *The Spectator*, CXVII (1916), 433–434; CXVIII (1917), 60.

The alternative plan worked out by the editor of the *Spectator* was based upon the re-establishment of the sanctity of treaties. Such a scheme, he held, was much better than a system of arbitration imposed from above. For in the first place there was always danger that the power against which the arbitration went would refuse to accept it. And secondly, a decision must be backed by force, with the possibility that other nations would be unwilling to use force in quarrels not their own. Therefore, the *Spectator* favored enforcement of the sanctity of international treaties by a universal boycott of any nation unwilling to carry out the obligations of a contract set forth in a treaty between sovereign states.[45]

By March, 1918, Strachey had espoused this new idea with some enthusiasm. On March 12, he wrote to President Wilson asking whether he was right in assuming that Wilson's views pointed to "an International system based upon Treaty obligations (*i.e.*, on contract) rather than on some scheme of Imperial or super-Imperial Federation." He reported that if he had interpreted Wilson correctly, he would feel encouraged in his efforts to get his view before the public mind. Wilson replied that it had been his opinion all along that it would be impossible to work out an elaborate and active league organization. In addition to supporting a mutual guarantee of political independence and territorial integrity, he favored Strachey's emphasis on the binding and sacred force of treaty agreements.[46]

Armed with such powerful encouragement, Strachey went ahead to elaborate his new project in a series of articles culminating on October 26 in a suggested constitution for a league of nations. Strachey's plan had three main features. It insisted that the league must not interfere with "national individuality," nor erect a tribunal with functions impinging on the independence and rights of sovereign states. Instead, it proposed a

[45] *Ibid.*, CXVIII (1918), 29, 308–309.
[46] Strachey to Wilson, March 12, 1918, Wilson to Strachey, April 5, 1918, in Ray Stannard Baker, *Woodrow Wilson, Life and Letters* (8 vols.; New York, 1927–1939), VIII, 73–74.

league to be formed with the object of binding its members never to make war upon a fellow member or an outside power without a year's notice abrogating any treaties in existence between the would-be belligerent and its prospective opponent. Such a scheme would involve not merely a year's notice of withdrawal from the league, but also a year's warning to the threatened state, since almost all nations had treaties of amity with one another. Finally, breach of the obligation of delay must not be dealt with by war, "for that would mean some system of international armies and fleets and air squadrons, which, men being what they are, would open up a hopeless vista of intrigue." The weapon by which the sanctity of treaties was to be upheld was rigid nonintercourse, going even farther than the simple imposition of economic sanctions. The proposed constitution was consciously modelled on the Articles of Confederation of the American states, drawn up in 1777. In some cases the actual wording of the Articles was adopted. The constitution outlined a detailed procedure for determining whether a particular nation had fulfilled its obligations and made provisions for the course of action to be taken if it had not.[47] In short, while the *Spectator* rejected the most generally accepted view of the league, it was at least interested in offering an alternative plan based upon a certain measure of international cooperation. In that position, it was far removed from the more intransigeant journals whose major tenets of faith were preparedness and reliance upon national strength in a world of international conflict.

The Conservative share in the development of the league of nations idea is on the whole not particularly impressive. Aside from members of the Government, few Conservative figures had much use for the notion of greater international organization. Those who did, like Lord Lansdowne, were rebuked by their fellows and subjected to violent attack in the Conserva-

[47] "A League of Nations," *The Spectator*, CXXI (1918), 37–38; "The League of Nations," *ibid.*, p. 444; "Suggestions for the Constitution of a League of Nations," *ibid.*, p. 445.

tive press. The press itself—if the important newspapers surveyed are considered as relevant examples—shied clear of the
league for years after the outbreak of the war. Only after the
government had accepted the league as an official part of its
war aims did papers like the *Times* and the *Telegraph* come to
give it a qualified approval. And even in 1918 the nationalist
Morning Post indicated the views of the "right wing" Conservatives by maintaining its opposition. Among the periodicals, a
somewhat similar situation prevailed. The more unbending of
Conservative journals—*Blackwood's,* the *Nineteenth Century*—
rejected the league as a snare and a chimera. Even the *Spectator,* which did work out a league scheme, took a position much
more cautious than that of most league advocates, and lost no
opportunity to denounce plans for fullfledged machinery of international organization. In the overall picture, therefore, the
Conservative attitude ranged from a cautious, hesitant acceptance of a limited league to an outright, unmistakable denial of
all the premises upon which the league project was based.
Clearly the major areas of league support were to be found elsewhere than among the Conservatives and their media of opinion.

The Liberal Contribution

THE ROLE OF THE Liberal party in the development of the
league idea contrasted sharply with that of the Conservatives.
Throughout the course of the war, the Liberals, far from
paralleling the hesitancy of most Conservatives, rivalled the
zeal of the Labor party in supporting projects of international
organization. On the plane of party action, it is true, the Liberals took a position somewhere between the Conservatives' dis-
inclination to make any party commitments and the Labor
party's elaboration of detailed proposals for the function of a
league of nations. The official Liberal party, led by Herbert Asquith, made it clear early in the war that a league was one of
the central planks in its postwar platform. But the working out
of schemes of organization and operation was left largely to individuals, either members of the party or closely connected with
it. It is necessary, of course, to keep clearly in mind that the
Liberals were not a united party in the war years. From December, 1916, the Asquith group was in opposition to the Coalition government, whose Liberal members and supporters followed the lead of David Lloyd George. The Coalition Liberals
were conditioned by the necessity of sharing power with a
dominant Conservative group; while the "regular" Liberals,
weakened by the split, had begun to take the hard road leading
away from effective political power. In addition, from the very
beginning of the war a group of Liberal public men—notably

those connected with the Union of Democratic Control—took the lead in questioning basic assumptions of the struggle, even when those assumptions were made by a Liberal government.

Previous chapters have already indicated the considerable part played by Liberals in developing independent schemes for the prevention of war. The Bryce group was primarily a Liberal gathering. The various league of nations societies owed much of their activity to the Liberals. Again, four out of five of the original founders of the Union of Democratic Control, which was one of the first British organizations to support the league project, were Liberals. Although some members of this group were gradually to find their way into the Labor party, in the early years of the war they represented the left wing of the Liberal party. Many of the Liberal personalities connected with these organizations were active in their own right as supporters of the league movement and, as we have seen, helped mold the characteristics of its propaganda.

Important as their work was, these various Liberals were after all only a handful of individuals. Their views, if unsupported by Liberal politicians, press, and periodicals, might fairly be felt to be unrepresentative of the attitude of the party. But a survey of the data brings home the fact that the Liberal party came during the course of the war to support some kind of league of nations. In some cases that league was conceived as a very limited body; in almost no instance did Liberals go far along the road to international government; but that the belief in the need for international machinery to prevent war was genuine cannot be doubted.

For the first two and a half years of the war, the Liberal party of Prime Minister Asquith was the dominant group in the government. During that period it took no official stand on the league question, but its two leading figures were not reluctant to approve the idea. As early as September, 1914, Asquith himself called for an Allied victory in order to achieve a European partnership "based on the recognition of equal right and es-

tablished and enforced by a common will." [1] True, Asquith was
an able politician and his vague suggestion may have had as
much relation to the building up of domestic morale as to any
clearly envisaged plan of world organization. But if so, his consistent advocacy of such organization as time went on revealed
that he had been won over to the idea.

Similarly, Viscount Grey endorsed the general idea in an in-
terview granted to Edward Price Bell on May 15, 1916. A few
months later, after President Wilson's spectacular espousal of
a league, Grey delivered an address before the Foreign Press
Association in which he gave emphatic welcome to the scheme.
Still later, he made his position incontestable in a telegram to
the American League to Enforce Peace which stated his belief
that such an organization was the best if not the only prospect
of preserving peace in the future. [2]

Meanwhile, Grey's Foreign Press Association speech was
quickly approved by the *Manchester Guardian,* the *Westminster Gazette,* and the *Daily News,* all of them prominent Liberal newspapers. [3] These three papers, which along with the
Daily Chronicle have been selected as samples of Liberal press
opinion, had already begun to turn to the consideration of future international organization. The *Guardian,* for example,
had greeted Wilson's League to Enforce Peace speech with
warm praise, pointing out that a league might deal with problems of international relations as they arose and before they
reached the acute stage. [4] The *Daily News,* a close supporter of
Asquith and Grey, had carried some material on the league as
early as 1915, but not until the Wilson speech did it make its
own position clear. Then the *News* gave unqualified approval

[1] The Earl of Oxford and Asquith, *Memories and Reflections, 1852–
1927* (2 vols.; Boston, 1928), II, 46–47.

[2] League of Nations Society, *Handbook for Speakers on a League
of Nations* (London, 1918), p. 85; *Manchester Guardian,* October 24,
1916.

[3] *Manchester Guardian,* October 24, 1916; *Daily News and Leader,*
October 24, 1916; *Westminster Gazette,* October 28, 1916.

[4] *Manchester Guardian,* October 28, 1916.

to the proposals as being rich in the hope of averting many threatened wars.[5] The *Westminster Gazette* likewise gave editorial support to Wilson's proposal and carried an article by Gilbert Murray showing that many prominent public figures in Great Britain already had indicated their acceptance of it.[6] Only the *Daily Chronicle,* which was considered to be the organ of the Lloyd George wing of the Liberal party, was somewhat less than enthusiastic about the American idea. It accepted the league scheme, but only after expressing surprise at its connection in Wilson's mind with the doctrine of freedom of the seas and with the warning that the prevention of war would only be possible when the leading nations had that "will to peace" so conspicuously absent in Berlin and Vienna in 1914.[7] With the exception of this single editorial comment the *Chronicle* paid little attention to the league before 1917.

The press, however, was considerably earlier than the Liberal periodicals in taking up the idea. An outstanding exception was *War and Peace,* a journal devoted to the study of international relations.[8] Beginning in January, 1915, *War and Peace* carried a

[5] *Daily News and Leader,* April 14, 1915, May 29, 1916; A. G. G[ardiner], "What Does America Stand For? The President's Policy," *ibid.,* June 17, 1916. Gardiner was the editor of the *Daily News.*

[6] *Westminster Gazette,* May 29, September 3, 1916.

[7] *Daily Chronicle,* May 29, 1916.

[8] This periodical went through a rather rapid series of changes in name and connections during the war. Until 1915 it was known officially as *War and Peace. A Norman Angell Monthly;* then the latter phrase was dropped and it became a magazine devoted to the study of "international polity and questions of war and peace." In this period it was associated with such groups as the Garton Foundation, whose directing board included Arthur Balfour and Lord Esher. In May, 1917, it became *War and Peace. The Nation Supplement. A Journal of International Politics, and the League of Nations.* Then in January, 1918, "The Nation Supplement" was dropped out of the title, and in September, 1918, it was renamed *War and Peace. The International Review.* With the end of the war a final change occurred, and the magazine from December, 1918, was called simply *The International Review.* Contributors included representatives of every side of politics, but the Liberal and Labor flavor of the journal is quite clear. Many of the Liberals were Radicals who were

series of articles discussing the subject, and in December, 1916, demanded the immediate calling of a conference in Paris to set up a league of nations to go into operation after the war.[9]

This bold suggestion, though it apparently gained little immediate support, may be taken as a prelude to the heightened Liberal discussion of a league which appeared in 1917 and rose to a crescendo in 1918. To a certain extent the increased interest may be laid to conditions already noted: the more active propaganda of the league of nations organizations and the gradual involvement of the United States in the war. In part it stemmed from the fact that the Asquith government had given way in December, 1916, to a broad coalition of Conservatives, Laborites, and Lloyd George Liberals. The result was considerably greater freedom for the Asquith Liberals, now the official opposition; while the followers of Lloyd George evidently felt it necessary to make concessions to the demands of labor and the position of the new American ally.

The American touchstone of Liberal thinking on a league was clearly revealed early in 1917. On December 18, 1916, President Wilson had addressed a note to the belligerents suggesting that they outline their war aims and the terms upon which they would consider peace. The Allied reply was dispatched to Wilson by the new foreign secretary, Arthur Balfour, on January 10, 1917. In its statement of war aims, it included the announcement that the Entente powers associated themselves whole-heartedly with the plan of creating a league

---

later, like Norman Angell himself, to find their way into the Labor party, but during the war the Liberal character of *War and Peace* tended to be more prominent—enough so that it was decided for convenience to discuss its contribution in this chapter. See Norman Angell, *After All. The Autobiography of Norman Angell* (New York, 1951), pp. 162–171.

[9] C. Ernest Fayle, "Some Factors of the Settlement: II," *War and Peace*, II (1915), 56; A. C. Pigou, "The Conditions of a Permanent Peace," *ibid.*, III (1916), 54–55; G. Lowes Dickinson, "The American 'League to Enforce Peace,'" *ibid.*, pp. 134–135; "A Paris Conference for a League of Nations or Failure of the War," *ibid.*, IV (1916), 34, 51.

of nations to ensure peace and justice throughout the world.[10] Curiously enough, the *Daily Chronicle,* probably the most regular supporter of the new Lloyd George Government, made no mention of this first official stand, but the *Manchester Guardian,* the *Daily News,* and the *Westminster Gazette* all applauded the statement as full of hope for the future.[11]

Acceptance of the league idea by the Liberal press was, however, rather cautious, as was revealed by the reaction to President Wilson's speech of January 22 before the United States Senate. The broad principle was given unqualified praise, but considerable scepticism greeted the idea of the freedom of the seas with which Wilson had associated it. The *Westminster Gazette* professed not to know what Wilson meant, and the *Daily News* likewise seemed at a loss to define the "precise significance of that undefined term." The *Daily Chronicle* was perhaps more candid when it stated that the phrase was not one that many Englishmen would be glad to hear.[12]

In any event, the actions of Wilson had served to focus attention on the conception of international organization, and in the subsequent year the Liberal press gave the question an ever-increasing amount of space. No particularly new ideas were added to the discussion, but it was made plain that the papers under consideration regarded the league as one of the key issues of the war. The respective papers tended to place slightly different emphasis on various parts of the scheme, but the overall effect was undoubtedly to bring it before more and more of the British people. The *Manchester Guardian,* for example, stressed the possibility of beginning to form a league

---

[10] *Documents and Statements Relating to Peace Proposals and War Aims (December 1916–November 1918), with an Introduction by G. Lowes Dickinson* (London, 1919), pp. 4–6, 11.

[11] *Westminster Gazette,* January 12, 1917; *Daily News and Leader,* January 12, 13, 1917; *Manchester Guardian,* January 18, 1917.

[12] *Westminster Gazette, Daily News and Leader, Daily Chronicle,* January 23, 1917.

of nations from the Allied coalition already in existence, and called upon British statesmen to develop the policy of inter-Allied consultation as a forerunner to a common and permanent council to handle the affairs of the world.[13] For the *Westminster Gazette,* disarmament was at the root of the matter. "If, after the war, armaments continue, and on the higher scale which will be set by the war, then our League of Nations will be, as the Prime Minister says, only a blessed phrase." [14]

While the *Daily News* revealed no such single minded approach, it probably represented better than any other Liberal paper the attitudes of the official Liberal party.[15] In general, the *News* took its cues from the lead given by President Wilson and former Prime Minister Asquith, giving especial endorsement to Asquith's views on the league.[16] The *News* summed up its own position as follows:

> Our business is to disarm the nations, to federate them in a new world order and to give them, great and small alike, the security of an international police that shall end forever the machinations of a brigand power. Certain things must be done first. The enemy who began the war must begin the peace by surrendering their "war map" and repudiating the desire of militarism that has flooded the world with woe. They must submit to the conditions that will make the new order possible. When that is done the problems of territory will solve themselves, for if the foundation is right the structure will not be wrong.[17]

Like the *Daily News,* the *Chronicle* predicated its acceptance of a league upon the complete defeat of Germany. But perhaps

[13] *Manchester Guardian,* May 16, 18, June 16, October 6, December 18, 1917.

[14] *Westminster Gazette,* December 15, 1917. See also *ibid.,* October 25, November 7, 1917.

[15] Irene Cooper Willis, *England's Holy War. A Study of English Liberalism during the Great War* (New York, 1928), xiv–xvi.

[16] *Daily News and Leader,* August 18, November 30, December 12, 1917.

[17] *Ibid.,* October 26, 1917.

because the *Chronicle* supported the government while the *News* tended to speak for the Asquith Liberals, the former gave greater prominence to the necessity of victory as an essential prerequisite than to the nature of the international organization itself. The *Chronicle*'s position was simply put:

> If we wish to secure a real peace for the after-years [declared a leading article], we must face realities now; and the fact which no eloquence can talk away is, that if Germany attempted a future aggression, the sole forces within the League of Nations which could restrain her are the forces which are attempting to restrain her now—there are no others. If these forces cannot now succeed in defeating her, does anyone suppose that they could be re-combined in an attempt to defeat her then? [18]

Such preoccupation with Germany as the sole future threat to peace was perhaps natural, but it would seem to have boded ill for the development of a genuine league of nations in contrast to a league of Allied nations intent on the perpetuation of a self-imposed *status quo*. But the *Chronicle*, whatever its connection with the government, probably represented the conventional Liberal point of view a good deal less than the *Guardian*, the *News*, or the *Westminster Gazette*, all of whose editors seemed less inclined to do their thinking in terms of war-engendered emotions. In any event, all four papers were outspokenly committed by the end of 1917 to at least the principle of a league of nations.

Meanwhile, two Liberal periodicals had begun to give the idea serious attention. The first article to appear in the leading Liberal magazine, the *Contemporary Review*, displayed an interestingly negative approach. In March, 1917, John Macdonell, analyzing various plans which depended more or less on force for the prevention of war, saw in the scheme for an armed league a danger that it might prove an obstacle to disarmament. "Real disarmament," he wrote, "will be the first visible sign of

[18] *Daily Chronicle,* December 1, 1917. See also *ibid.,* December 6, 1917.

permanent peace; and any project which would bar the way to or retard disarmament, or which would have the effect of 'shackling the new system with the old evil,' stands condemned." [19] In sharp contrast was an article by Sir Willoughby Dickinson. His discussion was essentially an outline of the League of Nations Society project, with its provision for machinery to settle international disputes and its insistence upon the need of force to ensure that such machinery would be used. [20]

Despite these articles, and others dealing with the colonial question, the *Contemporary Review* was not the most active periodical in the league discussion. That distinction belonged easily to *War and Peace*, a distinction it maintained all through the war. In January, 1917, it devoted its entire issue to a lengthy symposium on the use of force as a sanction for international government. Among the contributors were Charles Roden Buxton, Hugh Richardson, Bertrand Russell, J. A. Hobson, Arthur Ponsonby, G. Lowes Dickinson, and Henry T. Hodgkin. [21] There was very substantial agreement among these men on the necessity for providing machinery for the peaceful settlement of disputes, on the need, in other words, for some kind of a league of nations. But there was, of course, less agreement on the nature of that league. On the question of sanctions, for example, a sharp cleavage was apparent. Ponsonby, of the Union of Democratic Control, Russell, the Liberal philosopher, and Hodgkin, author of the "Community of Nations" pamphlet, all took exception to the use of military force. They felt that the future international organization must be based upon consent and moral sanctions, and that the use of military coercion would be a cure worse than the disease to which it was applied.

[19] John Macdonell, "Armed Pacifism," *Contemporary Review*, CXI (1917), 295, 298.

[20] W. H. Dickinson, "A League of Nations and Its Critics," *ibid.*, 666–669, 671–672.

[21] "Shall the Nations Enforce Peace?" *War and Peace*, IV (1917), 53–68.

Exactly the opposite point of view was taken by Dickinson and Hobson, who argued that to be effective international agreements must have collective force behind them. Hobson in particular attacked the doctrine that the imposition of economic sanctions was any more moral than the use of military coercion. He insisted unqualifiedly on the need for a police arm in any society.[22]

Having thus provided a forum for discussion of a league, the magazine itself continued to direct much of its effort to analyzing and supporting the idea. In May, 1917, *War and Peace* was taken over by the *Nation*, but the change in control made no difference in its policy. Almost every month witnessed the publication of articles on the league, some discussing the future international role of America, some arguing that postwar economic discrimination would militate against political internationalism, others taking up and answering the various objections that had been raised.[23]

War and Peace was especially critical of the approach presented in the *New Europe* and the *Edinburgh Review*, both of which, for want of a more precise classification, must be treated as Liberal periodicals. The *New Europe* was a journal inaugurated for the purpose of studying the various problems of European international relations and of advocating a postwar settlement based upon the principle of nationality. With relation to the league idea, the result was a curiously negative attitude. George Young, who had spent twenty-five years in the diplomatic service, insisted for example that the "League of Peace can only be begotten by sound vigorous national institutions on healthy young international institutions." How was this to be done? The only effective league must grow out of wartime alliances. The Allies had developed an imposing machinery for

---

[22] *Ibid.*, pp. 58–62.

[23] *E.g.*, "America and a League of Nations," *ibid.*, pp. 101–106; "The International Control of Supplies after the War," *ibid.*, V (1917), 107–111; "The Economic Task of a League of Nations," *ibid.*, pp. 128–130; "Opposition to the League of Nations," *ibid.*, pp. 11–12.

handling their world-wide economic problems. That machinery must remain in existence and serve as the nucleus for an international organization. The league, therefore, would be based not on ethical principles but on an economic monopoly of the world, from which exclusion would mean ruin. The enemy would have to come into the new combine, but on terms which Young was careful not to elaborate too specifically.[24]

Professor Ramsay Muir took a somewhat similar view. As he saw it, only states which could be trusted to fulfill their obligations could be admitted to the league. Germany must be excluded, as well as any state whose laws made it impossible to bind it beforehand to take military action. Therefore, America, with its check on foreign policy by the Senate, obviously could not make the required commitments. After the war a great Allied league of ten states would be in existence, and it could then devise means for the prevention of war among its members. Eventually other powers who could meet the test of trust and responsibility could be admitted.[25]

Another professor, W. Alison Phillips, was even less favorably disposed. His objections appeared in the *New Europe* and in the *Edinburgh Review,* whose long Whig tradition was apparently bending before the stresses of a changing world. In the *Review,* Phillips was particularly exercised over the possible interference of a league with the internal affairs of the nations. On a more general level, he believed that it could not work unless there were a world community of like ideas. Since no such community existed, he was very sceptical of the whole plan. In the *New Europe,* he took a different line. Reiterating his belief that a league was virtually impossible in practice, he nevertheless proposed only to criticize the assumption that the principle of international organization excluded that of the balance of

[24] George Young, "The League of Nations. (I) As a Progressive Principle," *New Europe,* V (1917), 290–291; *idem,* "The League of Nations. (II) As a Practical Procedure," *ibid.,* pp. 332–335.

[25] Ramsay Muir, "The Difficulties of a League of Peace," *ibid.,* II (1917), 69–73, 75–76.

power. The wartime experience of Britain, he asserted, offered painful experience of the grave peril of neglecting the balance of forces within the state, and of allowing excessive power to fall into the hands of certain organized groups in it. There was no reason to believe that the state and national groups within a universal league would not, on occasion, be as self-assertive. Therefore, if a league of nations were to be successful it must be based precisely on the principle of a balance of national forces within it, however the principle might be adjusted to the new scheme.[26]

The reaction of *War and Peace* to this type of thinking was immediate and direct. In answer to Professor Muir, it insisted that any very powerful combination which excluded other states would be, and would be regarded as, a menace to those states. It was essential for a real league of peace that it should admit any civilized state willing to agree to its terms.[27] C. Delisle Burns directed his attack especially against Phillips' doctrine of the balance of power within the league. Men like Phillips, he pointed out, were unwilling to give more than vague good wishes to an international organization. They did not really believe it was possible; therefore they held with all their might to the discredited, but old and authoritative "ready reckoning" of a balance of power.[28] Clearly, then, its work during 1917 stamped *War and Peace* as the outstanding Liberal advocate of a league of nations among the periodicals.

The following year witnessed a change in the Liberal periodical and newspaper campaign for a league that was more a matter of degree than of kind. As had been noted frequently, by 1918 the idea had grown to respectable stature in Britain. As

[26] W. Alison Phillips, "President Wilson's Peace Program and the British Empire," *Edinburgh Review,* CCXXV (1917), 233; *idem,* "National Federations and World Federation," *ibid.,* CCXXVI (1917), 1–27; *idem,* "The Balance of Power," *New Europe,* V (1917), 65, 74–75.

[27] "Anglo-Saxons and a League of Nations," *War and Peace,* V (1917), 27–32.

[28] C. Delisle Burns, "The Balance of Power," *ibid.,* pp. 147–148.

was to be expected, the Liberal newspapers which had accepted the idea in 1917 proceeded to broaden and deepen their support when it became apparent that some kind of league was to be one plank in the Liberal postwar platform. And as was also to be expected, Liberal periodicals, most of which had given scant attention to the idea hitherto, opened their pages to an ever-increasing discussion of the league as the war drew to an end.

Needless to say, *War and Peace* continued to be in the van of the league drive. Having been a pioneer in demanding immediate formation of an international body, the journal was gratified to see Liberal parliamentarians like C. A. McCurdy now take up the project.[29] But while supporting the "league now" scheme, it was more than willing to open its pages to a full discussion of its pros and cons. One of the results was the most thorough presentation of the various arguments on the subject to be elaborated during the war. In August and September an impressive list of league advocates–including Gilbert Murray, H. N. Brailsford, David Davies, J. A. Hobson, Arthur Henderson, Sir Willoughby Dickinson, and G. Lowes Dickinson–outlined their various positions on the question of timing.[30] Major Davies was of course the leading exponent of the plan, arguing that if the Allies did not have sufficient confidence in the principles of a league to apply those principles among themselves, they could hardly expect the people of autocratic and military states to believe that they genuinely desired international organization for peace. Hobson also favored immediate action, but not necessarily to form a league of Allied nations. He suggested an ingenious plan. First the belligerents –perhaps through neutrals–should agree upon the basic principle of settlement of the conflict. Next, they should make an armistice in order to hold a conference, whose chief work would be to construct the framework for a league of nations and to

[29] "Why Not a League Now?" *ibid.*, V (1918), 167–168.
[30] "A League of Nations Now? A Symposium," *ibid.*, pp. 305–309 and 326–328.

settle such concrete problems as proved capable of settlement at that stage. Then the neutrals should be invited to join the league, thus forming a full organization of neutrals and belligerents, the council of which would be entrusted with the handling of the issues still outstanding.[31]

Hobson's plan revealed that his approach to international government had not atrophied since early in the war. But none of the other writers in *War and Peace* took a similar position. G. Lowes Dickinson, for example, assumed a half-way stand. He wrote that if the league were to be a combination of the Allies based on the theory that Germany might enter only after formal repentance, a change of government, and years of penal servitude, it would simply be an organ to make peace impossible. If, on the other hand, the Allies drew up the covenants of the league, while publicly and emphatically announcing that enemy states were admissable as soon as they accepted those covenants, the way would be prepared for a true league to serve as a reconciling agency in the war-shattered world.[32]

Brailsford and Henderson expressed their views with less qualification. Their attitude illustrated the fact that labor was inclined to be more suspicious of the Allied governments than were most Liberals. If an attempt were made to form the league at present, they argued, the central powers would probably regard it as a move to weigh the scales against them; and Henderson also noted that the neutrals might fear that to join it would impinge upon their neutrality.[33]

The range of the *War and Peace* articles was extremely wide. The various schemes presented from time to time by groups or individuals were outlined and criticized. Thus the programs outlined by Aneurin Williams and Raymond Unwin of the League of Nations Society were rejected as too narrow in scope.[34] A. J. Jacobs' idea for a treaty of mutual defense was

[31] *Ibid.*, pp. 307–309.
[32] *Ibid.*, p. 308.
[33] *Ibid.*, pp. 306–307, 326–327.
[34] "Schemes of International Organization," *ibid.*, pp. 216–218.

greeted as an interesting and valuable suggestion, though *War and Peace* did not agree with it.[35] Labor's fear that the league might be a tool of capitalism was given serious consideration. The answer, as the Liberal journal saw it, was for the peoples of the world to work harder to make sure that it would not be so used.[36] Space was made available to Arthur Ponsonby and Maurice Hewlett in order that they might elaborate their opposition to a league whose sanction rested upon military coercion, although here again *War and Peace* declined to accept their particular point of view.[37]

As for *War and Peace*'s own attitude, though it continued to advocate the immediate formation of a league, it was aware that many who shared the same objective had considerably different motives. In September, 1918, a brilliant summary of the various suggestions for international organization pointed out that the proposals did not all mean the same thing. Even people who had always opposed international cooperation had suddenly become ardent champions of a league. But what kind of league? In the view of some, warned the journal, "at the end of the war the world is still to be divided into two great hostile alliances, but we shall call our alliance 'The League of Nations' and then, of course, everything will be all right, and the armament firms will flourish and the British Cellulose Company and the British Empire." [38]

In general, the *Nation,* another Liberal organ, took a similar position. But on the issue of when to organize a league, its editor, H. W. Massingham, diverged. In a series of articles, the *Nation* argued that no course of action could be more disastrous than to found a league during the war upon a war-alliance and to empower such a body to deal with vital economic prob-

[35] "A Treaty of Mutual Defence," *ibid.,* pp. 293–294.

[36] "Will a League of Nations Be a Tool of Capitalism?" *ibid.,* pp. 186–187; "Labor's Suspicions of a League of Nations," *ibid.,* pp. 226–227.

[37] Maurice Hewlett, "The Flaw in the Metal," *ibid.,* pp. 328–329; Arthur Ponsonby, "The Sanction behind a League of Nations," *ibid.,* pp. 329–330; "The Flaw in the Metal. A Reply to Mr. Hewlett," *ibid.,* pp. 354–355.

[38] "The League of Nations," *ibid.,* pp. 330–332.

lems of the world during the period of reconstruction. The *Nation* did not reject planning for the league that was to be set up after the war, but it placed itself definitely on record as opposing an Allied organization from which Germany was to be excluded. It also attacked the limited league proposed by the League of Nations Society and kindred organizations. Instead, it argued for a body whose broader economic aspects should be its most important feature. "We have the chance of creating by the fair diffusion of economic advantages a sense of loyalty to the League, an acceptance of it as a necessity in peace to every modern industrial State." Put positively, a world council might ration supplies of grain, cotton, and metals to each nation according to its needs; negatively, the withdrawal of these advantages would be its most effective means of reducing a disloyal or turbulent member to obedience.[39]

This broad view placed the *Nation* far in advance of most Liberal organs of opinion. Nevertheless, other important Liberal magazines continued to give consideration to the subject. The *Contemporary Review* augmented the coverage which it had begun in 1917. For example, John Macdonell, whose first article on a league had appeared in March, 1917, developed in a trio of articles his theme that it must come gradually.[40] Space was given to Arthur Henderson and Lord Parmoor for an explanation of labor's support,[41] nor was the Liberal position ignored. The *Contemporary*, for example, carried a pro-league

[39] "A League of Nations—When and How?" *Nation*, XXII (1918), 643–644; "The Two Paths," *ibid.*, XXIII (1918), 106–107; "The Two Policies," *ibid.*, pp. 188–189; "How to Form a League of Nations," *ibid.*, pp. 272–274; "Wrecking the League," *ibid.*, pp. 302–303; "War on the League of Nations," *ibid.*, pp. 465–466; "The Political Initiative," *ibid.*, pp. 516–517; "Faint-Hearted Leaguers," *ibid.*, pp. 615–616.

[40] John Macdonell, "Beyond the Battlefield," *Contemporary Review*, CXIII (1918), 14–21; *idem*, "Super-Nationalism," *ibid.*, pp. 250–256; *idem*, "The League of Nations in Jeopardy," *ibid.*, CXIV (1918), 126–133.

[41] Arthur Henderson, "The Outlook for Labour," *ibid.*, CXIII (1918), 129; Lord Parmoor, "Lord Lansdowne and the League of Nations," *ibid.*, pp. 8–13; *idem*, "President Wilson and the Peace Settlement," *ibid.*, CXV (1919), 10–14.

statement by T. McKinnon Wood, formerly a member of Asquith's first two wartime governments.[42] Likewise, in January,
1918, Walter Runciman, a prominent figure in the Liberal party,
insisted that a genuine league of peace with powerful sanctions
was one of its major war aims.[43] In contrast, Harold Spender
rejected the idea of coercion, though in a comparison of present
plans for a league with the seventeenth-century project of William Penn he found hope for its establishment.[44] Still other articles pointed to the moral value of an international organization
and to the conditions which gave hope for its success.[45] In general, the *Contemporary Review* presented no surprising or un-
usual plea for a league, but it was at least consistent in providing a means for publicizing the idea and in supporting by implication the general principle.

During 1918, the Liberal *English Review,* under the editorship of young, vigorous Austin Harrison, became one of the
foremost advocates of the league. In signed articles and editorial pronouncements, Harrison developed an interesting project for its immediate constitution, but one not based exclusively
on the wartime entente. As early as August, 1917, he had embodied his scheme in a so-called "International Magna Carta," [46]
and throughout 1918 he elaborated and explained what he had
in mind.[47] Because the idea was given such prominence in the

[42] T. McKinnon Wood, "A Necessary Guarantee of the Peace," *ibid.,*
CXIV (1918), 477–483.

[43] Walter Runciman, "The Radical Outlook," *ibid.,* CXIII (1918), 4.

[44] Harold Spender, "The League of Nations. A Voice from the Past,"
ibid., CXIV (1918), 407–414.

[45] Edward Winton, Bishop of Winchester, "The End of the War—
and After," *ibid.,* pp. 597–603; J. P. Malleson, "A League of Nations and
a Change of Heart," *ibid.,* CXV (1919), 83–88.

[46] "An International Magna Carta," *English Review,* XXV (1917),
146–154.

[47] The following articles by Harrison are illustrative: "Lord Lansdowne's Interrogation," *ibid.,* XXVI (1918), 76–92; "Ides of March,"
ibid., pp. 275–284; "For the Duration!" *ibid.,* 368–379; "League of Nations Again," *ibid.,* XXVII (1918), 297–306; "A World Declaration of
Rights," *ibid.,* pp. 369–378; "Towards the New Europe," *ibid.,* pp. 448–
457.

English Review, a summary which Harrison presented in April, 1918, merits fairly lengthy quotation:

> The Magna Charter scheme was a formula for the *immediate* formation of a League of Nations and the *immediate* setting up of Tribunals in the various countries to consider independently and collectively the manifold problems at issue, which total judgment would constitute the nearest human approach to civilized wisdom; and this judgment, when delivered, could either lay the foundations of similar Tribunals in the enemy countries, thus leading to an all-round constructive peace, or it would be used as a world-instrument of war, in which Japan, receiving world-sanction, would naturally cooperate at maximum strength, and Ireland, receiving from the Tribunals practically the maximum of her demands, might reasonably be expected to join cause with the Allies for the common welfare of humanity. But the indispensable principle was *sacrifice,* which is precisely what no Government is disposed to make. It differed from all previous suggestions of a League of Nations in that it was immediate, was a weapon of peace or war, and pre-conditioned a readiness to obtain a new orientation, in the first place by sacrifice, and in the second by wisdom as distinct from the secrecy of political Governments, thereby constituting a charter of international rights in the creation of which all nations would be united to co-operate.[48]

In addition to publishing Harrison's own articles, the *English Review* offered a prize of £100 for the best original essay on a league. Judges were the Master of Balliol, Lord Parmoor, General Sir Ian Hamilton, John Galsworthy, H. G. Wells, and Professor C. W. C. Oman.[49] They chose the essay submitted by H. N. Brailsford, whose activity as a pioneer has already been noted. Brailsford's contribution was printed in the August, 1918, issue [50] and shortly thereafter appeared as a separate pamphlet.[51] He argued that unless a real concept of internationalism

[48] "For the Duration!" pp. 376–377.

[49] *English Review,* XXVI (1918), 380–381.

[50] H. N. Brailsford, "The League of Nations Prize Essay: Foundations of Internationalism," *ibid.,* XXVII (1918), 87–101.

[51] *Idem, The Covenant of Peace: an Essay on the League of Nations* (New York, 1919).

was developed, no league could be effective. The international organization must be one which could ensure that necessary changes would be effected before any people was driven by an intolerable grievance, or even a reasonable ambition, to force change by arms.[52] This broad view was substantially echoed by George Aitken, author of the second prize study.[53] While these essays did not necessarily parallel the *English Review*'s position, their insistence that machinery to prevent war was not enough coincided with the views of that journal's editor. Harrison's conception of the international charter was certainly well in advance of most Liberal thinking on the subject.

Unlike the journals which made their own position clear, the *Fortnightly Review* merely opened its pages to a rather widespread debate. The widely-read *Fortnightly*, judged in the light of its career under John Morley, must be considered a Liberal periodical, but from 1894 under the editorship of W. L. Courtney, its Liberalism was often somewhat difficult to distingush.[54] Thus, with regard to the league, the *Fortnightly* carried both sides of the argument. Several early articles[55] paved the way for a discussion in 1918 when the magazine became the medium of a vigorous controversy. On the one side, J. B. Firth attacked the league with wholehearted enthusiasm by pointing out the various difficulties involved. An international army was impossible, while national contingents might not be available when necessary. Large nations would not submit to arbitration by smaller states, and judges would be motivated by national and political considerations. The league could not provide for

[52] "Foundations of Internationalism," pp. 92–94.

[53] George Aitken, "A League of Peace," *English Review*, XXVII (1918), 171.

[54] Courtney, for example, kept his editorial connection with the *Daily Telegraph*, the important Conservative newspaper. Arthur Waugh, *A Hundred Years of Publishing, Being the Story of Chapman and Hall, Ltd.* (London, 1930), pp. 169–173.

[55] Sir Frederick Pollock, "What of the Law of Nations?" *Fortnightly Review*, CVI (1916), 902–904; James D. Whelpley, "America's Weapon for Peace," *ibid.*, CIX (1918), 116–123.

colonial expansion by large progressive nations and keep the "natural appetite" of a nation satisfied to prevent it from seizing what it wanted by force. The phrase was now a popular catchword and in any forthcoming general election all parties and candidates would have to agree to support any practicable scheme that might be put forward. But unfortunately, that would not bring the league one step nearer practical realization.[56]

Several authors undertook to refute these arguments. J. Swift MacNeill and William Archer, for example, pointed out that most of the objections were to matters of detail that could be worked out and that none of the obstacles was insuperable.[57] In addition, several other contributors gave more or less substantial support to the league idea.[58]

Actually, therefore, the *Fortnightly Review* accepted more material favoring the league than otherwise. But in his regular feature, "Obiter Scripta," the veteran Frederic Harrison demonstrated how far he had come from his radical days of the eighteen-seventies. Which, he asked, were to be considered real nations? Russia? China? Those under foreign domination? How would it be possible to apportion the vote of each nation? Would the league have coercive powers? Was it to include the present enemy states? What was to take the place of the battered system of international law? The answers to these questions seemed so difficult that Harrison saw no hope for a league. But apparently his lack of hope was conditioned by positive aversion. "It is one of the many devices," he wrote, "to draw off our minds from the one task that admits of no delay and no in-

[56] J. B. Firth, "An Illusory League of Nations," CX (1918), 44–51; *idem*, "The Government and the League of Nations," *ibid.*, pp. 367–370.

[57] J. Swift MacNeill, "Is a League of Nations Illusory?" *ibid.*, pp. 300–301; William Archer, "The Obstacles to a League of Nations," *ibid.*, pp. 569–572.

[58] See, for example, E. J. Dillon, "The Empire and the World League," *ibid.*, pp. 489–501; Mona Caird, "The Greater Community," *ibid.*, pp. 742–755; Sidney Low, "The Conference of Nations," *ibid.*, pp. 865–873.

terruption—the final and utter defeat of the enemy of mankind." [59] Clearly, Harrison had little use for the idea.

The approach of the *Round Table,* another monthly journal of considerable importance, was quite cautious. The *Round Table* was the organ of a group of young men whose chief concern was with the British Empire and its future interrelationships. It was not strictly tied to any party, but its moving spirits were close to the Lloyd George wing of the Liberals. Philip Kerr, for example, left the editorship of the *Round Table* to become secretary to Lloyd George, and his successor, Lionel Curtis, was said to be chiefly responsible for the Montagu scheme for Indian reform.[60] The *Round Table* did not really take up the league question until after the war had ended. Then in December it published two articles outlining its views.[61] At the suggestion of the Research Committee of the League of Nations Union these essays were reprinted as a pamphlet. Despite an introduction by Viscount Grey, however, *The Peace Settlement—and After* was a striking example of the limited league the government Liberals had in mind.[62]

The *Round Table* suggested that the way to inaugurate a league was for the original conference not to dissolve, but, "so far as the Great Powers are concerned," simply to adjourn to some date within a year of its rising. The representatives of all the signatory powers might meet at intervals of four or five years, while the premiers and foreign secretaries of the great powers would meet annually as a kind of executive committee for the league as a whole. This interstate conference of foreign ministers would be a re-establishment of the old Concert of Europe, "out of which alone, as the wisest of nineteenth century

[59] Frederic Harrison, "Obiter Scripta," *ibid.,* CIX (1918), 647; CX (1918), 161–169, 321–329.

[60] *Lord Riddell's War Diary,* pp. 264, 340.

[61] "Windows of Freedom," *Round Table,* IX (1918), 1–47; "Some Principles and Problems of the Settlement," *ibid.,* pp. 88–120.

[62] *The Peace Settlement—and After* (London [1919]). Citation is to this pamphlet edition.

statesmen were always aware, true international co-operation could be expected to spring."

The journal was not alone content to provide for complete great power control of the league; it severely limited the functions of that league as well. It provided for the conventional division of disputes into justiciable and non-justiciable types, but was only willing to compel acceptance of an international decision in the former case. To ask the powers to bind themselves to accept the award of a council of conciliation was to throw too great a strain on the growing international organism; while to provide for compulsory reference to conciliation with the possibility that the award might be disregarded risked bringing the new international authority into contempt. The proposal, admitted the *Round Table,* would not satisfy many of those who looked for the immediate birth of a fullfledged league of nations. But it was the only practicable way to begin. The world would eventually see a government speaking and acting in the name of mankind. "It is the only intelligible goal of practical politics. But the hour is not yet." [63] Whether the *Round Table* scheme would ever bring a "government speaking and acting in the name of mankind" was at the least open to serious question.

Among the Liberal newspapers surveyed, no such sharp divergence of opinion was evidenced as, for example, between *War and Peace* and the *Round Table*. The *Daily Chronicle,* in fact, stood close to the limited views of the *Round Table,* but on the other hand, none of the three other papers seemed prepared to go so far as *War and Peace*. Nevertheless, all four papers did advocate some kind of a league, and their work during 1918 is of some interest in tracing the areas of Liberal support for that body.

The *Manchester Guardian* repeatedly declared that it did not wish to see the league become a coalition of the Allies directed against Germany. The object of a league of nations, it insisted,

[63] "Windows of Freedom," pp. 22–23; "Some Principles and Problems of the Settlement," pp. 65–67.

was to maintain peace, and it must seek therefore to include all nations. The paper also made a particular point of opposing an economic boycott of Germany to further the economic interests of the wartime Allies. With the end of the war, it began to work for the inclusion of a league as an integral part of the peace settlement. Disarmament and conscription, it argued, required an authority to see that terms agreed upon were carried out. Minorities could be protected only by an international body that set the conditions of protection and to which appeals might be made. The solution of a host of other problems postulated a league of nations, not as an afterthought, but as the very foundation of the whole edifice of peace.[64]

The position of the *Westminster Gazette* was substantially that of the *Manchester Guardian*. It held that there would be no real guarantee of peace until German militarism was discredited, but it rejected the contention that a league of the Allies must be the goal of government planning. It agreed, likewise, that discriminating tariffs and boycotts of a defeated enemy had no place in any scheme of international organization.[65]

The *Daily News* echoed the *Guardian* and the *Gazette*. Its advocacy of a league followed very closely the line set by Herbert Asquith and Viscount Grey, the leading figures of the official Liberal party. The editor, in fact, called upon Grey, as the man with the greatest moral stature in Europe, to take the lead in the drive to exorcise war. And in that drive, said A. G. Gardiner, there was no room for half measures. War must be labelled a crime and its preparation fought with political ostracism and economic strangulation; national armaments, secret diplomacy, secret treaties must all be outlawed and the exercise of force in international affairs committed to the international instrument of peace. Despite this sweeping presentation, Gardi-

[64] *Manchester Guardian*, March 16, 20, May 18, June 8, 21, 28, July 9, August 17, December 4, 19, 1918.

[65] *Westminster Gazette*, May 4, July 11, August 1, 2, September 16, 17, 27, 1918.

ner in practice went no further than the editors of other Liberal papers. For he, too, urged the constitution of a league of nations immediately. If all the Allies were not ready, then the English-speaking world could make a beginning. France and Italy could come in when they wished, and the neutrals would then follow. The essential thing was to get the new organization established. Gardiner also repeated the insistence that the league must not be used for economic warfare after the close of hostilities, but agreed that it must control the world's major commodities, shipping, raw materials, and the like.[66] And nowhere was the curious dichotomy between a league with broad functions but limited in membership really grappled with and fully resolved. The *News* also served as a forum for a host of Liberals and a few Laborites who supported the movement. Gilbert Murray, Lord Buckmaster, Arnold Bennett, Silas K. Hocking, and H. G. Wells were among those represented.[67] Whatever the nature of the league that emerged from the pages of the *News*, there was no question but that the paper was sincere in its support of the general principle.

The *Daily Chronicle* hewed even closer to an official line than the other three Liberal papers. Virtually no flights of idealistic thinking were to be found in its editorial columns. Instead it followed the safe policy of fulsome praise each time a leading Liberal or a member of the Government spoke in general terms in favor of a league.[68] Actually, the most unqualified support to appear in the paper came not in its editorials but in articles contributed by H. G. Wells, Arthur Henderson, Sidney Webb, Silas Hocking, and a few other new converts.[69] Altogether, though it accepted the league, the *Chronicle* itself seemed

[66] *Daily News and Leader,* January 1, 1918; *Daily News,* May 11, June 1, 20, July 5, November 9, 28, 1918. On April 14, 1918, the paper became the *Daily News.*

[67] *Ibid.,* January 1, 7, August 7, 19, November 7, 8, 1918.

[68] *Daily Chronicle,* January 7, 11, March 14, June 20, 27, 28, December 31, 1918.

[69] *Ibid.,* February 25, April 30, June 12, August 1, October 3, November 5, 1918.

ready to drift whichever way governmental winds might happen to blow.

Aside from the formal direction provided by the Liberal leaders, the Liberal press was more active in taking up the league idea than were the party's politicians. That is not to say that the Liberals did not play a prominent part in what parliamentary discussion there was of the scheme. But in the early years of the war that part was largely the work of a few radical members of the party, men closer in spirit to the Union of Democratic Control, for example, than to the Liberalism of the Asquiths and Greys. Only toward the end did Liberal M.P.'s come to the defense of a league in any appreciable numbers.

Until the end of 1917, Liberal parliamentary support was confined largely to two members of the left wing of the party, H. B. Lees Smith and Richard Lambert.[70] Their statements were actually only an incidental part of a parliamentary campaign carried on by the radical Liberals for a statement of war aims and a definite disavowal of imperialist ambitions and secret diplomacy. Members of Parliament like Arthur Ponsonby and Charles Trevelyan carried the brunt of that campaign and though both were league supporters they found little time to develop their advocacy in the House of Commons. But on December 19, 1917, their efforts did show some result. During the course of a debate in which Ponsonby attacked the secret treaties, the leaders of the Liberal party rose to define British war aims. Looking back to his Dublin speech of September, 1914, Asquith made the rather amazing statement that Britain had entered the war to ensure the setting up of a league of nations. This had been the purpose of the British government from the first, of the people of Britain, and of the people of the Empire.[71]

Asquith's speech marked a change in parliamentary consideration of a league. It was soon followed by an official statement

[70] *Parliamentary Debates,* Commons, LXXXVIII (December 21, 1916), 1728; XC (February 12, 1917), 353; XCVIII (November 6, 1917), 2011–2013, 2022–2023.

[71] *Ibid.,* pp. 2229–2230.

of British war aims by Lloyd George, a statement which included reference to a league as an objective of British policy. The result was that in 1918 several debates on the question were possible in the Commons, and in the House of Lords as well. In the lower chamber the first major discussion took place on May 16, 1918, when a group of Liberals presented their arguments. Herbert Samuel, one of the leading supporters of Asquith, insisted that a league of nations could only be based upon military victory. Once a reasonable settlement had been achieved, it could then serve as the guarantor with some hope of success. Josiah Wedgwood and others carried this idea one step further, arguing that a militaristic peace imposed by either side would be disastrous to the league policy. The idea of a "league now" also entered the debate, its leading advocates, Charles McCurdy and Major David Davies, declaring that immediate constitution would demonstrate to the world that the Allied governments gave more than lip-service to the ideal.[72]

An even lengthier debate took place on August 1. Once again, familiar Liberal names appeared as the chief advocates. Charles McCurdy, Sir Willoughby Dickinson, and Aneurin Williams offered the soothing assurance that the members of the league would still remain sovereign nations, though they entered into an agreement to settle disputes among themselves peaceably. Other Liberals who spoke generally tended to take this cautious view rather than the more sweeping stand of Josiah Wedgwood, who noted that the league involved a definite surrender of national sovereignty. It meant that international rule would have to take over contested spots of the world when there was conflict. It required that people outside the British Empire have some say in how the various parts of the Empire were to be governed in the future. "It is nasty medicine to take," he warned, "but I believe that to swallow it is the only way out." [73] Wedgwood, it must be remembered, although

[72] *Ibid.*, CVI (May 16, 1918), 587–588, 597–604, 608–610, 626–627.

[73] *Ibid.*, pp. 680–685, 693–696, 705–706, 717–719, 727–728, 732–734.

nominally a Liberal, was already on his way from Liberalism into the ranks of the Independent Labor party.

Real consideration of a league in the House of Lords was confined to a fullfledged debate touched off by a motion of Lord Parmoor expressing support of the house for the idea. The debate began on March 19 and was continued on June 26. Although its chief feature was Lord Curzon's exposition of the Government position, Liberals like Viscount Bryce, Earl Lore burn, and Lord Parker carried the brunt of the discussion. On March 19, Loreburn tied his advocacy to an idea usually associated with the Union of Democratic Control—the thesis that secret diplomacy must go and that foreign affairs must be placed directly under parliamentary control.[74] But easily the most interesting argument was made by Lord Parker, one of the law lords. Parker took exception to the views of the American League to Enforce Peace and the British League of Nations Society, which attempted to classify disputes into various categories but did not exclude the possibility of war as a method of solving certain problems. Instead he offered an alternative plan, similar in many ways to that outlined by A. J. Jacobs earlier in the war. Parker proposed simply to form a league, the members of which would recognize that war for whatever reason was a danger to civilization and was to be acted against. As he saw it, the world was not yet ready for the institution of fullfledged instruments of international cooperation. Acting, therefore, on the idea that the posse had existed before the codification of municipal law, he suggested a transfer of the same system to international affairs. Once it had become established that war was outlawed, international institutions of a more elaborate sort could be expected to develop.[75]

When the debate was resumed on June 26, Viscount Bryce, Earl Russell, and Lord Shaw—all Liberals—outlined the reasons for the necessity of a league, indicated why it would be possible at the end of the war, and pleaded with the house to

[74] *Parliamentary Debates*, Lords, XXIX (March 19, 1918), 488–491.
[75] *Ibid.*, pp. 499–510.

accept the idea at least in principle. In keeping with this latter plea, the House of Lords concluded the debate by passing a resolution: "That this House approves the principle of a League of Nations, and commends to His Majesty's Government a study of the conditions required for its realisation." [76] On the whole, a study of the debates in the Commons and Lords indicates that only a relatively small number of Liberal members of parliament were sufficiently concerned to press for a league with vigor and persistence. On the other hand, the attitude of leaders such as Asquith and Samuel makes it clear that the principle had, by the end of the war, been accepted in general terms as a tenet of Liberal politics.

Meanwhile, the Liberal party had been slowly moving toward an official declaration of policy. Herbert Asquith, as titular head of the party, took the lead in setting the course. In speeches and interviews he continued to stress the need for machinery to settle international quarrels without war. But, he added, the nations from the very beginning must develop something more than the negative functions of policing the world and preventing breaches of the peace. Their goal should be nothing less than "a partnership of the nations in the joint pursuit of a freer and fuller life for the countless millions who, by their efforts and their sacrifices, generation after generation, maintain the progress and enrich the inheritance of humanity." [77]

These noble, if somewhat vague, sentiments were translated into official policy for the first time in January, 1918, when the executive committee of the National Liberal Federation took advantage of speeches by Lloyd George and President Wilson to pass unanimously the following resolution:

That this Executive Committee of the National Liberal Federation, convinced that the future security of the world and of civilization depends upon the overthrow of Prussian militarism and the institution of a League of Nations, under which the law of Public Right will replace the exercise of force, heartily en-

[76] *Ibid.*, XXX (June 26, 1918), 384–392, 413–418, 420, 429.
[77] *Handbook for League of Nations Speakers*, pp. 72–74.

dorses the statements of Allied war aims made by the Prime Minister on January 5 and by the President of the United States on January 8, 1918.[78]

During the next few months, the leaders of the party kept the idea in the forefront,[79] and finally in September action was taken at the annual meeting of the National Liberal Federation at Manchester. At this gathering Herbert Samuel moved a resolution which, after urging wholehearted prosecution of the war, supported the league project in the following terms:

> The Committee [of the National Liberal Federation] further declares its conviction that the establishment of a League of Nations to protect the equal rights of States, great and small, to prevent future conflicts, and to secure the limitation of armaments, is the greatest and most urgent constructive work of the statesmen and peoples of the world.

After some debate and the defeat of an amendment proposing that the league be an essential condition of the terms of peace, the original resolution was carried unanimously.[80] The Liberal Federation published and circulated a booklet outlining these proceedings, and at about the same time issued a series of articles on Liberal policy in which the league figured prominently.[81]

[78] The *Times*, January 19, 1918.

[79] *Ibid.*, July 11, August 5, September 14, 1918; *War after War: The Inaugural Meeting of the League of Free Nations Association Held in the Town Hall at Northampton, on September 13th, 1918. Speech by Viscount Bryce.* (LNUP, Ser. 2, No. 13) (London, 1918).

[80] National Liberal Federation, *Proceedings in connection with the Meeting of the General Committee of the National Liberal Federation, Held at Manchester, September 26th and 27th, 1918, with the Resolutions and Speeches including that Delivered by the Right Hon. H. H. Asquith, K.C., M.P. in the Free Trade Hall* (London, 1918), pp. 18, 24–27.

[81] *Liberal Policy in the Task of Political and Social Reconstruction* (London, 1918). Reprinted in *Pamphlets and Leaflets for 1915–1918, Being the Publications for Four Years of the Liberal Publication Department* (London, 1919).

In the election campaign at the end of the war, the league again played a major role as a tenet of Liberal policy. Liberal candidates in general, and the Liberal leaders in particular, hammered home in speech after speech that international organization had always been a Liberal goal, and that the party stood foresquare behind the demand for a league of peace. Asquith, Grey, Sir John Simon, Major Davies, and Richard McKenna were among the many Liberals who spoke out in positive terms of support.[82] Although the Liberal party was crushed at the general election, Asquith for one demonstrated that its position had not been merely an election expedient to be discarded once the ballots were counted. He continued to take an active part in the agitation for the league and to urge support of President Wilson in his efforts to make that institution a reality.[83]

By the end of 1918, then, the league of nations had become an integral part of the Liberal program. The precise nature of that program is, however, somewhat difficult to gauge. In general, it seems accurate to say that the leaders of the Liberal party and its official organization were more inclined to give general support to the idea than to elaborate far-reaching schemes of international organization. Emphasis was laid upon the contention that a league would not interfere with national sovereignty, that its task was to prevent the outbreak of war, and that further functions of a league might perhaps develop in the course of time.

The Liberal press tended to follow the lead of the party, though it should again be pointed out that in the early years of the war greater attention than was evident in political circles was given to the idea by such papers as the *Manchester Guardian,* the *Westminster Gazette,* and the *Daily News.* The *Daily Chronicle,* closely in tune with the Lloyd George segment of the Liberals, was even less bold than its fellows. After Lloyd

[82] The *Times,* October 11, November 3, 24, December 7, 1918.
[83] *Ibid.,* December 30, 1918, January 13, February 1, 1919.

George had taken over the premiership in December, 1916, it held to the course of official Government policy with little deviation.

In Parliament, where a comparatively small group of Liberals undertook to advocate a league, a few aberrations from the usual approach were to be noted. Examples were Lord Parker's scheme for the outlawing of war and the radical wing's insistence upon economic cooperation as a fundamental basis for international organization. But aside from these exceptions and Asquith's league speech of December 19, 1917, Liberal parliamentary discussion of a league was relatively unimportant.

The greatest range of ideas was to be found among Liberal and quasi-Liberal periodicals. Some, like the *Edinburgh Review* and even the *Round Table,* either rejected the idea or whittled it down to very narrow limits. Others, like the *Contemporary Review* or the *Fortnightly,* provided a forum for discussion but took no editorial stand in favor of a league. Still others, notably *War and Peace,* the *Nation,* and the *English Review,* advocated an international body whose functions went considerably beyond the mere prevention of war. But it seems clear that they did not reflect the sentiments of most Liberal public figures. Regardless of that fact, it is important that the Liberal party, however limited and cautious its policy may have been, did advocate some kind of a league and did set itself the task, in the last year of the war, of working for its realization. That position was in sharp contrast with the attitude of the Conservative party, though it did not go nearly so far as the stand eventually taken by the political organization of British Labor. A survey of the Labor attitudes toward a league must, therefore, be made to indicate the areas in which they differed from those of the other two parties.

Labor's Conception of a League

THE POLICY OF THE Labor party and its affiliated societies is in some respects a great deal easier to trace than that of the Liberals. Periodic conferences of the party and of the Independent Labor party met throughout the war, and their proceedings and resolutions served as landmarks in defining the official labor attitude toward international organization in general and the league of nations in particular. These conferences were doubly important in indicating labor's position because organs of labor opinion were so few. After 1915 not a single daily labor newspaper was printed in Great Britain. Of the two outstanding weeklies, the *Herald,* while close to the Labor party, often displayed, under the editorship of the pacifist George Lansbury, a point of view other than that of the party's leadership. The Independent Labor party, though constituting a tiny proportion of labor's voting strength, was better served by the press. H. N. Brailsford, the *Herald's* most outstanding writer on international affairs, was himself a member of the I.L.P., and that group had its own official organ in the *Labour Leader.* Other labor weeklies, such as the *Bradford Pioneer* and the Glasgow *Forward,* were likewise connected with the I.L.P. Among the periodicals, the I.L.P. had a medium in the *Socialist Review,* and the much more widely read *New Statesman* represented, though unofficially, the outlook of the Fabian Society. Expressions of labor opinion were also to be found, of course, in speeches and interviews and occasionally in the parliamentary debates, but the official attitude was best revealed in the meetings and conferences held during the war.

The Labor party, based mainly upon the trade union movement, and the Independent Labor party, eclectic in membership and strictly socialist in outlook, reacted to the outbreak of the war in similar fashion. The executive committee of the Labor party passed a resolution indicting the conflict as due to secret diplomacy and the principle of the balance of power and reiterating the opposition of the labor movement to that principle.[1] The national administrative committee of the I.L.P. issued a manifesto on the same model, but with the addition, among other features, of support for the idea of a United States of Europe.[2]

In short order, however, this parallelism of outlook tended to disappear. The Independent Labor party remained consistent, urging the early conclusion of a negotiated peace and working out attitudes far beyond any position acceptable to the Labor party. The trade union majority of the Labor party repudiated the resolution of its executive committee by accepting the official view of the war. Although the Fabian Society, as has already been seen, outlined one of the earliest fullfledged schemes for a league of nations, nevertheless it joined with the Labor party in supporting the war. And on the extreme right a group led by Havelock Wilson of the Seamen's Union became exceedingly patriotic and bellicose.[3] Since this latter group

[1] Philip Snowden, *An Autobiography* (2 vols.; London, 1934), I, 354; *Labour Leader*, August 13, 1914; Independent Labour Party, *The War in Europe. Manifesto of the Independent Labour Party* (1914).

[2] *Labour Leader*, August 13, 1914.

[3] The right-wing position was most vociferously outlined in the pages of the *British Citizen and Empire Worker,* a weekly which came into existence on August 25, 1916, to represent the point of view of "National" Labor. Its first notice greeted the American League to Enforce Peace as a "world-wide intrigue in the interests of a German Peace," but by the end of the war, it was willing to accept a stronger Commonwealth, tied closely with France and the United States, as the "germ of the League"—but only after national territorial ambitions had been satisfied.

played no particular part in the discussion of a league it can safely be ignored in the account that follows.

These attitudes of the respective wings of the labor movement made it inevitable that the Independent Labor party should be the most active, early in the war, in developing bold plans for postwar international organization. On October 1, 1914, the first concrete step was taken in the form of a peace program outlined in the *Labour Leader*. The program advocated settlement of frontier problems on the basis of nationality and proposed that subject peoples be given self-government. It demanded the nationalization of armaments, the end of secret diplomacy, and parliamentary control of foreign policy. The policy of the balance of power, it declared, should be superseded by a league of Europe, of which all nations should be members and one of whose purposes should be to judge all quarrels and differences. "The ideal towards which we should move," concluded this sweeping plan, "is a United States of Europe, ultimately of the world, in which national armies and navies are replaced, until absolute disarmament is possible, by

---

British Citizen and Empire Worker, December 2, 1916, August 8, November 2, 1918. While the *Clarion,* edited by Robert Blatchford, one-time pioneer of British socialism, was perhaps as anti-internationist as the *British Citizen,* it was willing to concede the possible usefulness of a league of the victorious Allies, after Germany had been defeated. But its leading writers differed among themselves on the question of whether such a body could be successful unless and until the causes of war (which they defined differently) were dealt with. *Clarion,* October 27, 1916, January 26, October 12, 1917, June 21, October 4, 1918.

On the other hand, on the extreme left-wing of the labor movement, the tiny, antiwar, Marxist British Socialist party took the position that a league would be the tool of capitalist governments to suppress revolutionary movements and retain imperialist spoils. One editorial in the party's weekly declared that a "capitalist 'League to Enforce Peace' stands as much chance of realization as a thieves' league to enforce honesty." *Call,* November 9, 30, 1916, April 12, October 4, December 28, 1917.

Clearly, the constructive contribution of any of these groups to the development of the league idea was negligible.

an International Police Force." [4] In subsequent issues, the *Labour Leader* repeated and explained the program. [5] Among the explanations was one by Arthur Ponsonby, who apparently found that the I.L.P. was more sympathetic to his ideas than his own Liberal party. [6]

The policy outlined in the *Labour Leader* was formally adopted at the I.L.P. conference at Norwich in April, 1915. An omnibus resolution, embodying the various ideas detailed earlier, was carried unanimously. Its section on international organization demanded that British foreign policy be directed in the future towards "establishing a federation of the nations, and the setting up of an International Council, whose decisions shall be public, together with the establishment of courts for the interpretation and enforcement of treaties and International Law." Immediately upon passage of this resolution another was adopted expressing the opinion that an international arbitration court should be established, with power, as an alternative to war, to enforce its decisions by declaring a postal, commercial, transport, and financial boycott against any dissenting nation. [7]

The principle of a federated world fitted in well with the type of internationalism espoused by the I.L.P. The picture of international organization painted in the party weeklies, in leaflets, and in the *Socialist Review* continued to spell out its details. The I.L.P. advocated the setting up of an international parliament, recognizing the autonomy and independence of nations but designed to maintain international law and substitute arbitration for war. [8] It argued that the history of international cooperation in the past indicated that such an international parlia-

[4] "Review of the Week." *Labour Leader,* October 1, 1914.

[5] *Ibid.,* January 7, March 4, 1915.

[6] Arthur Ponsonby, "The Case for a United Europe," *Labour Leader,* April 1, 1915.

[7] Independent Labour Party, *Report of the Annual Conference Held at Norwich, April, 1915* (London, 1915), p. 88.

[8] "Review of the Week," *loc. cit.,* February 24, 1916. See also *Labour Leader,* May 11, 1916; *The I.L.P. Attitude* ("I.L.P. Road to Peace Leaflet," No. 5) (1915); *Bradford Pioneer,* November 5, 1915.

ment was quite possible.[9] Self-government, nationalization of the armament industry and eventual disarmament, democratic control of foreign policy, free trade—these were some of the elements upon which world federation was held to depend.[10] But it was recognized that such a far-reaching scheme had little hope of any immediate realization. J. Bruce Glasier, one of the leaders of the I.L.P. and for a time editor of the *Socialist Review,* repeated in the *Labour Leader* that international federation, with some kind of world council, was essential to any system of disarmament upon which real security could alone be based. But, he stressed, the advocates of federation must welcome as a beginning any provisional tribunal for the establishment of international law and arbitration.[11] This view provided a link with the more cautious schemes for a league of nations soon to become prominent in Great Britain, though it should be emphasized that the I.L.P. never showed any great enthusiasm for the doctrine of a limited league except as perhaps a temporary way station on the road to world federation.

During 1916 and well into 1917, the I.L.P. pursued the policy outlined, with little addition of new proposals. The high point in 1916 was a report issued in response to a manifesto of the International Socialist Bureau, asking socialist groups to indicate their position on peace terms. Once again, the I.L.P. stated its familiar conditions, including a demand for an international court and council to administer international law.[12]

The note on peace addressed by President Wilson to the bel-

---

[9] F. W. Pethick Lawrence, "Towards a Federated World," *Socialist Review,* XII (1915), 740–742.

[10] "Review of the Week," *loc. cit.,* February 24, 1916.

[11] J. Bruce Glasier, "VII. The Case for Disarmanent," *ibid.,* May 20, 1915.

[12] *Labour Leader,* October 12, 1916; *Bradford Pioneer,* March 17, June 16, 1916; *A People's Peace* ("I.L.P. Women's Peace Crusade Leaflet," No. 6) (1916); *Report of the Independent Labour Party to the Executive of the International Socialist Bureau in response to the Manifesto Issued on May 1st, 1916* (London, 1916); *Report of the Annual Conference of the I.L.P.* (London, 1917), appendix I, pp. 29–31.

ligerent powers in December, 1916, lifted the hopes of the
I.L.P. for a negotiated peace which might lead to a decent international settlement. Francis Johnson, secretary of the party's
National Administrative Council, was directed to send a letter
to Wilson. Included in this communication was the statement
that the president's appeal had "raised a fervent hope that
negotiations may be begun now which will lead to a settlement
on such terms as will be just and honourable to all the countries
involved, and which will begin the formation of a League of
Nations for maintaining Peace, to which idea you have given
such valuable support." [13]

But Wilson's view of the league was not quite that of the I.L.P.
The gulf between the two was clearly evidenced in the
publications of Ramsay MacDonald, who was still, despite the
difficulties resulting from his attitude toward the war, the most
important figure in the party. In one of his earliest comments,
MacDonald admitted that the movement to establish a league
to enforce peace had something to be said in its favor. But there
were certain considerations connected with it which demanded
serious discussion before men of pacifist determination could
support it. First of all, he noted, there was the question of its
composition and support. Among the promoters of the league
there were people with whom the I.L.P. could honestly cooperate, but there were others with whom Labor could have
little in common. Secondly, the idea of an armed league of
nations was so simple, so accommodating to every existing interest and tradition, so acceptable to both militarist and pacifist,
that its very all-things-to-all-men aspect must make it suspect
to those who were determined to strike militarism at the root.
Finally, the force provided for the league would be controlled
by the men who had controlled the governments of the world
hitherto. "They are not to abandon their methods, their traditions, their conceptions of policy." A league, for example, which
united the governing authorities of the European states might

[13] I.L.P., *Report of the Annual Conference. . . . April, 1917,* pp.
8–9.

well be an anti-democratic alliance. The present conflict proved that so long as there were armaments there would be war. The need, therefore, was for disarmament, the end of the prevailing political system of Europe, open diplomacy, and the genuine internationalism of socialism.[14]

As time went on, MacDonald indicated what he thought might be done from a constructive point of view. He suggested the summoning of an international conference—as contrasted with the peace conference of government officials—to formulate the new international policy. There should be an international court of arbitration, he declared, which would adjudicate disputes when they had arisen. An international council of conciliation, elected by the various parliaments with departmental officials serving only as advisers, should be established. To this body should be assigned the task of preparing international laws affecting commerce and labor, and all treaties and agreements should be referred to it for consideration and report. No treaty or agreement not sent to it should be regarded by any nation as binding, and ministers making such agreements should be indicted. In addition, it would be necessary for the socialist parties in each parliament to keep closely in touch with their fellows in order to foster common international policies. "If these things are done," MacDonald declared, "we shall want no League of Nations to Enforce Peace, with its dangers and surrenders to militarism."[15]

The position outlined by MacDonald was incorporated in an official statement of policy at the annual I.L.P. Conference at Leeds in April, 1917. Taking the view that suggestions thus far enunciated proposed an armed alliance of capitalist governments which might threaten the workers, the I.L.P. advocated

[14] J. R. MacDonald, "Thoughts on a League to Enforce Peace," *Labour Leader*, December 14, 1916; *idem, National Defence. A Study in Militarism* (London, 1917), pp. 56–64.

[15] *Idem*, "Peace Guarantees," *Socialist Review*, XIV (1917), 29–30. See also *idem, Labour and International Relations* (Burton-on-Trent, 1917), pp. 5–7.

a "world-wide alliance of the common People." The proposed league of nations, it was admitted, represented a substantial advance, but the conference doubted the possibility of securing peace by the threat of war. Accordingly, it advocated that the new league of peoples be based on mutual trust rather than on force.[16] This attitude, embodied in a resolution passed by the conference, was of considerable significance. For by it, the I.L.P. became the first, and the only, important political group in England to reject the idea of military sanctions as the guarantee of the new international organization.

The I.L.P.'s stand on international organization was thus indicated in its publications and at its formal meetings. In Parliament, its few members were apparently too busy demanding a restatement of war aims in terms of abandonment of imperialist conquests and aggrandizement to have much time for the league of nations scheme.[17] Occasionally the leaders of the party would bring up the idea. Thus Philip Snowden argued that a league depended upon a fair postwar settlement, and Ramsay MacDonald declared that it must represent not governments but parliaments and public opinion.[18] The absence of a concerted parliamentary campaign did not, however, detract from the fact that the I.L.P. had by the end of 1917 given outstanding support to a plan for a democratic league, based on disarmament and open diplomacy and sanctioned by public opinion rather than by armed force.

The Labor party, of which the I.L.P. was a constituent segment, was a great deal more diffident in the early years of the war. After the original blast delivered by its executive committee against the diplomacy that had fostered the conflict, it took up an attitude in support of the war that reflected the

[16] I.L.P. *Report of the Annual Conference. . . . April, 1917,* p. 72.

[17] See *Labour Leader,* May 24, 1917, for an outstanding example of this activity.

[18] *Parliamentary Debates,* Commons, XCIII (May 16, 1917), 1634–1635; XCVIII (November 6, 1917), 2037.

views of the majority of its members.[19] Perhaps the best indication of this attitude was the fact that the party permitted several of its members, including Arthur Henderson, to accept portfolios in the Coalition government formed by Lloyd George in December, 1916.

At a conference held in Bristol in January, 1916, F. W. Jowett of the I.L.P. attempted to persuade the Labor party to accept that group's approach to international organization. In a composite resolution, he called for parliamentary control over foreign policy; the reduction of armaments, their nationalization and the prohibition of their export from one country to another; adoption of the principle that no territory should be transferred without the consent of the people living there; and finally, the establishment of a concert of Europe and the setting up of an international council.

In proposing this resolution, Jowett especially attacked secret diplomacy. In refutation, David Gilmour of the Miners charged that the whole scheme savored too much of the views of the I.L.P. and the Union of Democratic Control. Some parts of the motion might be acceptable, he felt, but the clauses on secrecy seemed designed to embarrass the Government in its prosecution of the war. That the majority of the delegates at the conference agreed with this view was evidenced when Jowett's resolution was defeated by a vote of 1,045,000 to 688,000.[20] With its defeat, for the time being, went Labor party support for a league of nations.

By the time the annual Labor party conference met a year later, however, the league as a technique of international organization had begun to catch on with all elements of the party. At Manchester in January, 1917, the new orientation was first revealed when George J. Wardle included in his presidential address a plea for a combination or federation of nations which

[19] Brand, *op. cit.*, p. 59.
[20] *Report of the Fifteenth Annual Conference of the Labour Party, Bristol, 1916* (London, 1916), pp. 132–133.

would act, by force if necessary, to preserve the future peace of the world. Later in the course of the conference a resolution was presented which put forward the following demand:

> . . . the formation of an International League to enforce the Maintenance of Peace on the plan advocated by the President of the United States and approved by the British Foreign Secretary; each affiliated nation to co-operate to restrain by any means that may be necessary any Government or Nation which acts in violation of the Laws and Judgements of the International Court.

The resolution was carried unanimously,[21] and although it was clearly not so far-reaching in implications as the I.L.P. scheme it demonstrated that the Labor party was beginning seriously to consider the need for postwar international organization.

This change was already being reflected in the *Herald*. The labor weekly welcomed the idea of a league to enforce peace, even though it recognized the dilemma involved for those who, like its editor, hated the use of force. Ultimately, an editorial noted, nothing would ensure world-wide peace but a world-wide "will to peace." Nevertheless, faced with a practical situation, it admitted that an international league would be powerless to enforce peace in a world of capitalist and militarist competition unless it was prepared to back the demand for peace with the threat of war. A little later, the *Herald* hailed the speeches delivered at the first public meeting of the League of Nations Society, reserving special approbation for Lord Buckmaster's warning that without the inclusion of Germany any league was impossible. Still another idea appeared in an editorial signed by H. N. Brailsford, who insisted that labor must not be satisfied with a conservative peace based on the *status quo*. Change was necessary in international affairs, he emphasized, but it must henceforth come through a league of nations rather than by war.[22]

[21] *Report of the Sixteenth Annual Conference of the Labour Party, Manchester, 1917* (London, 1917), pp. 84, 135.

[22] *Herald*, October 28, 1916, May 19, July 7, 1917.

Brailsford was a member of the I.L.P. and the fact that his admonitions to labor appeared in the *Herald* was an indication that the socialist left wing of the Labor party was still intent on compelling that party to take a broader view of its postwar international aims. The Fabians, too, contributed their share of new suggestions during this early period of the war. They did not go formally beyond the scheme for a limited league that they had published in 1915. But their organ, the *New Statesman,* gave more than passing attention to some of the wider functions that a league might undertake. On July 14, 1917, it began a series of six articles on the league with an introductory sketch tracing the rapid and hopeful development of the league idea.[23] This was followed by a demonstration of the fact that the international economic policies of any particular nation might often be used as a potent and unwarranted weapon against the commerce and economy of other nations. Previous attempts to regulate such matters, declared the *New Statesman,* had been spasmodic and unsatisfactory.[24] The postwar world required that there should be a guarantee of complete freedom for goods in transit, including freedom from duties and from hostile discrimination by administrative measures such as the manipulation of railway freight rates. Such a system, it was argued, could only be coordinated through the agency of a league of nations. The *New Statesman* suggested the creation of a permanent "right of way" commission by the council of a league for the purpose of watching over the carrying out of the provisions of the treaty establishing freedom of economic communications. It would also be the duty of the commission to frame proposals relating to these matters. These proposals would be submitted to the council of the league.[25] Other pos-

[23] "A League of Nations. I.—Introductory," *New Statesman,* IX (1917), 342–344.
[24] "A League of Nations. II.—Economic Rights of Way," *ibid.,* pp. 368–369.
[25] "A League of Nations. III.—Economic Rights of Way (continued)," *ibid.,* pp. 392–393.

sible functions of the league were outlined by the *New States-man*, including the task of overseeing the administration of colonial areas,[26] and of serving as the central coordinating body for the different international bodies which had already sprung up to meet actual international needs.[27] This latter function was also stressed by Leonard Woolf, chief author of the Fabians' *International Government,* in a little volume which analyzed some of the major plans drawn up by the end of 1916.[28]

From the beginning of 1917 the Labor party began to move towards accepting the broader outlook on international organization expressed at I.L.P. conferences and in the I.L.P. weeklies, the *Herald,* and *New Statesman.* The reasons were numerous, but certainly the attitude of the majority in the party was influenced by fear of a military stalemate and by distaste for the supposedly imperialist objectives of the Government.[29] The first significant evidence of the new policy appeared in the work of a special conference of the party held at Central Hall, Westminster, on August 10, 1917. This conference was especially notable because of its decision to send representatives to Stockholm to confer with Allied, neutral, and enemy socialists on problems of the forthcoming international settlement. The Government's refusal to let the British labor delegates go to Stockholm resulted in the withdrawal of some of Labor's representatives from the Coalition cabinet. The resignation of Arthur Henderson was particularly important, since he took advantage of his freedom from official responsibility to encourage the party to take an independent line on matters of future world organization.[30]

Actually, that independence was demonstrated at the confer-

[26] "A League of Nations. IV.—Overseas Possessions," *ibid.,* pp. 416–418.

[27] "A League of Nations. V.—The Need for International Co-operation," *ibid.,* pp. 440–441.

[28] Woolf, *The Framework of a Lasting Peace, passim.*

[29] Brand, *op. cit.,* pp. 55–56.

[30] Paul Kellogg and Arthur Gleason, *British Labour and the War* (New York, 1919), pp. 12–16.

ence of August 10. Previously, the Labor party and the Trade Union Congress had agreed to sponsor a joint Inter-Allied Labor and Socialist Conference in February, 1918. At the special conference, therefore, they drew up a statement of war aims to be presented to the Inter-Allied conference. Among other things, the statement demanded that a league be provided for in the treaty of peace, to act as a supernational authority. All the present belligerents were to be adherents of the league and every other sovereign state was to be pressed to join. The statement then supported the immediate establishment of an international high court by the league for settlement of justiciable disputes, and the setting up of effective machinery for mediation in non-justiciable disputes. The influence of the socialist Left was to be seen in the plea for formation of an international legislature, with representation from all the states, and for the beginning of codification of international legislation. The states were to pledge that they would submit all disputes for settlement and that they would make common cause against any state that failed to carry out its commitments. One important feature of this "Draft Memorandum on War Aims" was its sharp rejection of an economic "war after the peace." [31]

This document served as the basis for the "Memorandum on War Aims" drawn up by a committee whose most important members were Arthur Henderson, Sidney Webb, and Ramsay MacDonald.[32] The cooperation of the three indicated how much closer the policies of the I.L.P., the Labor party, and the Fabian Society were drawing than in the previous period of the war. The "Memorandum on War Aims" was approved by the executive committee of the Labor party and the parliamentary committee of the Trade Union Congress, with a recommendation that it be endorsed by all sections of the British labor movement. Accordingly, when the special conference reconvened on December 28, Arthur Henderson pressed for acceptance of the

[31] The *Times*, August 11, 1917.

[32] Mary Agnes Hamilton, *Arthur Henderson. A Biography* (London, 1938), p. 175; Van der Slice, *op. cit.*, pp. 102–103.

statement and it was adopted almost unanimously.[33] Shortly thereafter, the memorandum, with an introduction by Henderson, was published as *The Aims of Labour*.[34]

In the meantime and before the Inter-Allied Labor and Socialist Conference towards which all this activity was directed, a number of other developments served to clarify labor's attitude. The reaction to the Lansdowne letter of December, 1917, was unqualifiedly favorable. The *Herald* printed long lists of public figures who had expressed their approval of Lansdowne's position and in a two-page spread announced that despite previous quarrels labor supported him to the utmost. The British people, it declared, had been told over and over again that they were fighting for the establishment of public right and a league of nations, but when Lansdowne suggested a means of achieving that end he was rebuked by the leaders of the Government. Similarly, Mr. Asquith had reiterated his desire for a league, but "M. Clemenceau and Sir Edward Carson ignorantly and impudently reject the idea of a League of Nations—and Mr. Asquith is not in power, and *they are*." [35]

Further evidence of labor's new determination to force the government to abandon generalities and adopt a fullfledged league program soon appeared. Impelled by a number of circumstances to make a statement on war aims, Lloyd George on January 5, 1918, outlined the first detailed official pronouncement on war aims before a special trade union conference. But although he repeated that the Government advocated a league of nations, labor was no longer content with broad general platitudes. The *Herald* welcomed his support for an international organization, but pointed out that its success depended upon a host of other problems. Thus, it asked, if the natives of German colonies were to be protected from European exploitation, as suggested by the Prime Minister, why not those under British control? What about Egypt? And India? As for his state-

[33] The *Times*, December 29, 1917.
[34] Arthur Henderson, *The Aims of Labour* (London, 1918).
[35] *Herald*, December 8, 15, 1917.

ment that Britain would use its control of raw materials to supply itself and its friends first, the *Herald* editorial and an article by H. N. Brailsford attacked it with no little vigor. As an alternative, they proposed the equitable regulation of the supply of raw materials under a league of nations, as recommended in the labor memorandum. A few days later, the *Herald* argued that the future settlement depended largely on the development of free interchange of goods in all areas of the world. Sharply in contrast with the position taken by Lloyd George was its statement that with international free trade, "a true world democracy and an effective League of Nations are at least possibilities, without it they are foolish dreams." [36]

President Wilson's enunciation of war aims in his Fourteen Points was afforded better treatment than the address of the Prime Minister. The parliamentary committee of the Trade Union Congress and the executive of the Labor party were joined by the Cooperative Parliamentary Representation Committee in a statement issued on January 9. It endorsed Wilson's outline of war aims, especially the league of nations and freedom of the seas, which it considered a necessary corollary of the league. [37]

But even Wilson's declaration was not accepted blindly, as was indicated in the Labor party conference at Nottingham a fortnight later. That conference passed a resolution offered by Arthur Henderson welcoming "the statements as to War Aims made by the British prime minister and President Wilson," but only "in so far as they are in harmony with the War Aims of the British Labour Movement and make for an honorable and democratic peace." At the same time the Labor party asked for a joint statement of war aims by all the Allies. [38] Still another indication that the Labor party had moved close to the inter-

[36] *Ibid.,* January 12, 19, 1918; H. N. Brailsford, "Tearing Off the Mask," *ibid.,* January 12, 1918.

[37] *The Times,* January 10, 1918.

[38] *Report of the Seventeenth Annual Conference of the Labour Party, Nottingham and London, 1918* (London, 1918), pp. 55–56.

national position developed by the I.L.P. appeared in its new constitution adopted early in the year. Included in the list of party objects was the following:

> To co-operate with the Labour and Socialist organizations in other countries and to assist in organizing a Federation of Nations for the maintenance of Freedom of Peace, for the establishment of suitable machinery for the adjustment and settlement of International Disputes by Conciliation or Judicial Arbitration, and for such International Legislation as may be practicable.[39]

The changes in the attitude of the Labor party were apparently an accurate reflection of those of the trade union rank and file. Early in the war, the Trade Union Congress turned down resolutions calling for an international council of the nations to take the place of the old balance of power, for reduction of armaments, for the nationalization of the armaments industry, and for a prohibition of the export of arms.[40] And as late as its Blackpool meeting of September, 1917, the Congress almost completely ignored the league question. At the Blackpool gathering the only reference to the league was in a speech by Arthur Henderson, who was not a delegate but only a "fraternal delegate" from the Labor party.[41] But the Trade Union Congress did cooperate with the Labor party in planning for the Inter-Allied conference and in outlining a broad list of British war aims in preparation for that conference. Despite the Congress's silence on the subject in September, therefore, there seems no reason to doubt that it had been won over to the idea of a league with wide powers. At the special conference of December 28, 1917, it had approved the "Memorandum on

[39] *Ibid*, Appendix I, p. 141.

[40] *Report of Proceedings at the Forty-Seventh Annual Trade Union Congress held in Association Hall, Bristol, on September 6th to 11th, 1915* (London, 1915), p. 79.

[41] *Report of the Proceedings at the Forty-Ninth Annual Trade Union Congress held in the Palace Hall, Blackpool, on September 3rd to 8th, 1917* (London, 1917), p. 273.

War Aims" and had accepted responsibility along with the Labor party for the convocation of the Inter-Allied conference, with the view of obtaining international agreement on the basis of the memorandum as that conference might choose to amend it.[42]

The Inter-Allied Labor and Socialist Conference which met in London late in February, 1918, was an extremely important gathering. For it gave the sanction of large segments of international labor to the British declaration on war aims. With a few minor exceptions, the most notable of which dealt with the control of African territories,[43] the Inter-Allied body accepted the British memorandum. The document which emerged may therefore be taken as the most complete statement of the ideas of the British labor movement on the question of future international organization.

The section devoted to a league in the Inter-Allied memorandum was headed "Making the World Safe for Democracy." Whatever may have been the objects for which the war was begun, it declared, the conference supported the continuance of the struggle primarily to ensure the exorcising of future war from the world.

> Whoever triumphs [it went on], the peoples will have lost unless an international system is established which will prevent war. It would mean nothing to declare the right of peoples to self-determination if this right were left at the mercy of new violations, and was not protected by a super-national authority. That authority can be no other than the League of Nations, which not only all the present belligerents, but every other independent State, should be pressed to join.

[42] Inter-Allied Labour and Socialist Conference, *Memorandum on War Aims Agreed upon at the Central Hall, Westminster, London, S.W., on February 20th to 24th, 1918* (London, [1918]), p. 3. The text, with a few changes, was printed by C. A. McCurdy, as a justification of the Allied position in the war, in a pamphlet called *A Clean Peace. The War Aims of British Labour* (New York, [1918]).

[43] See Chap. VIII.

The constitution of such a league of nations, according to the statement, implied the establishment of an international high court, not only for the settlement of all justiciable disputes, but also for prompt and effective mediation in other issues. The league, it insisted, was the only body suited to carry out the principle of self-determination. It should establish the procedure of international jurisdiction in such cases, fix the methods to guarantee free and genuine elections, restore the political rights of individuals injured by violence and conquest, repress any attempt to use pressure or corruption, and prevent any subsequent reprisals. In addition, the document also urged that it would be necessary to form an international legislature, in which all civilized states were represented, and to push forward the development of international legislation. The members of the league, it stated, must bind themselves to submit every issue to arbitration. Refusal to accept arbitration or to submit to the settlement proposed would imply deliberate aggression, in the face of which all the nations would have to make common cause by using all their economic or military resources against the offending state.

The memorandum did not even stop there. It argued that the sincere acceptance of the rules and decisions of the supernational authority entailed the complete democratization of all countries; the removal of all arbitrary powers which until now had assumed the right of choosing between peace and war; the maintenance or creation of legislatures elected by and designed to express the will of the people; the suppression of secret diplomacy in favor of legislative control of foreign policy; and the publication of treaties, none of which must contravene the stipulations of the league of nations. Again, the league, in order to prepare for the abolition of conscription in all countries, must first take steps to prohibit fresh armaments and limit those already existing, as well as to control manufacture of the implements of war. The states, it added, must undertake such manufactures themselves, so as to abolish the profit motive in war scares and competition in armaments. In order to give effect to all the principles noted, the conference declared that the rules upon which the league was to be founded must be included in the treaty of peace at the end of the war.

The Inter-Allied statement also noted specific areas in which the league of nations would be required to play a significant role. With regard to territorial questions, for example, it postulated that the establishment of a system of international law, and the guarantees afforded by a league of nations, ought to remove the last excuse for insistence on the possession of strategic territories. Similarly, the conference expressed its belief that the main lines of maritime communication ought to be open to vessels of all nations under the protection of the league. It attacked all projects, "now being prepared by Imperialists and capitalists," for an economic war after the peace.[44]

On any showing, the Inter-Allied Memorandum on War Aims was a remarkable document. Since it was in large measure the work of the British labor movement, it demonstrated the fact that British Labor was ready to go all the way in its demand for a league with real and widespread functions. During 1918, the various wings of the labor movement continued unflaggingly to discuss the ideas presented at the Inter-Allied conference, to support them and even occasionally to claim that they did not go far enough. This discussion was carried on at conferences, in Parliament, on the lecture platform, in the labor press and periodicals, and through the medium of special pamphlets.

The Independent Labor party met in conference at Leicester in April, 1918. At this meeting, a revised constitution was adopted by the party. Included in the constitution was the following restatement of the I.L.P.'s international outlook:

> Realizing that war is not only an appalling crime, but constitutes the greatest menace to civilization, the I.L.P. believes that no higher duty rests with the Socialist and Labour movement than that of rendering war impossible. It demands the abolition of Conscription and opposes militarism in all forms.

[44] *Memorandum on War Aims,* pp. 8–10, 13.

It opposes the appropriation of territories and the subjugation of native peoples, the imposition of tariffs, secret treaties, and all policies calculated to provoke animosity and strife between nations. It warmly supports the establishment of International Law and the International Federation of States. For these ends and for the unification of world-wide forces of Socialism and democracy the I.L.P. works in co-operation with the Socialist International.[45]

The I.L.P. conference did not merely indicate its general views on the league. It undertook to examine the "Memorandum on War Aims" passed at the Inter-Allied meeting. In a statement of its position, it expressed its belief that there was much in the memorandum of the utmost value. It particularly endorsed those sections dealing with a league of nations, the repudiation of economic warfare, and the economic reconstruction of the world. But it declared that the party could not commit itself unreservedly to those parts concerned with territorial readjustment. Its main criticism of the memorandum was that "while it accepts the principles of self-determination and the right of nationalities to self-government, it applies these principles only to territory in the possession of the Central Powers, and appears to tacitly deny the rights of subject races and peoples to self-government and self-determination who are under the domination of the Allied Governments." On the understanding, however, that the memorandum was a contribution to the discussion of the peace settlement and not an irreducible minimum, the I.L.P. expressed its pleasure that it had been produced.[46]

The *Labour Leader* served as a medium for additional expressions of the I.L.P. point of view. Philip Snowden, who wrote a regular weekly column for the paper,[47] was particularly

[45] Independent Labour Party, *Report of the Annual Conference held at Leicester, April, 1918* (London, 1918), p. 94.

[46] *Ibid.*, pp. 17–18.

[47] The "Review of the Week" column began to be signed by Snowden from September 14, 1916.

outspoken, for example, on matters of economic policy and territorial aggrandizement. He feared that the Government looked with favor upon a postwar scheme of protectionism and upon the exclusion of Germany from sources of essential raw materials. Such a policy, he warned, was utterly inconsistent with the idea of a league of nations and destructive of the possibility of reducing armaments. It could only be carried out by maintaining the old and vicious system of competing alliances, and by the use of diplomacy to secure spheres of commercial influence for a particular nation. Snowden also accused Arthur Balfour, the foreign minister, of taking the position that a military victory by which one side could impose its conditions upon the other was essential to the establishment of a league. On the contrary, he maintained, a victory by which the Allies were enabled to impose conditions based upon the secret treaties would leave such a feeling of humiliation and irritation as to make friendly international relations impossible.[48]

The *Herald* likewise demonstrated its resolution not to be taken in by a makeshift league totally unconcerned with such problems as territorial aggrandizement and economic warfare. In some cases, particularly in the articles of H. N. Brailsford, it was closer to the I.L.P. position than to the slightly less far-reaching stand of the Labor party. Brailsford's reaction to the Inter-Allied memorandum was typical. Much of it he found admirable, "above all those sections which really are the work of our Labor Party," that is, the outline of a league and the provisions for economic peace. But, like the I.L.P., he was sceptical about the territorial clauses of the plan. Not even the enemy socialists could regard these clauses as a possible basis for peace.[49] Somewhat later, he blasted the definite adoption of the policy of imperial preference by the cabinet. Such a scheme, he charged, would mean a split and atomized world.

[48] Philip Snowden, "Review of the Week," *Labour Leader*, June 20, 27, August 8, 1918.
[49] H. N. Brailsford, "Maximum or Minimum?" *Herald*, March 2, 1918.

We stand to-day confronted with a choice—the only choice which will decide the issue of this war. We shall at the end of it make a single League of Nations, or we shall fail. To succeed in this is victory; to fail in it is defeat. What do we mean by this League? Some mean by it that a collection of States, each isolated, each lonely and repellant in its individualism, shall be linked up for the enforcement of peace by the external tie of a treaty of arbitration. That is a childish and mechanical thought. That League would be a scrap of paper. The League which will be powerful and authoritative when some sudden crisis confronts us with the danger of war, is the League which has made itself influential and important in the normal years of peace. . . . You cannot allow States to go on in the old way, from year to year, with no occasion to remember that a league exists, and then expect them to bow to it when you wave a musty parchment in front of their raging passions.

Brailsford therefore reiterated the argument he had made elsewhere, that the league must develop an economic organization which would assure to each nation, without struggle, its equitable share in the world supply of essential foods and raw materials. It would thus make itself so necessary and so beneficent that it would readily be obeyed in time of crisis. "There is talk of substituting economic boycotts for war. A boycott would have no terror for States living in habitual economic independence of each other." [50] Throughout the year, Brailsford continued to urge a labor policy towards a league based upon the arguments outlined in the foregoing articles, and the end of the war only stimulated him to press his views more vigorously.[51]

Editorials in the *Herald* echoed the analysis made by Brailsford. They too implied that the Inter-Allied conference had not gone far enough in its suggestions for future international settlement. "Let us extend to Ireland, India, Egypt," the *Herald*

[50] *Idem*, "Free Trade for Socialists," *ibid.*, August 10, 1918.
[51] See, for example, "Bulgaria's Surrender," *ibid.*, October 5, 1918; "Wilson on Balfour?" *ibid.*, November 2, 1918; "The Coalition and Peace," *ibid.*, November 30, 1918.

demanded, "the same principles which we profess to want to see adopted in the Austrian and Turkish Empires." All through 1918, it pressed for a policy based upon a league with wide economic functions, the abandonment of economic warfare, the repudiation of the secret treaties, self-determination, disarmament, freedom of the seas, and international control of backward areas.[52] When the war ended, and labor was preparing for the general election, the *Herald* issued a supplement making plain that the league it advocated had little in common with that accepted by the British Government and its supporters. "The League of Nations which Labour seeks," it declared, "is a League, not of capitalist Governments, but of peoples, a League set, not on stemming the tide of world revolution, but on the speedy realization of Social Democracy over all the world." [53]

Despite the criticisms of the I.L.P. and the *Herald* noted above, there was substantial agreement in the labor movement toward the end of the war on the general nature of the league desired. This fact is perhaps nowhere better illustrated than in the pages of the *New Statesman*. The Fabian Society's original plan called for a league with limited functions. Yet in 1918, the *New Statesman's* articles gave support to an international organization many of whose tasks were very like those suggested by the I.L.P., the Labor party, the *Labour Leader* and the *Herald*. The Fabian journal also took issue with the advocates of the plan to set up a league of Allies immediately. Some, it claimed, wanted such a body because they hoped it would persist and so prevent the creation of a new international system embracing all the present belligerents in a league of peace. Others, it was granted, believed that it was better to have an incomplete league than none at all. The real objection to such a procedure was not merely that it would create suspicion among those states outside the league, but that an alliance for

[52] *Herald*, March 23, June 15, 29, October 12, 19, November 9, 1918.
[53] "Why Labour Left the Coalition" (Supplement), *ibid.*, November 30, 1918.

war could not turn gradually into an organization for peace. In the words of the *New Statesman,* "You cannot cast out the Devil by entering his service and wearing his livery." [54]

While the *New Statesman* continued to insist that the league's chief function must be to provide machinery for the prevention of war, it agreed with the Inter-Allied Labor and Socialist Conference on the importance of economic functions. It advocated a systematic control of the exportable surpluses of the various countries, in order to prevent economic boycotts or other policies that might endanger peace or good order. And it quoted directly from the Inter-Allied memorandum in stressing that the league must consider "the need for an international agreement for the enforcement in all countries of the legislation on factory conditions, a maximum eight-hour day, the prevention of 'sweating' and unhealthy trades necessary to protect the workers against exploitation and oppression, and the prohibition of night-work for women." [55] A league with such tasks obviously had more in common with that of H. N. Brailsford than with the organization proposed in the more conventional schemes.

A comprehensive scheme for the league to act as the vehicle of international intercourse had thus been worked out by labor bodies and organs of opinion. Individual leaders of the labor movement were no less active as the war drew to a close, except in the halls of Parliament where their role in the discussion of a league was minor during 1918. Lord Parmoor at this time can hardly be called a leader in the labor movement, or indeed even a representative of labor, but since he was in attitude well on the way to his later membership in the first Labor Government by the end of the war, his views and activity may perhaps be indicated here. As has already been noted, Parmoor had participated early in the work of the League of Nations Society. In addition, he took various occasions to reiterate his views. In

---

[54] "How to Make the League," *New Statesman,* IX (1918), 365–366.
[55] "The League of Nations," *ibid.,* XII (1918), 125–127.

November, 1917, he delivered the Rhodes lecture at University College, advocating a league with an authoritative tribunal and adequate sanctions.[56] He prompted the important debate in the House of Lords which began on March 19, 1918, with his resolution in favor of a league. In proposing the resolution, Parmoor noted that the league offered the only substitute available for the discredited policy of the balance of power. If the league had existed in 1914, he declared, it was virtually certain that war would not have broken out. In providing machinery for the settlement of disputes, he warned, the league must be in a position to limit the rights of national sovereignty. He recognized that many would object to this, but he felt it necessary to make the issue clear. He went on to argue that in order for a league to be effective it must rest on some system of relative disarmament, so that no individual nation would be in a position to menace the force of the whole organization. Finally, Parmoor re-emphasized his belief that a genuine league of nations must be prepared to use military force if it were to carry out its functions.[57]

Later, in a lecture before the Grotius Society, Parmoor again outlined his proposals for a league of nations to prevent the outbreak of war.[58] In general, his scheme was the cautious one of the League of Nations Society, but it should be noted that his emphasis upon disarmament went farther in its implications than many of the Society's members were willing to go. Actually, when the negotiations to amalgamate the Society with the League of Free Nations Association were in progress, Parmoor objected. He denounced the alliance with a group that

[56] The *Times,* November 27, 1917; Lord Parmoor, *A Retrospect; Looking Back over a Life of More than Eighty Years* (London, 1936), p. 124.

[57] *Parliamentary Debates,* Lords, XXIX (March 19, 1918), 476–488.

[58] Lord Parmoor, "The League of Nations (An Address Delivered by Lord Parmoor in Gray's Inn Hall on April 10th, 1918)," *Transactions of the Grotius Society,* IV (Problems of the War: Papers Read before the Society in the Year 1918) (London, 1919), xvii–xxiii.

was in favor of a premature league of Allied nations, and preferred to wait and make a more generous and all-inclusive league.[59] Such objectives were, of course, disregarded, but Parmoor continued to advocate his own views of a league.[60]

Labor's role in parlimentary discussion of a league was minor during 1918. In general, the small labor delegation in Parliament was too busy working out plans for reconstruction after the war and dealing with problems peculiar to the workingman to give any great consideration to the league. In addition, of course, the time allotted to the Labor minority for debate was necessarily short. A rather striking exception to this picture was a speech made by Ramsay MacDonald in the House of Commons on August 1. MacDonald denounced the idea that a league of nations could enforce the peace. It could only make arrangements, he argued, which would prevent the conditions under which war became possible. Peace would be maintained, he insisted, when international affairs were made responsible to the public opinion of the world, and the league's task must therefore be to instruct public opinion. "The good sentiment, the tremendous genuine desire to end all this kind of conflict, is not going to be done merely by creating the machinery of a League of Nations." An organization developed by the Allies, and excluding Germany, could not be called a league of nations. The league, MacDonald said, must not be merely European or American, but must embrace the whole world. And finally, he reiterated the view of the I.L.P. on the nature of the League:

> It cannot be a league of Governments; it cannot be a league of Diplomatists; it cannot be a league of Foreign Offices. It must be a league of Parliaments. You must have popular representation. Your League of Nations must not be a part of the machinery of Governments—of national Governments. Your

[59] Letter of Parmoor to *Manchester Guardian*, October 2, 1918.
[60] *E.g.*, Lord Parmoor, "President Wilson and the Peace Settlement," *Contemporary Review*, CXV (1919), 10–14.

League of Nations must be part of the general political life of
your nations. Without that you are bound to fail.[61]

A few other Labor M.P.'s spoke in support of a league of
some kind, but added little in the way of new ideas.[62] Outside
Parliament, labor spokesmen were a great deal more vocal.
Arthur Henderson, J. H. Thomas, and J. R. Clynes helped
spread the idea in speeches delivered before and after the conclusion of the war. Even G. N. Barnes, whose views were
drawing further and further away from those of the labor rank
and file, made speech after speech in favor of a league. The
nature of his league, however, was radically different from that
projected by his former Labor colleagues. Barnes tended to accept the "league now" argument, but favored eventual inclusion
of Germany in order better to control her.[63]

A trio of interesting pamphlets was further evidence of labor's genuine concern about future international organization.
Labour and the New Social Order was the fruit of the collaboration of Arthur Henderson, Ramsay MacDonald, and Sidney
Webb, which had already resulted in the British "Memorandum
on War Aims." [64] The pamphlet was a statement of the program
of the Labor party—as seen by the leaders of its major constituent groups—for the postwar world. In its passage on international relations, it declared that labor disavowed any claim
to an increase of British territory and disclaimed all idea of
economic war. It expressed the opposition of the labor movement to the "old entanglements and mystifications of Secret
Diplomacy and the formation of Leagues against Leagues." Instead, it reiterated the labor proposal for a universal league of

[61] *Parliamentary Debates,* Commons, CIX (August 1, 1918), 720–
724.

[62] *Ibid.,* p. 699; CIX (August 8, 1918), 1579–1592.

[63] *Liberal Magazine,* XXVI (June, 1918), 236; *The Times,* January 2, June 17, August 6, 18, October 6, November 22, December 4, 1918;
Forward, July 27, 1918.

[64] Hamilton, *op. cit.,* p. 175.

194 The League of Nations Movement in Great Britain 1914-1919

nations, with an international high court to try all justiciable disputes; an international legislature to enact such common laws as could be mutually agreed upon; and an international council of mediation to endeavor to settle without conflict non-justiciable disputes. "The world," concluded this statement of policy, "has suffered too much from war for the Labour Party to have any other policy than that of lasting peace." [65]

Arthur Henderson contributed an essay to the league of nations series of the Oxford Press. In it, he set forth in simple, direct terms the main elements of the league as conceived by labor. He was especially emphatic in warning that the league must be a federation of all the nations, not excepting Germany. And when Germany was included, it must be on terms of equality with other nations. If the league was to have any hope of success, Henderson stressed, everything must be done to prevent the division of Europe into two separate and hostile economic camps after the war. "What is to be thought of a statesmanship," he asked, "which invites the German people to form part of a Federation of Nations for the maintenance of world peace, and at the same time proclaims the intention of constructing a Federation of Allies for no other object than the setting up of a commercial boycott of Germany?" Such a proposal, he charged, was not only dangerous but criminal, and the sooner it was repudiated the better it would be for the Allied cause. [66]

The third pamphlet, entitled *Memoranda on International Labour Legislation: The Economic Structure of the League of Nations*, was not published until 1919, when the peace conference was in session. But it was composed of memoranda written earlier under the direction of the Labor party's research department, and was issued as a summary of the party's position

[65] Labour Party, *Labour and the New Social Order, A Report on Reconstruction* (London, 1918), pp. 22–23.

[66] Arthur Henderson, *The League of Nations and Labour* (London, 1918), pp. 45–46, 49, 53.

during the war on the subjects dealt with. As a compact statement of that position, the pamphlet throws considerable light on the views developed by the labor movement.

Three of the memoranda on international labor legislation dealt especially with the league of nations. The tenor of the one which took up a "Parliament of the League of Nations" may be inferred from its initial statements that the "development of practical internationalism during the War has forced the idea of a League of Nations far beyond the original conception of an organization to ensure peace" and that "apart from its functions as a legislator and an arbitrator, its administrative tasks will make it in a real sense a World Government." The labor memorandum recognized that it was virtually certain that the league would contain a sort of executive composed of officials of the Allied great powers and that its "general conference" would consist of delegates appointed directly by the various governments. Such a plan, it noted, provided for no body to act as a real critic of the executive or to subject its conduct to the test of public opinion. The only body which could do that would be a genuine parliament based on proportional representation. Such a body would at once bring together common opinions. A Socialist party would at once be formed, then, perhaps, a Clerical party, and gradually other shades of opinion would coalesce. "The class line of cleavage would be seen to be international, and a great step would be gained in emancipating the workers from the obsessions of a narrow nationalism. Perhaps for this reason our opponents will resist, and we ought to promote the idea." The parliament might be chosen by direct election, or, what was undoubtedly easier, the popular house in each national parliament might elect the national delegation by proportional representation. If the national parliament was fairly created, the result would be a reasonably exact mirror of national opinion. To implement its idea, the memorandum drafted the following recommendation which was addressed to the "conference" of the league:

That the Conference shall propose the inclusion in the governing machinery of the League of Nations of a Deliberative International Parliament, composed of delegations chosen by proportional representation from each national Parliament. Its functions should be to create an international public opinion, to bring to bear upon the Executive and Commissions of the League in their administrative action, and to prepare drafts or suggestions of international legislation for the Conference of the League.[67]

The other two memoranda were concerned with the economic functions and structure of the league of nations. They argued in forceful terms that the league must not be merely an *ad hoc* association for the prevention of war by conciliation or arbitration, but at least the groundwork of a real system of international cooperation as well. Its economic functions must, therefore, be clearly defined and it must have permanent machinery to ensure the continuance of economic cooperation. The necessary functions of the economic section of the league, as conceived by the Labor party, formed an imposing list:

1. To assist in the maintenance of credit, *i.e.*, purchasing power, in the various countries at such a level as will ensure (a) a fair allocation of supplies of materials, etc.; (b) stimulation of supply of important materials by promoting production in the various countries; (c) no unnecessary disturbance of world market conditions through a breakdown of purchasing power in a particular country owing to preventible causes.

2. To prevent exploitation by trusts, operating in the world market, whether of interests concerned in production, transport, or distribution, and to control the operations of international firms and combines.

3. To regulate the granting of concessions in undeveloped countries, and to safeguard such countries from unfair exploitation or monopolization by particular interests.

4. To secure the enforcement of international conventions,

[67] Labour Party, *Memoranda on International Labour Legislation: The Economic Structure of the League of Nations* (London, 1919), pp. 1, 27-28.

in the matter of the open door and other matters, and to prevent their evasion by secret rebates, concessions, etc.

5. To promote international economic conventions based on the widest possible measure of international co-operation, e.g., commercial treaties, Labour conventions, traffic agreements, and so forth.

6. To undertake the international allocation of supplies of which there is a shortage, or which are in danger of being monopolized by a particular nation or interest to the detriment of others.

7. To promote the formation of international conferences or councils in various industries and economic groups, in order to secure the greatest possible measure of co-operation in each industry or group.[68]

This elaborate series of suggestions was paralleled by an equally detailed scheme for the economic structure of the league, along lines designed to provide machinery for carrying the recommendations into effect.[69] Clearly, the Labor party had come a long way from its cautious acceptance of the league idea early in the war.

All through 1918 various groups affiliated in one way or another with the labor movement added their voices to the clear-cut demand for a league of nations. In May, for example, the Cooperative Congress passed a unanimous resolution in favor of the league. Several months later, the National Union of Railwaymen in preparing for the Trade Union Congress reiterated its support of the league and emphasized its condemnation of the secret treaties and secret diplomacy. And immediately upon conclusion of the war a Labor Emergency Conference was called by the Labor party at which a declaration was made in favor of a world Labor congress "with a view to the foundations of an effective League of Nations being laid upon a genuinely democratic basis." [70] It goes without saying that in the election

[68] *Ibid.*, pp. 28–30.
[69] *Ibid.*, pp. 30–31.
[70] *Labour Leader*, May 23, 1918; *The Times*, August 24, 1918; *Manchester Guardian*, November 14, 1918.

campaign of December, 1918, support for a league was a principal plank in the Labor platform.[71]

By the end of the war, then, British Labor was a most important political force behind the drive for a league of nations. It had made a slow start, for while the Fabian Society had published its plan early in the war and the Independent Labor party had taken a broad view of future international organization from the beginning, the moderate majority based on the trade unions did not really accept the need for a powerful league until well into 1917. By then, however, the Labor party came to adopt most of the basic proposals outlined at I.L.P. conferences, in the I.L.P. press, and sometimes in the *Herald* as well. The result was a conception of the league of nations as the central core of international intercourse. Labor saw it as an organization whose major function was to be the regulation of the peacetime activities of the world—especially the economic activities—in order to ensure conditions which would make war unlikely. The labor movement did not reject the idea that the league must provide machinery for the peaceful settlement of disputes; it merely insisted that such a function was only one of the tasks of the international body. It produced a number of cogent documents outlining its position, and in its official utterances showed a willingness to commit itself to a comprehensive league scheme far beyond the generalities indulged in by other political groups. Its stand was more definite and more concrete than that of the Liberal party, and it pressed its position with considerably more vigor. In any assignment of credit for the development of the league idea, therefore, British labor must be ranked well ahead of the Liberals and, of course, far ahead of the Conservatives.

[71] *Why Women Should Join the Labour Party and Vote for the Labour Candidates* (Labour Party Leaflet, No. 3, new series); *Why Labour Supports a League of Nations* (Labour Party Leaflet, No. 17, new series); *Why I Shall Vote Labour* (Labour Party Leaflet, No. 26, new series); *The Labour Party* (unnumbered Labour Party Leaflet), all of 1918.

The Idea of Colonial Trusteeship

ONE TANGENTIAL CURRENT of discussion requires attention in order to round out the picture of the development of the league of nations idea. The concept of trusteeship over colonial areas was one of the most significant outgrowths of the campaign, and its development throws into sharp focus the attitudes of various groups towards the league itself. In a sense, the degree of willingness to accept such a concept which implied a broadly-conceived and powerful league was a test of the kind of league envisaged by the particular proponents and, as we shall see, revealed much the same pattern as has already been outlined earlier in this study.

The idea of trusteeship was most fully worked out in Great Britain, whose status as a colonial power inevitably directed attention to the question. In Britain, the man most intimately associated with the idea was General Jan Smuts. There has been a tendency, in analyzing the mandates system, to trace its origins to him, or at the most to a few groups believed directly to have influenced his thinking. Actually, discussion of trusteeship developed in Britain long before Smuts expressed himself on the matter, and in fact the major possible lines of approach had already been outlined before his suggestions appeared. To be sure, as has recently been pointed out,[1] the roots of the idea go back at least as far as the eighteenth century. Nevertheless, it

[1] H. Duncan Hall, *Mandates, Dependencies and Trusteeship* (Washington, 1948), pp. 18, 92–93.

seems quite clear that the conception developed between 1914 and 1919 was a reaction to the conditions revealed by the war and took its character from the contemporary response to those conditions.

To a generation not far removed from the scramble which had led in its most spectacular aspect to the partition of huge portions of Africa it appeared axiomatic that rivalry over economic opportunities in colonial areas was one of the chief causes of war. During the great league debate in Great Britain, most attention was directed to the problem of providing instruments for the settlement of colonial disputes—or any disputes— once they had arisen. But a few organizations and individuals went further. In Liberal and above all in Labor quarters, an attempt was made to define the terms under which equitable access to colonial markets, resources, and investment facilities might be made compatible with international cooperation and peace. This point of view first appeared as a modest demand for the application of the open door principle to "backward" areas whose resources were essential to an industrialized Europe. Gradually, however, concern for the protection of colonial natives developed into an integral part of the argument. As a result, the doctrine of tutelage or trusteeship became the pivot of "progressive" thinking on the colonial question. Though there were, of course, differences of opinion as to the techniques of application, this doctrine of trusteeship gained influential support and was eventually written into the League Covenant as the mandates articles.[2]

As early in the war as 1915 a number of writers began to urge the adoption of the open door policy. In the pages of the *New Statesman,* organ of the Fabian Society, a long discussion of the fate of the German colonies was carried on by Sir Harry Johnston, the noted African explorer, G. Lowes Dickinson, and E. D. Morel. Dickinson and Morel, the latter already well-known for his campaign to better native conditions in Africa, both argued

[2] Elizabeth Van Maanen-Hellmer, *The Mandates System in Relation to Africa and the Pacific Islands* (London, 1919), pp. 29–30.

that it would be unwise to deprive Germany of her colonies. Dickinson proposed agreements whereby equality of economic opportunity should be guaranteed to all nations in all colonial areas. Morel, at this time a pacifist Liberal but soon to join the ranks of Labor, added a significant plea for the preservation of native rights to the land in those same areas.[3]

At about this same time, the empire-minded *Round Table* group, which was to have an important role in the development of the mandates idea, first appeared on the scene. C. E. Fayle, after studying various articles in the *Round Table* and consulting with C. R. Buxton and J. M. Keynes,[4] suggested that some attempt should be made by the powers to secure agreement on the policy of freedom of trade and cooperation in the opening up of undeveloped territory. Looking ahead to the possible breakup of Asiatic Turkey, Fayle reasoned that the only way to avoid a struggle over the spoils would be "an equitable and friendly agreement by the Powers for the protection of their joint and several interests."[5]

As yet the issue of international supervision, as contrasted with international agreement, in colonial matters had not been raised. But in *The War of Steel and Gold,* a cogent, and widely-read, analysis of the economic causes of war, H. N. Brailsford outlined a "Sketch for a Federal League" which added the element of an international organization. Brailsford indicated that such a league might carry on trade with the colonies of the member states, control the competition for concessions and spheres of influence, and finally see to it that trade with colo-

[3] *New Statesman,* V (July 31–October 2, 1915), 445, 644–645, *passim.*

[4] P. B. Potter, "Origin of the System of Mandates under the League of Nations," *American Political Science Review,* XVI (1922), 573.

[5] Fayle, *The Great Settlement,* pp. 194–196. It is difficult to agree with Potter that "the general drift of the thought" in the direction of international control "can be clearly detected." Potter, "Origin of the System of Mandates," *loc. cit.,* p. 573. Fayle did, however, suggest international supervision in January, 1919. Cf. *The Fourteenth Point,* pp. 335–336.

nies remained open to all league members on the same terms as the trade of the mother country.[6]

In sharp contrast to the somewhat vague suggestions of the writers already noted, J. A. Hobson's *Towards International Government* considered the concrete problems of control and offered several positive proposals. Hobson rejected the old sphere of influence theory and advocated instead that the future international council effect a partition "which, having regard to the special political and economic interests of particular nations by virtue of accessibility or established connections, would acknowledge a special right of intervention and even of political control, but with an express agreement to maintain an open door and equality of opportunity for the capital and trade of other nations." He pointed out that the principle had been embodied in recent treaties such as the Algeciras agreement, but that none had contained adequate guarantees for the performance of its undertakings. "If," he argued, "a standing International Council could be empowered to negotiate such partitions, with periodic arrangements for revision, the dangerous collisions of economic interests which have underlain the policy of political and economic expansion in the past might be reduced to a minimum."[7]

As one student of the mandates system has pointed out,[8] Hobson's proposals contained most of the elements of that system—the selection, by an international organization, of states which should have the right of administering certain areas, but in a way not prejudicial to the interests of other nations. But as yet the idea of the protection of inhabitants of colonial territory was not a part of the newly-postulated schemes for international control. That lack was remedied in 1916, somewhat vaguely by P. H. Kerr (later Lord Lothian), at that time editor of the *Round Table,* more explicitly by Hobson himself. Kerr's

[6] H. N. Brailsford, *The War of Steel and Gold* (London, 1915), pp. 335–336.

[7] Hobson, *Towards International Government,* pp. 138–142.

[8] Maanen-Hellmer, *op. cit.,* p. 32.

contribution in April was a chapter entitled "Political Relations between Advanced and Backward Peoples" in a little volume on international relations. In the course of his general survey of political relations with backward groups he insisted that the only real justification for alien rule was the well-being of the natives. To that end, he laid down the principle that "so long as there are peoples seriously behind the present level of the most civilized, commercial intercourse is bound to lead to evils which can only be ended by a more civilized people assuming charge of the government of the more backward race." But, he added, "when this has been done the ruling people ought to govern the dependency as trustees for all mankind, having as their ultimate aim the raising of the inhabitants to the level at which they can govern themselves and share in the greater responsibilities of the world." [9] Here then was the idea of obligations toward the natives, but expressed in terms of a somewhat tenuous "trusteeship for all mankind," with no mention of an international body selected to watch over the trustees. In the light of Kerr's later close connections with the development of the mandates idea it is perhaps not difficult to assume that his 1916 discussion implied such an international organization, but a close reading of the argument fails to reveal that implication.[10]

Hobson was much more explicit in his contribution to a series of essays written mainly by outstanding Liberals and members of the *Round Table* group, but edited by C. R. Buxton, who was already moving from the ranks of Liberalism towards the Independent Labor party. Hobson saw the problem faced by European nations as twofold: how to secure the reasonable rights

[9] P. H. Kerr, "Political Relations between Advanced and Backward Peoples," in Grant and others, *An Introduction to the Study of International Relations* (London, 1916), pp. 170–179.

[10] Both Maanen-Hellmer and Potter appear to have read between the lines and assumed that Kerr's idea of trusteeship implied some enforcing authority, but the text of his argument gives no such hint. Cf., Maaner-Hellmer, *op. cit.,* p. 32 and Potter, "Origin of the System of Mandates," *loc. cit.,* p. 574.

of the inhabitants of undeveloped countries against a policy of plunder, servitude, and murder; how to secure equal economic opportunities for the members of the more advanced nations in those areas. In the case of territories already possessed, the solution, he thought, might be found in a simple agreement by all the powers to offer equal economic access to their colonies to members of all nations. But in the case of still unappropriated territories he went much further, suggesting two possible means of attack. One was the establishment of a joint international protectorate, exercised by a commission appointed by whatever international organization was set up. The other was the delegation of the duty of protection by the international authority to some single nation, and the apportionment of such protectorates among the various "civilized" nations.[11] In either case, Hobson's argument was based on the idea of responsibility to the native as well as on that of economic arrangements which would help keep peace among the more powerful nations. E. D. Morel likewise reiterated his concern for the interests of colonial inhabitants, but as yet connected it only with the project for the immediate neutralization of Central Africa.[12]

Finally, in September, the *New Statesman* fused the ideas of neutralization and internationalization. In a consideration of the question of German colonies, it proposed that all international fences be abolished in the tropics. All Central Africa should be neutralized and administered by an international commission for the benefit primarily of the native groups and secondarily of the traders of all countries on equal terms. Recognizing the difficulties of international administration, the *New Statesman* tackled the problem in a truly Fabian spirit:

> If the Allies determine at the end of the war to retain control of the German Colonies, they might and ought to give a solemn undertaking to hold those territories in trust for civilization, to

[11] J. A. Hobson, "The Open Door," in C. R. Buxton (ed.), *Towards a Lasting Settlement* (New York, 1916), pp. 105–107.

[12] E. D. Morel, "Towards a New Europe," *Labour Leader,* January 20, 1916.

treat the interests of the natives therein as paramount, and to preserve in perpetuity the principle of the Open Door in the fullest sense of the term. If at the same time France and Great Britain consented to make their own tropical dependencies in Africa subject to the same trust, the moral effect of the undertaking as a demonstration of our good faith would obviously be enormously enhanced. The sacrifice, if any, would be small, whilst the principle thus established of giving all countries an equal place in the sun (as far as this great area is concerned) would be of inestimable value as a step towards the permanent solution of the African problem. The further step of international control would be merely one of machinery.[13]

By the end of 1916 the essential features of the idea of trusteeship had been developed. In the discussion that followed there was general agreement as to the two aims of such trusteeship, but there was a certain amount of disagreement as to whether colonial territories should be administered directly by an international body or controlled by a single nation under international supervision. Throughout 1917 and well into 1918 the question was kept alive mainly by the efforts of the labor movement. The British Labor party executive, the Independent Labor party, members of the Fabian Society, individual Labor party members, and even labor-minded publicists like H. G. Wells contributed their ideas. In view of the volume of discussion it is rather surprising to find that most accounts of the development of the mandates scheme skip hurriedly over the role of Labor in order to direct attention to the *Round Table* and General Smuts.[14] The explanation is probably to be found

[13] "An Allied Peace III.—The German Colonies," *New Statesman,* VII (1916), 582–583.

[14] This is true of the works of Maanen-Hellmer and Potter cited above, and to a certain extent also of Quincy Wright's *Mandates under the League of Nations* (Chicago, 1930). See, for example, pp. 21–22. On the other hand, Ray Stannard Baker, who was close to President Wilson, believed that Smuts had been greatly influenced by the work of the Inter-Allied Labor and Socialist Conference of 1918. Cf. Baker, *op. cit.,* I, 227. Brand, *op. cit., passim,* outlines most of the official Labor proposals.

in the fact that the most immediate sources of General Smut's inspiration—and through him of President Wilson's views— were an article published in December, 1918, in the *Round Table* and conversations with members of the group responsible for its policies.[15] Nevertheless, once the idea took shape, and almost until the end of the war, it was Labor that consistently furnished the impetus to the campaign for the principle of trusteeship.

The general nature of Labor's approach to the colonial question was outlined by the *Herald*, in May, 1917. In a signed editorial, H. N. Brailsford attacked the proposal that the German colonies be annexed and Germany's industry crippled by the monopolization of indispensable tropical raw materials. What was needed, he declared, was an international charter, based upon amicable agreement between competing groups of European capitalists and prohibiting the confiscation of native land and its produce. A league of nations might be able to succeed "where the old Europe of the armed peace and the competing alliances failed and was bound to fail." [16]

Labor's drive for international control of colonies received its official start in August. In anticipation of the pending Inter-Allied Labor and Socialist Conference the Labor party executive drew up and published a statement of war aims in nineteen articles, two of which addressed themselves to the colonial problem. With regard to all the colonies—German and Allied—in tropical Africa north of the Zambesi River and south of the Sahara Desert, the statement proposed that, together with the "nominally independent" republic of Liberia, they be turned over to the proposed supernational authority or league of nations. That body would then appoint an imperial tribunal, with its own trained staff, to administer them as a single independent African state. In the state, the open door and equal freedom of enterprise for the traders of all nations were to be enforced. Na-

[15] Potter, "Origins of the System of Mandates," *loc. cit.*, p. 575; Wright, *op. cit.*, pp. 22–23, note 53a.
[16] *Herald*, May 26, 1917.

tives were to be protected against exploitation and oppression, and their tribal interests preserved. All revenues raised were to be expended for the welfare and development of the African state itself. Finally, the area was to be permanently neutralized. The statement also pointed out that it would be unwise to return Armenia, Mesopotamia, and Arabia to the inefficient rule of Turkey. Instead, if those areas proved incapable of self-government, they should be dealt with in the same way as the colonies of tropical Africa, and placed for administration in the hands of a commission acting under the league of nations.[17]

The far-reaching aims of the executive committee were clear. Not only did it advocate international control of African colonies, but it suggested, for the first time, a scheme for international administration that went far beyond any previous plan. In little more than a fortnight the Independent Labor party, having considered the proposal of the executive committee, responded to it with a "Note by the Independent Labour Party on the Memorandum of the Labour Party Executive." In parallel columns, it printed the original suggestions and its own comments on them. While supporting the demand for the internationalization and neutralization of tropical Africa, the I.L.P. indicated some of the difficulties presented by the scheme.

> The first [the Note pointed out] is that the proposal, if carried out, would deprive the Central Powers of all sovereignty in any part of Africa, and would take away from the Allied Powers, with the exception of Great Britain, the sovereignty of most of their present Colonies, while leaving the British Colonies in South Africa and South-West Africa still under the sovereignty of Great Britain. This seems to us to be an unreasonable proposal, and one which cannot be defended as being consistent with the accepted principle of "No conquests as the outcome of this war." Further, we have grave doubts as to the practicability of any League of Nations at present being able thoroughly to administer such an enormous area as the whole of Central Africa, a country without roads or railways. For the

[17] *The Times,* August 11, 1917.

time being we think it would be better if direct responsibility for the administration of divided areas were laid upon individual European states under the supervision of an International Commission charged with the oversight of the observance of the principles 1, 2, 3 and 4 laid down in the paragraph of the Memorandum.[18]

Here was a fundamental divergence of views on the techniques of internationalization. The Labor party executive had proposed direct and complete international administration; the Independent Labor party had countered with a trusteeship plan which most nearly approximated that of J. A. Hobson. The British Socialist party, which also prepared a program for submission to the Inter-Allied Conference, went further than either of the other two organizations. It proposed that all "unsettled," that is, colonial, areas yielding raw materials required by civilization, no matter by whom at present held, should be placed under the control of an international commission. But at the same time it demanded that Mesopotamia should be transferred to Turkey and the German colonies returned to Germany.[19]

For a few months the official Labor controversy over the type of colonial administration dropped out of sight. Then, on December 28, 1917, the executive committee of the Labor party presented its "Memorandum on War Aims" to a special conference of the labor movement held at Central Hall, Westminster, in London. The text of the colonial articles had undergone some minor revisions, but the gist of their contents was substantially the same. No concessions had been made to the I.L.P. proposal for national administration under international supervision; full international administration remained the pivot of the idea.[20] It was accepted without amendment by the special conference.

Once again the Independent Labor party took up the argument. Writing his regular "Review of the Week" in the *Labour*

[18] *Ibid.*, August 29, 1917; *Labour Leader*, August 30, 1917.
[19] *The Times*, August 27, 1917.
[20] Henderson, *The Aims of Labour*, pp. 86–87.

Leader, official organ of the I.L.P., Philip Snowden noted that
the strongest criticism of the memorandum could be based
upon the fact that it was a statement of war aims from the British rather than an international point of view. "While proposing to liberate subject races everywhere who happen to be under enemy control, the document is singularly silent about the
liberation of subject peoples under French, British, Italian, and
American authority," [21] Snowden was silent on the subject of
the mechanics of trusteeship, but that the I.L.P. argument had
not been discarded was soon to be demonstrated.

The Inter-Allied Labor and Socialist Conference met in London, February 20–23, 1918. The delegates proceeded to amend
the memorandum of the Labor party executive and the resulting colonial articles represented a triumph for the Independent
Labor party. The wording of the section on Turkey remained
substantially the same, as did the paragraphs denouncing colonial imperialism. But in the vital area of administrative recommendations there were drastic changes. The draft finally accepted ran as follows:

> With respect to these colonies [in tropical Africa] the Con-
> ference declares in favor of a system of control, established by
> international agreement under the League of Nations and main-
> tained by its guarantee, which, while respecting national sover-
> eignty, would be alike inspired by broad conceptions of eco-
> nomic freedom and concerned to safeguard the rights of the
> natives under the best conditions possible for them, and in
> particular:
> (1) It would take account in each locality of the wishes of
> the people, expressed in the form which is possible for
> them.
> (2) The interests of the native tribes as regards the owner-
> ship of the soil would be maintained.
> (3) The whole of the revenues would be devoted to the well-
> being and development of the colonies themselves.[22]

[21] *Labour Leader,* January 3, 1918.
[22] *The Times,* February 25, 1918.

Although one of its major proposals had been accepted by the Inter-Allied Conference, the Independent Labor party was far from satisfied. At its annual conference in April, 1918, the delegates adopted a resolution deploring the attempt of the Socialist movement to commit itself in advance to detailed territorial readjustments, and objecting that the memorandum still appeared to deny the right of self-determination to subject peoples under Allied domination. Nevertheless, the memorandum was in general welcomed as a major contribution to the discussion of the peace settlement.[23]

While the official Labor debate was in progress, there was no moratorium on other discussions of the problem of colonial administration. One of the most striking proposals appeared in the August 4 issue of the *New Statesman.* After expatiating at length on the evils of unchecked imperialism, this article went on to propose the establishment of a permanent commission of the league, divided as experience dictated into sub-committees with competence in different political or economic spheres. The commission should have the power of (a) allocating among the different nations spheres for investment of capital; (b) arranging the terms upon which different national groups should share either in loans or railway enterprises or other concessions; (c) adjudicating upon appeals from a state in behalf of its nationals claiming participation in financial, commercial, or industrial enterprises; (d) recommending a case for adjudication either by a tribunal or council of conciliation of the projected league of nations; (e) protecting native interests; (f) framing general proposals to be submitted to the council of the league for the regulation of native interests.

The *New Statesman* plan went on to declare that on the sub-committees national financial and commercial groups might be represented in addition to governments, and that native interests must be officially represented. In the case of advanced countries such as China, Turkey, Persia, or Siam, native repre-

[23] Independent Labour Party, *Report of the Annual Conference* . . . April, 1918, pp. 17–18.

sentatives would probably be able to defend the interests of their fellow countrymen. But the same would not be true for tropical Africa. Here the difficulty might be met "by the appointment of a certain number of men or women who had devoted themselves to the protection of native interests, whether as missionaries, writers, or in other ways." [24]

The article did not make it clear whether colonial administration was to be handled by the various states or whether international administrative units were to be set up, but a week later the *New Statesman* definitely rejected the idea of international administration.[25] The most interesting feature of its proposals was the role assigned to a permanent commission. This commission was to serve as a coordinating body for the subcommittees. It was to exercise a kind of trusteeship based on control over the resources, trade and investment opportunities of colonial areas. The central idea undoubtedly stemmed from the very early argument in favor of enforcing equality of access to the colonial economies, but in its *New Statesman* form it had been so elaborated and developed as to mark a virtual departure from previous thinking on the subject. Perhaps for that reason it did not reappear—barring one possible exception —in the discussion of trusteeship under a league of nations.

Various individuals helped elaborate the Labor viewpoint. E. D. Morel continued his defense of native interests in Africa. In a little book published by the I.L.P.'s National Labour Press, he accepted the idea of European trusteeship in tropical Africa, but seemed to envisage that trusteeship merely as an international guarantee of proper administration by the various states in their own colonies. His program was a threefold one: the neutralization of tropical Africa, the internationalization of European commercial activities in that area, and the enforcement of certain basic principles of administration designed to preserve native institutions and protect the native in the possession

[24] "A League of Nations IV.—Overseas Possessions," *New Statesman*, IX (1918), 418.
[25] *Ibid.*, IX (1918), 437.

of his land.[26] While Morel's plan was vague in matters of technique, its insistence upon native rights blended effectively with the general Labor argument as to the purposes of European control in the colonies.

In a second and revised edition of a *League of Nations,* which had been first published in February, 1917, H. N. Brailsford was much closer to one of the official points of view. The new edition, dated November, 1917, echoed the arguments which the Independent Labor party had made the previous August. On the subject of colonies he addressed himself first to the original suggestions of the Labor party executive, as yet unmodified by the decisions of the Inter-Allied Labor and Socialist Conference. Analyzing the proposal for a single, internationalized Central African state, he concluded that it erred by excess.

> The burden is too heavy, the task too large to thrust upon a League which has yet to be created. It is easy to construct on paper an International Civil Service, composed of Englishmen, Frenchmen, Germans and Americans, but it would start work without a common tradition, or rather with a set of extremely various traditions. . . . There are other objections to the plan. It would wipe out the German Colonial Empire while leaving to us and the French most of our valued possessions.

In place of the Labor scheme Brailsford suggested a plan whereby the various nations, including Germany, would retain their colonies subject to the acceptance of certain principles of administration. Those principles were the familiar ones: recognition of the native's right to his property, prevention of economic discrimination, internationalization of capital investments in new railroads, prohibition of the arming and training of native levies, neutralization of tropical Africa. In order to insure their observance, Brailsford advocated a permanent African commission under the league of nations, with power to send inspectors into Africa and to deal with complaints.[27]

[26] E. D. Morel, *Africa and the Peace of Europe* (London, 1917), pp. 52–53, 119.

[27] Brailsford, *A League of Nations* (2nd ed.), pp. 283–285.

Brailsford returned to the argument for a league commission with his essay, first published in the summer of 1918, which won the *English Review* prize for the best short study of the idea of a league of nations. This time, however, he was chiefly concerned with the economic phase of the colonial question. As in his earlier work, *The War of Steel and Gold,* he stressed the function of a league in enforcing the open door in all the colonies of member states.[28] Beyond that he did not venture.

Redoubtable support for the official Labor policy came from H. G. Wells, ex-Fabian and more recently a founder of the Socialist National Defence Committee. As early as 1917 the well known author had written, in a letter rejected by the *Times* and printed in the June 4 issue of the *Daily Chronicle,* that what was needed in Africa was international control to override nationalist exploitation. A little later he published an article in the *Daily News* which was reprinted by a free trade organization and of which more than 200,000 copies were distributed. Here he argued that the solution to the problem of German colonies in Africa "is neither to return them to her nor to deprive her of them, but to give her a share in the pooled general control of mid-Africa." [29]

Wells' most fully worked out argument for the Labor plan appeared in his book, *In the Fourth Year,* first published in London in 1918. In his view, certain broad ends must be achieved if Africa were not to remain a festering sore on the body of mankind. The militarization of the black must be prevented, the sale of arms and liquor to the natives must be halted, slavery or forced labor must be abolished, and finally international trade rivalry in the area must be checked. To that end, Wells insisted that the league of nations must appoint what he called a "public trustee for the world" whose function it would be to call upon the nations to give an account of their stewardship. Not only would such a commission regulate commercial activities, but it would serve as a common authority to which the na-

---

[28] *Idem, The Covenant of Peace,* p. 24.
[29] Wells, *In the Fourth Year,* pp. 51, 55–57, 62–63.

tives might appeal for justice. And this, as Wells saw it, was the gist of the Labor proposal. Writing shortly after the publication of the Inter-Allied Labor and Socialist Conference memorandum, he declared:

> This—and no more than this—is what is intended by the "international control of tropical Africa." *I do not read that phrase as abrogating existing sovereignties in Africa.* What is contemplated is a delegation of authority. . . . I understand the Labour proposal as meaning that we should delegate to an African Commission the middle African Customs, the regulation of inter-State trade, inter-State railways and waterways, quarantine and health generally, and the establishment of a Supreme Court for middle African affairs. . . . Upon that Commission the interested nations . . . might all be represented in proportion to their interest. . . . Now beneath the supervision and restraint of such a delegated Commission I do not see why the existing administration of tutelage Africa should not continue. I do not believe that the Labour proposal contemplates any humiliating cession of European sovereignty.[30]

Whether or not Wells' analysis was a completely accurate reading of the Labor point of view, it represented support for the principle of trusteeship. By any standards, it was an important contribution to the colonial discussion.

Although the *New Statesman* had been prominent in its advocacy of the trusteeship idea, individual members of the Fabian Society were not altogether in accord as to its precise definition. Their writings mirrored the controversy over international administration versus international control. R. C. Hawkin was one of the earliest proponents of an international state of Central Africa, governed from Brussels under the presidency of the Belgian king and by an international commission. During 1917 and early in 1918, he sent a number of communications to the *Daily News* and *Daily Chronicle*, outlining his scheme and defending it. The international executive, as he saw it,

[30] *Ibid.*, pp. 38–39, 41–49.

would be composed of the states now controlling territory in Central Africa—Great Britain, Germany, France, Italy, Portugal, and Belgium—together with trustees to represent native and Mohammedan interests. Its task would be to maintain peace and neutrality, to control the liquor trade and the introduction of munitions, to secure free trade, freedom of religion and native rights, and finally to create an international police force to implement its authority in the area. Hawkin argued that since the international commission which controlled the Danube had succeeded, there was little reason to believe that a similar body for Central Africa would fail.[31] In the summer of 1918, he published for the Fabian Society a pamphlet entitled *Central Africa and the League of Nations.* In it, he suggested the calling of a world conference, which would take steps immediately to neutralize the area as the first move towards internationalization. While Hawkin failed to suggest a concrete plan of control, it was clear that he had not retreated from the scheme expounded previously, for he saw the objective of his proposal as "the development of an international State subject to the control of the League of Nations."[32]

On the other hand, Sir Sidney Olivier, former Governor of Bermuda and also a member of the Fabian group, took the opposite stand in *The League of Nations and Primitive Peoples,* published as one of the Oxford Press pamphlets on the league. Arguing from history that unchecked national possession had not worked successfully, Olivier suggested a series of safeguards of native interests, to be enforced by a league of nations, whose major features echoed the demands of such earlier projects as those of Morel, Wells, and certain Labor periodicals and spokesmen. But on the question of international administration he was sceptical. Noting the nature of existing territorial possession, he concluded:

[31] *Daily News,* January 12, 26, June 7, 1917; *Morning Chronicle,* January 4, 1918.
[32] R. C. Hawkin, *Central Africa and the League of Nations, Fabian Tract No. 186* (London, 1918), pp. 3, 14.

It is not advisable when such overlordship exists to assign control to committees of different Powers. Joint sovereignties have not worked satisfactorily. What it seems most desirable to aim at is the reposing of undistributed local authority in whatever government may be the trustee of sovereign power, with responsibility for observance of principles laid down, enforceable through appeal to the court of the League.

Olivier noted that the more successful colonial powers would have little to fear from such a system, while its enforcement by a league of nations would serve to improve the administration of the less efficient.[33] Similar arguments were repeated in the *Labour Leader* and in the *Contemporary Review*.[34] In at least its superficial features, the project was similar to that which was written into the League of Nations Covenant.

A third Fabian scheme took a somewhat different approach, but the objective was similar. Noel Buxton, a member of the Society, elaborated his views in the *Contemporary Review* for November, 1918. Arguing against international administration, he proposed to leave national sovereignties untouched, but to extend the area of neutralization as laid down in the Berlin Act of 1885 to include all of tropical Africa. The enforcement of such neutralization would be entrusted to the league of nations, operating through a special commission. The league might then set up other commissions to guarantee native rights and ensure European access to raw materials. Finally, the league would have as its representative in Africa a permanent commission, which would send out inspectors to report on the conditions of the natives under the various administrations, and it would establish a court of appeals before which breaches of the general African treaty would be brought for judgment.[35] Although the

[33] Sir Sidney Olivier, *The League of Nations and Primitive Peoples* (London, 1918), pp. 13–14.

[34] *Idem*, "The German Colonies," *Labour Leader*, November 7, 1918; *idem*, "The Repartition of Africa," *Contemporary Review*, CXV (1919), 15–22.

[35] Noel Buxton, "The International Factor in the African Settlement," *Contemporary Review*, CIV (1918), 514–515.

suggestion of multiple commissions was somewhat of an innovation, having been previously elaborated only by the *New Statesman,* the main features of the projects of Olivier, Brailsford, and Wells remained.

Parliamentary discussion of trusteeship was conspicuous by its paucity. Among the Labor members of Parliament, Ramsay MacDonald was the only one to take it up, and even his single mention of the subject was extremely general. On August 1, 1918, in the course of a debate on the league, he declared that such a body might well be used as the responsible authority in certain imperial matters. In Central Africa, for example, "the league of nations might be regarded as the authority on tropical economic products and distribution, the protector of peoples, and so on." [36]

But if its parliamentary spokesmen displayed no great enthusiasm for speaking on trusteeship, the Labor party continued to bring the matter up in its publications. In 1919, it reprinted under one cover a series of memoranda prepared with the help of the Labor Research Department by various advisory committees. The memoranda, which were addressed to the Paris peace conference, had this to say on the colonial problem:

> While the League of Nations may only be able at first to recommend reforms to the various Eastern Governments, a more imperative procedure might be followed, if it appoints certain Powers as its "mandatories" to administer certain areas, e.g. Syria and Mesopotamia in the East. It might be laid down as a condition to be accepted by these Powers that they will carry out in these areas every recommendation on Labour legislation, made by a Council, Conference, or Commission of the League. In other words, what the League recommends as an ideal to other Powers should be imposed as an obligation upon "mandatory" Powers in "trustee" areas. If that principle could be established, our best strategy would then be to demand that the older Dependencies of the colonising Powers should also be brought under the mandatory system. [37]

[36] *Parliamentary Debates,* Commons, CIX (1918), 724.
[37] *Memoranda on International Labour Legislation,* p. 23.

Taken as a whole, the Labor contribution to the development of the trusteeship idea was an outstanding one. Seizing upon the first proposals for such trusteeship, the labor movement gave the general scheme widespread publicity. It conducted a public debate designed to arrive at the most effective techniques for international control of colonial areas in the interests of European peace and the protection of colonial inhabitants. By late 1918, when the *Round Table* group turned once again to the problem, Labor had already defined the possible solutions. As a result, the letter, if not the spirit, of some of the official and unofficial Labor recommendations found expression in the mandates articles of the League Covenant.

During 1917 and 1918, then, British Labor bore the brunt of the fight for international trusteeship. In some quarters, of course, the whole concept was scouted as ridiculous. The conservative *Morning Post,* for example, attacked it in editorial after editorial, while the *Daily Mail,* one of the Northcliffe papers, relegated the idea to the far-distant future.[38] Even among Liberals, the debate over whether Germany's colonies should be seized or returned to her was still being waged as late as September, 1917. W. H. Dawson made the case for return of the colonies subject to certain guarantees, while Sir Harry Johnston suggested "buying" them through the medium of a smaller postwar indemnity. Johnston, incidentally, was so vehement in his opposition to international administration that he declared he would prefer to see the colonies returned to Germany rather than sanction the internationalization project.[39]

The *Round Table,* to which has been ascribed so much of the credit for the mandates idea, was curiously silent. But a few

[38] *Morning Post,* January 17, February 1, June 30, 1917, July 16, December 27, 1918; *Daily Mail,* January 30, 1918.

[39] W. H. Dawson, "The Future of the German Colonies, II. The Case of Conditional Return," *Contemporary Review,* CXII (1917), 256–263; H. H. Johnston, "The Future of the German Colonies, I. The Case for Retention," *ibid.,* pp. 250–255; *idem,* "The Labour Party and Tropical Africa," *Daily Chronicle,* January 3, 1918.

Liberal voices were heard to mitigate the lack of any but Labor
discussion. Ernest Barker provided a slogan for the national
trusteeship point of view: "national administration: international criticism." In his pamphlet entitled *A Confederation of
the Nations,* Barker adduced the moral argument, rather than
the charge of inefficiency, in declaring against international
government. He doubted whether an international body would
have as acute a conscience or show as keen a sense of responsibility as a national administration whose members felt themselves responsible to the public opinion of their country. The
government of separate spheres by separate nations was pref-
erable because each nation "will feel immediate responsibility
for the sphere of its control; and the judgment of the world will
be able to affix responsibility for error and wrong upon each
controlling nation." Such a solution would not eliminate the
need for an international commission to deal with such evils
as exploitation of the natives, gun-running, drink-running, and
the like. The commission, acting under the league and subject
to an appeal from its findings to the league, might play a great
part in helping to ensure that, in regions under its control, all
nations had fair access to all necessary resources, and that no
national administration had a lower standard in its dealings
with the natives than the rest.[40] Here again was the idea of trusteeship, of national responsibility to an international organization for the proper administration of colonial areas.

An even more prolific exponent of the trusteeship idea was
the Reverend John H. Harris, organizing secretary of the Anti-
Slavery and Aborigines Protection Society. Most of Harris' suggestions were elaborated in Liberal papers and periodicals,[41]

[40] Barker, *op. cit.,* pp. 32–33.

[41] J. H. Harris, "The German Colonies, II.—One Way Out," *Daily
News,* January 11, 1918; *idem,* "Colonial Dependencies: 'Possession' or
'Trusteeship'?" *Contemporary Review,* CXIII (1918), 207–212; *idem,*
"Self-determination and the British Commonwealth, V Equatorial Africa,"
New Europe, VI (1918), 173–179; *idem,* "Tropical Colonies—'Interna-
tional Government,'" *Fortnightly Review,* CII (1917), 742–747.

but at least one article was accepted by a Conservative periodical as well.[42] The most systematic statement of his position was printed in the *Fortnightly Review.* Harris drew upon past experience to support his contention that international administration would be sheer madness. But, by the same process of arguing from history, he found that the colonizing nations had been moving, in terms of international agreements, gradually toward the establishment of international control. The problem, therefore, was more fully to extend these international agreements into the spheres of colonial labor, land titles and commerce, and to cap the structure of agreements by an international organ of supervision. Whatever the composition of the organization, it must provide for (a) the periodic revision of international engagements on colonial questions, (b) the collection of data on tropical diseases, alcohol traffic and the like, and (c) the judicial hearing of appeals upon alleged violations of international agreements.[43]

The only Liberal periodicals to contribute editorially to the development of the trusteeship idea were *War and Peace* and the *Nation,* whose international policies were a great deal less cautious than the official Liberal line. In August, 1917, *War and Peace* came to the support of the scheme for national control of backward areas, but under the restriction of international supervision. All the elements emphasized in Labor projects were included in that of *War and Peace:* protection of native rights and land, equal opportunities for all nations, and the view that control was "not a lucrative privilege, but a painful duty, no more to be coveted than it is to be shirked." [44]

War and Peace's parent magazine, the *Nation,* did not enter the campaign for trusteeship as early, nor did it work out as de-

[42] *Idem,* "Germany's Colonial Empire: Seven Reasons against Restoration," *Nineteenth Century and After,* LXXXI (1917), 1157–1163. See also *idem,* "Labour Party and the German Colonies," *Morning Post,* January 5, 1918.

[43] *Idem,* "Tropical Colonies," *loc. cit.*

[44] "The Organization of Africa," *War and Peace,* V (1917), 64–65.

tailed a program of control. Nevertheless, in 1918 it took the opportunity to declare itself in favor of the rationing of colonial products, such as cotton, grain, and metals, by a world council, and insisted that the league of nations must regard immature native populations as its wards, whom it must protect from exploitation.[45] It was clear that the *Nation* agreed substantially with *War and Peace*, whatever might be its attitude toward the machinery of administration.

There were other evidences that the idea of national control of colonial areas under world supervision had gained considerable Liberal support by the end of 1918. For a pair of Liberal newspapers gave editorial backing to the trusteeship idea. How, inquired the *Manchester Guardian*, could the interests of the native races in tropical possessions, especially in the conquered German colonies, be defended if there was to be no international authority to defend them? And moving out of the tropical sphere, the editorial went on to ask:

> How are the great protectorates over lands not barbarous but not yet capable of standing alone—Mesopotamia, Syria, Palestine,—which ought to be held simply as trusts, to be prevented from degenerating into unqualified possessions in breach of this trusteeship if there is no one to see that the trust is observed and that the local autonomies are not violated? [46]

The reference to Mesopotamia, Syria, and Palestine seemed to demonstrate that earlier Labor concern with the subject nationalities of Turkey as well as with Central Africa was beginning to affect Liberals as well.

The *Daily News*, close to Herbert Asquith's wing of the Liberal party, announced its position earlier than the *Guardian* by applauding the trusteeship clauses of the Inter-Allied Labor and Socialist Conference "Memorandum on War Aims." In the view of the *News*, "the new arrangements contemplated are

[45] "How to Form a League of Nations," *Nation*, XXIII (1918), 273; "The Political Initiative," *ibid.*, p. 517.

[46] *Manchester Guardian*, December 4, 1918.

practical and ingenious, and rest upon a very clear-eyed appreciation of the facts of very tangled problems." [47] But that there was no unanimity in the Liberal press was demonstrated by the *Daily Chronicle*, which supported Lloyd George's Coalition Liberals. In a series of editorials, the *Chronicle* displayed much greater concern for seizing the German colonies than for an international control of areas held by any of the belligerents. [48]

Perhaps indicative of the strength of the trusteeship movement is the fact that the great Conservative journal, the *Quarterly Review*, contained a brief word on the idea—though not until several months after the war was over, and after General Smuts had presented his proposals. In an article on the league of nations, Lord Phillimore, whose official connection with governmental studies of the league idea may have caused him to speak with caution, declared in favor of league supervision of backward peoples and of areas where the interests of several nations might collide. Such supervision, Phillimore thought, might give the league positive duties and regular employment which would keep it active and vital. [49]

But the Conservative contribution to the trusteeship debate was negligible. Full-scale Liberal discussion was not so scarce, and the idea did at least gain general support in what might be called semi-official quarters of Liberal opinion. As in the case of a majority of Laborite spokesmen, Liberal preference, insofar as it was expressed, favored the principle of supervised national control over that of international government, a preference which the Liberal imperialists of the *Round Table* were to echo, when that journal turned to the problem.

Not till June, 1918, however, did the *Round Table* take up the question of trusteeship, and even then in a strikingly negative manner. In an article considering the fate of the German colonies in the Pacific, the New Zealand correspondent of the magazine expressed serious concern over the Labor party's rec-

[47] *Daily News*, February 25, 1918.
[48] *Morning Chronicle*, February 12, June 12, October 24, 1918.
[49] Phillimore, "A League of Nations, *loc. cit.*, pp. 226–227.

ommendations for colonial areas. He reported that New Zealand was alarmed lest the same international authority proposed for the African colonies should also be given jurisdiction over the Pacific islands.

> We should be sorry indeed to see the Empire exchanging the substance of possession for such a shadowy security as this. If the experiment were needed to provide for the conflicting claims of our Allies, the case would, of course, be different. But neither the benevolence which seeks to placate Germany by offering her a share in what, under the most favorable conditions, is a dubious and risky enterprise—a condominium—nor the false modesty which refuses to take the boon that the kindness of fortune and the needs of self-defense have placed in our hands seems to be sound business.[50]

In simple terms, the New Zealand *Round Table* group rejected the idea of international administration for the German colonies in the Pacific, but did not suggest national trusteeship as an alternative. Instead, it wanted outright ownership, basing its claims on the right of conquest and the requirements of defense.

No further mention of the trusteeship idea appeared in the *Round Table* until December, when "Windows of Freedom," the article which General Smuts is said to have had before him when he drew up his mandates proposals,[51] was published. Explaining that in tropical Africa, as in the Pacific, the only hope of groups which could not yet govern themselves was in the tutelage of some great democratic nation, the *Round Table* article proposed to indicate how such tutelage would operate. It assumed that the supervision of German East Africa had been assigned to Belgium, and that the charge had been brought that Belgium had excluded British, French, or German traders, that forced labor had been introduced, that the natives were being demoralized by liquor, or that black troops were being organ-

[50] "The German Colonies in Africa," *Round Table*, VIII (1918), 656–658.
[51] Wright, *op. cit.*, pp. 22–23, note 53a.

ized for some ulterior purpose. In such a situation, the accusation of violation of her trust would be brought against Belgium at a meeting of the inter-state conference, *i.e.* the league of nations. That body would conduct an inquiry to get at the facts, and propose reforms to the Belgium government. If the reforms were not carried out, then the league might take the supervision of the area away from Belgium and transfer it to some other nation.[52] Interestingly enough in the light of later developments, the articles insisted that the principle outlined could be successfully applied only if the United States participated as a trustee power. This was a point to which Viscount Grey called special attention in his introduction to a pamphlet [53] made up of reprints of "Windows of Freedom" and of another article from the same issue of the *Round Table*, which also argued for trusteeship on the basis of individual national control.[54] Perhaps even more interesting was the fact that "Windows of Freedom," written by editor Lionel Curtis, was willing to place the Pacific islands under trusteeship, but specifically excepted German South West Africa, where Germany had "established peace by creating a solitude." [55] Whatever the nature of the "solitude," it had apparently impressed General Smuts, for he too exempted South West Africa from his mandates proposals.

These proposals were made in Smuts' *The League of Nations, a Practical Suggestion,* which appeared on December 18, 1918. In this little volume, the South African member of the War Cabinet outlined a series of suggestions designed to offer the framework for a new system of colonial administration. Because so much of his argument appeared verbatim in the League Covenant, it may be useful to outline its major elements. In the first article dealing directly with the mandates idea, Smuts advanced the theory that "so far at any rate as the

[52] "Windows of Freedom," *loc. cit.,* pp. 27–28.

[53] *The Peace Conference—and After,* p. 4.

[54] "Some Principles and Problems of the Settlement," *loc. cit.,* pp. 96–97.

[55] "Windows of Freedom," *loc. cit.,* pp. 33–34.

peoples and territories belonging to Russia, Austria-Hungary and Turkey are concerned, the League of Nations should be considered as the reversionary in the most general sense and as clothed with the right of ultimate disposal in accordance with certain fundamental principles. Reversion to the League of Nations should be substituted for any policy of national annexation." Explaining why he had excepted German territory from his general principle of league control, the general argued that Alsace-Lorraine must be returned to France as a matter of moral justice, while the German colonies in Africa and the Pacific were inhabited by barbarians utterly incapable of the first notion of self-government. His mandates principle, in other words, was to be applied to those areas either virtually capable of self-government now or receptive to instruction in self-government. Whether the proximity of the major German colonies to the South African Union influenced the analysis is an intriguing question, but one that can hardly be answered from the documents.

Having laid down his general premise, Smuts went on to explain that in none of the territories mentioned must there be annexation to the victorious powers, and that in their future administration either the principle of self-determination or at least the consent of the governed to their form of government must be decisive. He pointed out that in some cases the league might recognize territories as independent under governments of their own choosing while at the other end of the scale—in Palestine, for example—administration would have to be undertaken to a very large extent by some external authority. That being the case, he then went on to examine the nature of such administration and proceeded to develop the basic thesis that "any authority, control or administration which may be necessary in respect of these territories and peoples, other than their own self-determined autonomy, shall be the exclusive function of and shall be vested in the League of Nations and exercised by or on behalf of it."

Taking up the question of the nature of the "authority, control or administration" of the league, Smuts declared that any joint international administration, insofar as it had been applied in the past, had not been successful. Personnel taken from different nations found it difficult to work smoothly or loyally together; the native inhabitants of the territory either found the situation confusing or, if they were sufficiently developed, made use of the differences to play off one set of nationals against the others. The only successful administration of undeveloped or or subject peoples had been carried on by states with long experience and with staffs whose training and singleness of mind fitted them for the task. Consequently, he suggested that "it shall be lawful for the League of Nations to delegate its authority, control or administration in respect of any people or territory to some other state whom it may appoint as its agent or mandatary, but that wherever possible the agent or mandatary so appointed shall be nominated or approved by the autonomous people or territory." General Smuts was extremely positive in his insistence that wherever possible the views of the subject peoples with reference to the mandatory power must be respected. He also pointed out that his proposal for national trusteeship under a league rather than genuine international administration was actually a compromise, made partly to conciliate the great powers and partly in view of the administrative inexperience of the league at the beginning. But he insisted that the authority and control of the league must be real and effective, and expressed the hope that mandates under individual nations would prove to be only a temporary expedient.

Meanwhile, in order to implement the proposed system it was necessary that "the degree of authority, control or administration exercised by the mandatary state shall in each case be laid down by the League in a special act or charter, which shall reserve to it complete power of ultimate control and supervision, as well as the right of appeal to it from the territory or people affected against any gross breach of the mandate by the mandatary state." The mandatary state, in other words, should look upon its position as a great trust and honor, not as an opportunity for profit or private advantage. And in the case of flagrant violation of this trust, the league should be able to assert its authority to the full, even to the extent of entrusting the mandate to some other state. This proposal paraphrased very closely the *Round Table* plan outlined in December, just before the publication of the *Practical Suggestion.*

Finally, Smuts addressed himself to the economic and military aspects of the colonial problem which had formed the basis of so much previous discussion of trusteeship. Here he simply proposed that "the mandatary state shall in each case be bound to maintain the policy of the open door, or equal opportunity to all, and shall form no military forces beyond the standard laid down by the League for the purposes of internal peace." [56]

Whatever the genesis of Smuts' plan, it clearly incorporated most of the suggestions thrown out in the course of the trusteeship debate. Even in the case of international administration, the *Practical Suggestion* seems to reject it regretfully, with the hope that eventually national feelings and international experience would permit its application. The major importance of Smuts' mandates scheme, of course, lay in the fact that President Wilson, who had already been exposed to American ideas of trusteeship, took it over, extended it to the former German colonies, and used it as a basis for the discussion of colonial administration at the peace conference. [57] While substantial changes were made, the final mandates articles owed more to the *Practical Suggestion* than to any other single source.

Would the new mandates system meet the need which had given rise to it? The Labor party did not think so. Soon after the publication of the Versailles treaty, it raised serious objections. It declared that no provision had been made in the treaty to prevent the application, in recently conquered African territories, of the same policy of preference, exploitation, and exclusion which had characterized past administration. Australia, New Zealand, and South Africa had in reality annexed the Ger-

[56] Smuts, *The League of Nations, a Practical Suggestion*, pp. 9–24.
[57] Baker, *op. cit.*, I, 226–227.

man colonies nearest them, while even in the case of the other mandates large areas had been added to Allied control under a somewhat thin disguise. "A greater air of impartiality," at the very least, "would have been given to the transaction if the burden of Empire had been a little more evenly distributed by giving some mandates to neutral states." [58] All in all, the new system was a great disappointment to the Labor party.

The attitude of that organization after the signature of the treaty pointed up the central fact of the trusteeship discussion from 1914 through 1918. Early in the war and again toward its very end, members of the *Round Table* group undertook to discover the most effective means of colonial administration and hit upon the idea of national control under international supervision. A few Liberal publicists came up with similar answers and were echoed in various areas of Liberal opinion. General Smuts, after the war had ended, elaborated the plan that most nearly shaped the mandates articles. But, during most of the war, the labor movement and its supporters gave the widest circulation to the twin demands for protection of native rights and for machinery to ensure equal economic opportunities—all under international supervision. Even when there were differences of opinion as to techniques, those two aims were postulated by the various disputants with a consistency that revealed their fundamental agreement on basic premises. Without question, the idea of international responsibility for colonies and their inhabitants gained its most persistent and most powerful organized support in this quarter. Regardless of the nature of the final scheme embodied in the League Covenant, the key role of British Labor appears as the outstanding feature of the wartime campaign for the principle of trusteeship.

[58] Labor Party, *Labour and the Peace Treaty* (London, [1919]), pp. 47–48. H. N. Brailsford bitterly recorded a later view in 1932. "The Allies carved up Turkey, and Mr. Wilson said grace before meat. It was then found that Providence had thoughtfully arranged that the wishes of the victors, recorded in the Secret Treaties, should harmonize exactly with the preferences of the inhabitants of these regions." Brailsford, *If We Want Peace* (London, 1932), pp. 36–37.

IX

The British Government and
the League

THE PRECEDING CHAPTERS HAVE attempted to sketch the manner and the arenas in which the league of nations idea developed in Great Britain. It is necessary, in order to complete the picture, to indicate the reactions of the British Government to the scheme and to outline the official steps taken to bring it near realization. The early statements of the two leading figures in the cabinet which held office until December, 1916, have already been noted in Chapter VI. Herbert Asquith and Sir Edward Grey both supported the league idea. Grey in particular encouraged the work of such men as Gilbert Murray and G. Lowes Dickinson, and in his relations with such Americans as Colonel House and Theodore Marburg emphasized his own support for a league of nations. He was equally clear, however, that the British Government could not make any formal declaration in its favor without consulting its Allies. For that, he wrote to Theodore Marburg, "there is not time while we and they are still in the very crisis of the war." [1]

The league idea appears to have been first presented to the cabinet in a memorandum sent by Lord Haldane on April 8, 1915, a few weeks before he left office. In the course of his analysis of the future relations of the great powers, Haldane suggested an association of nations somewhat on the same lines

[1] Trevelyan, *op. cit.*, pp. 270–271, 312–313; Grey to Theodore Marburg, September 16, 1916, in Latané, *op. cit.*, I, 163–164.

as the later world organization.[2] But there is no evidence that the Haldane proposal was considered seriously, nor any, in fact, to indicate that it was considered at all.

The actual focusing of the attention of the Government on the league was in large measure the work of Lord Robert Cecil. In 1916, he took office in the first Coalition cabinet formed under the leadership of Prime Minister Asquith and soon submitted a memorandum on "proposals for diminishing the occasion of future wars." [3] The Cecil note argued that the increasing horror of war made imperative the substitution of some other way of settling international disputes. Arbitration he rejected as impractical, but he felt that the submission of disputes to a European conference had possibilities, if some sanction were provided to ensure the use of the conference method. Economic and financial pressure might provide the sanction, for the two combined would be too much for any modern state to resist. Cecil also indicated that he had considered provisions for the limitation of armaments, since he believed that such limitation would greatly increase the chances of success for his scheme. But, he declared, he had omitted that proposal in the light of the "convincing criticism" made by Sir Eyre Crowe of the foreign office.

The concrete recommendations of Cecil were embodied in three resolutions labelled "Proposals for Maintenance of Future Peace." The first dealt with adjustments in the postwar territorial settlement. The other two, because they represent the first real league plan to be presented to the British Government, merit quotation in full:

> If any difference or controversy shall arise between any of the High Contracting Powers, with respect to the meaning of any of the articles of this treaty, or with respect to the rights

[2] Sir Frederick Maurice, *Haldane, 1915–1928* (London, 1939), pp. 15–16.

[3] Viscount Cecil, *A Great Experiment* (London, 1941), p. 47; David Lloyd George, *The Truth about the Peace Treaties* (2 vols.; London, 1938), I, 31.

of any of the parties thereto, or with respect to any other matter, a conference of Powers shall forthwith be summoned, and the controversy shall be submitted to it, and no action shall be taken by any of the parties to the controversy until the conference has met and considered the matter, and has either come to a decision thereon or has failed for a period of three months after its meeting to come to such a decision. Any decision agreed upon at such a conference shall be maintained and enforced by all the High Contracting Powers as if it were one of the articles of this treaty.

Each of the High Contracting Powers guarantees and agrees to maintain the provisions of this treaty if necessary by force of arms, and in particular undertakes that if any Power shall refuse or fail to submit any controversy to a conference as provided in the last preceding article of this treaty, each of the High Contracting Powers shall thereupon cut off all commercial and financial intercourse with any other Power, whether a party to this treaty or not; and it is hereby further agreed that for the purpose of enforcing this provision, any of the High Contracting Powers may detain any ship or goods belonging to any of the subjects of the wrong-doing Power or coming from or destined for any person residing in the territory of such Power, and with the same object may take any other similar step which may seem desirable or necessary.[4]

There was no cabinet discussion of these proposals, but they were exposed to sharp criticism in a memorandum by Sir Eyre Crowe. He first made a number of general observations concerning the projected conference of nations. He noted (a) that it must include not only the powers signing the peace treaty, but the neutral powers as well; (b) that it would have to possess a permanent headquarters and organization in order to be able to deal with each concrete issue that arose; (c) that it would be a formidable means of obstruction and delay, but would be feeble in promoting definite progress; and (d) that the readiness of all countries to join and to pledge themselves to united action could not be taken as certain.

[4] Cecil, *op. cit.*, appendix I, pp. 352–357.

Crowe then went on to elaborate his criticisms. Assuming that all nations united in such a solemn league and covenant, he asked, would they keep it? Nations would only be willing to prevent the violation of the territorial settlement, for example, so long as they felt it to be a just one. Since no territorial settlement could be permanently just, there was no certainty that an attempt at revision would be actively resisted by the rest of the world. Failing active resistance, would the nations of the world impose a blockade and economic boycott? Probably not, thought Crowe, if they were in any danger of being overrun as a result by powerful neighbors. At most, the proposed conference would be a mitigating influence against hasty aggression. It could not eliminate it. And, he added, it could not compel nations to compromise on issues they regarded as vital to their national existence or interest. Great Britain in particular would be exposed by the scheme, for a substantial majority could be found among the powers at almost any time for measures supposedly designed to serve the cause of peace, but actually aimed at curtailing British supremacy at sea.

Thus, declared Crowe, the nations would continue to seek alliances to attain the ends they regarded as vital. The balance of power remained the fundamental problem. To prevent aggression and domination nothing would serve but adequate force. He rejected the idea of disarmament, not only because of technical difficulties, but because the good faith upon which it must rest did not exist and was not likely to exist.[5] In fine, this response to the Cecil memorandum revealed that there were currents in the British Government not at all favorable to the league idea.

Shortly after the preparation of these two notes the Asquith Government fell and was replaced by a second Coalition cabinet

[5] Crowe's memorandum of October 12, 1916, is summarized by Lloyd George in his *War Memoirs* (6 vols.; Boston, 1933–1937), IV, 58–62. Though Lloyd George's recollections often have to be viewed with caution, the memorandum coincides so well with the general opinions expressed by Crowe that its substance can be accepted as accurate.

led by Lloyd George. The new Government was almost immediately faced with President Wilson's inquiry to the belligerents concerning the terms upon which they would consider peace. It consulted with its Allies and a joint note was prepared which was dispatched to Washington on January 10, 1917. The Allied reply contained the first official acceptance of the league of nations project, though only in the vaguest terms.

> In general, [declared the Allied governments] they make a point of declaring that they pay homage to the loftiness of the sentiments inspiring the American Note, and that they associate themselves whole-heartedly with the plan of creating a League of Nations to ensure peace and justice throughout the world. They recognize all the advantages that would accrue to the cause of humanity and civilization by the establishment of international settlements designed to avoid violent conflicts between the nations—settlements which ought to be attended by the sanctions necessary to assure their execution, and thus to prevent fresh aggressions from being made easier by an apparent security.

On the other hand, the Allied reply continued, a discussion of future arrangements designed to assure a lasting peace presupposed a satisfactory settlement of the present conflict.[6] The Allied governments, and thus the British, were not yet willing to commit themselves unreservedly to a league of nations.

Clearly, however, the idea had to be considered seriously. In the autumn of 1916 Lord Robert Cecil had proposed that an interdepartmental committee be set up in the foreign office to prepare a draft agreement binding nations not to use war as an instrument of policy and to suggest measures for the prevention of aggression. In January, 1917, soon after Lloyd George took office and after he had consulted with Cecil, he appointed a committee to work out a practical scheme for a league. Its

[6] "Allied Statement of War Aims, January 10, 1917," *Documents and Statements relating to Peace Proposals and War Aims (December 1916–November 1918), with an Introduction by G. Lowes Dickinson* (London, 1919), p. 11.

chairman was Lord Phillimore, one of the judges of the High Court. The other members of the committee were three historians, A. F. Pollard, J. Holland Rose, and Sir Julian Corbett, and three officials of the foreign office, Sir Eyre Crowe, Sir William Tyrrell, and C. J. B. Hurst. The Phillimore Committee considered a great number of suggestions, but did not report a plan to the cabinet until March 20, 1918.[7]

Meanwhile, the league idea was further discussed in the Imperial War Cabinet that had been set up. On April 26, 1917, the conclusions of a committee, headed by Lord Milner, on the economic desiderata in the terms of peace were presented to that body. The "Milner Report" commented somewhat unenthusiastically on the various proposals for a league of nations with broad powers. It declared:

> The Committee were directly impressed with the danger of the complete destruction of civilised Society which threatens the world if the recurrence of a war like the present cannot be prevented, and with the necessity of devising means which would tend, at any rate, to diminish the risk of such a calamity. They felt, however, that any too comprehensive or ambitious project to ensure world peace might prove not only impracticable, but harmful. The proposal which seems to promise the best results proceeds along the path of consultation and conference for composing of differences which cannot otherwise be adjusted. The Treaty of Peace should provide that none of the parties who are signatories to that Treaty should resort to arms against one another without previous submission of their dispute to a Conference of the Powers. The Committee thinks that the details of such a scheme should be discussed with our Allies and especially with the United States of America, before the conclusion of the war.[8]

In the discussion which followed, Lloyd George remarked that the Milner Committee had rather thrown cold water on the

[7] Cecil, *op. cit.*, p. 60; Lloyd George, *The Truth about the Peace Treaties,* I, 605–607; D. C. L. and Lord Phillimore to editor, *The Times,* March 20, 24, 1920.

[8] Lloyd George, *War Memoirs,* appendix D, IV, 64.

idea of a league of nations. Milner defended the report, arguing that all that was possible was an agreement by which the
nations bound themselves not to go to war without first submitting their cause to a conference. He did not think that the
conference could be an international court, binding the nations
to enforce its decisions. But, he added, a conference such as he
had outlined would probably have prevented the outbreak of
the present war. At the same meeting, Lord Robert Cecil,
though he spoke more positively in terms of a league of nations,
nevertheless supported substantially the same view as that expressed by Milner—delay until an international conference
could consider the cause of potential conflict.[9]

The subject was again taken up at the next meeting of the
War Cabinet on May 1. Lord Robert Cecil read to the cabinet
the terms of a rudimentary league scheme which he had first
drawn up in 1916. This appears to have been the first official
presentation of the plan to the cabinet. With regard to the provisions outlined by Cecil for economic sanctions, General Smuts
declared that the precise nature of the sanctions would have to
be worked out later. At present, it would be enough for the
Imperial War Cabinet to express itself in general terms in favor
of the principle of sanctions. The cabinet concurred in the view
expressed by Smuts. The meeting also took up the question of
disarmament, in which connection Arthur Henderson disagreed
with some of the doubts expressed by Lord Milner and others.
He declared, however, that he was convinced that it was necessary first of all to see what results could be achieved in the direction of a league of nations, for disarmament policy would
have to depend on the nature of the international relations set
up after the war.[10]

These cabinet discussions, while they reveal a cautious approach to the league idea, at the same time indicate that the
British Government felt it to be important enough not to be
ignored. On a more informal level, Lord Robert Cecil, who was

[9] *Ibid.*, IV, 23–26.
[10] *Ibid.*, IV, 26–28.

in touch with Colonel Edward House, reported the formation of the Phillimore Committee, obviously for the information of President Wilson, and suggested that a joint Anglo-American commission might be formed to consider the league problem.[11]

Whether Cecil's suggestions represented indirectly the wish of the British Government is difficult to judge. Walter Hines Page, the American Ambassador to Great Britain, was convinced of Lord Robert's sincere advocacy of a league, but had reservations about Lloyd George. In a letter to President Wilson, Page remarked that the Prime Minister had not thought out the project further than to see its difficulties. Lloyd George's main concern, Page believed, was that control of the British fleet might be turned over to the league in some possible crisis, a contingency that was impossible to any red-blooded son of the British Isles.[12]

In any event, President Wilson was unreceptive to the idea of a joint committee, just as he was unwilling to acquiesce in the proposal to publish the suggestions of the Phillimore Committee.[13] That committee had held nine meetings in which it had studied sixteenth and seventeenth century proposals for a league of nations as well as the projects of the war period.[14] On March 20, 1918, it presented its conclusions to the secretary of state for foreign affairs in an "Interim Report," made up of a draft convention for a kind of league of nations together with an explanation of its provisions. In May, the "Interim Report" was printed for the War Cabinet and circulated among its members. It was not published during the war because of the opposition of President Wilson, but it received the support of

[11] Cecil to House, September 6, 1917, February 16, 1918, in Seymour, *op. cit.*, IV, 6–7, 9.

[12] Page to Wilson, March 17, 1918, Library of Congress, Woodrow Wilson Papers, file II.

[13] Seymour, *op. cit.*, IV, 17.

[14] *Interim Report*, p. 1. All page references are to the copy of the report sent to President Wilson and found among his papers: file II, July 17, 1918.

various members of the British Government, though not formally adopted as an official policy.[15] A "Final Report," which
was made on July 3, 1918, by the Phillimore Committee, merely
elaborated its earlier analysis of the various projects of a league
of nations.

The actual plan outlined by the committee was a curious attempt to reconcile the league idea with conventional diplomatic
procedures and techniques. As Sir Alfred Zimmern has noted,
the result was "an unsatisfactory hybrid." "The officials," he
has written, "succeeded in checking the juridical inclinations of
the Chairman: but the Chairman and his colleagues were
clearly in no mood to consider far-reaching political alternatives." [16] The plan conceived of the future international body as
an "alliance" rather than a league. No mention was made of the
exact composition of the organization, but the committee
clearly envisaged a league of wartime allies. Article 17 of the
"Draft Convention," for example, provided that the conference
of powers in the postwar organization consider applications for
membership and determine whether they should be granted
and whether it would be necessary to impose any terms. The
explanatory notes of the "Interim Report" pointed out that this
ability to impose terms upon prospective members would enable the league "to require reparation for past outrages, or to
insist upon partial disarmament if the military or naval forces
of the applicant were disproportionate to those of the States already in the League." [17]

The core of the Phillimore draft convention was Article 1. It
provided that each of the parties to the convention should agree
not to go to war with any other signatory (a) without first submitting the matter in dispute to arbitration or to a conference

[15] Lord Reading to Wilson, July 3, 1918, Library of Congress, Woodrow Wilson Papers, file II.

[16] Sir Alfred Zimmern, *The League of Nations and the Rule of Law,
1918-35* (London, 1935), p. 180.

[17] *Interim Report,* pp. 4, 7.

of the Allied states, and (b) until there had been an award or a report by the conference. In addition, each state was to undertake not to go to war with another of the Allied states which complied with the award or the recommendation (if any) made by the conference in its report.

Even these provisions were greatly limited by the proposal that any disputing state might apply to the conference to be relieved of the moratorium imposed in Article 1, on the ground that there was a continuing injury or on the ground that unless prompt provision for reparation or restitution were made the injury would be irreparable. The conference was to be empowered to relieve the applicant state from the provisions of the moratorium if it judged that procedure wise.

Having provided for a severely restricted area of international action in the case of disputes, the Phillimore plan undertook to ensure that its limited "league" would function. In the event that one of the Allied states broke the covenant contained in Article 1, it would be *ipso facto* at war with all the other Allied states, who were to agree to take all military, naval, financial, and economic measures best designed to prevent breach of the covenant. Financial and economic measures were to include the severance of all trade and financial relations with the covenant-breaking state.

The Phillimore Committee classified international disputes not as justiciable and non-justiciable, but as arbitrable and non-arbitrable. Its members were apparently unwilling that a permanent international court should judge questions relating to international law, the interpretation of treaties, and the like. Instead they proposed that such cases be handled by the more flexible processes of arbitration. When the disputants could not agree as to the composition of the tribunal of arbitration or when they did not agree that the dispute was suitable for arbitration, any one of them might apply to the conference of the Allied states to take the matter under consideration. The function of the conference was to ascertain the facts in the dispute, and make a recommendation calculated to ensure a just and lasting settlement. The recommendation was not to have the force of a decision.[18]

The scheme, considered carefully, represents only a slight advance over the various arbitration treaties in force before the war. It rested upon the belief that delay would usually be sufficient to prevent a dispute from breaking into open warfare. With the causes of international disputes it was not concerned. It made no provision for a permanent organization to act as a constant instrument of international intercourse. The members of the conference were to be the diplomatic representatives accredited to a state unnamed in the convention, and the president or sovereign of the state was to call the conference into session when a dispute had to be considered.[19] Provisions were made for the functioning of the conference once called, but fundamentally the Phillimore plan was an attempt to revitalize the old Concert of Europe by outlining a regular procedure for its convocation and demanding that it be employed before the outbreak of war. Its importance lies in the fact that many of its suggestions were later embodied in the actual League of Nations Covenant.[20]

While the Phillimore plan was never officially adopted as the policy of the Government, a league of nations of some kind was constantly kept before the Allied and enemy public in 1918 as one of the British postwar objectives. The ministry of propaganda under Lord Northcliffe, for example, appointed a committee headed by Dr. J. W. Headlam and H. G. Wells to prepare propaganda literature for Germany. The committee drafted a memorandum which included the idea of a league of free nations among British war aims. The memorandum suggested that the league comprise all the nations of the world, including a Germany purged of military aggressiveness, and that it should have an international congress to revise, codify, and

[18] *Ibid.*, pp. 4–6.
[19] *Ibid.*, p. 5.
[20] David Hunter Miller, *The Drafting of the Covenant* (2 vols.; New York, 1928), I, 9.

extend international law, as well as an international court for the handling of disputes. The suggestions were sent to Arthur Balfour for the endorsement of the foreign office. While that section of the Government took no action with regard to this plan, it was nevertheless used for some time as the basis of propaganda directed towards the enemy. Similarly, it was announced in June that the Government had given Viscount Grey's pamphlet on a league wide circulation in neutral and enemy countries. No mention was made of its circulation at home.[21]

Meanwhile, however, it was authoritatively announced to the British public that the Government favored a league. On January 5, 1918, Lloyd George addressed a special conference of trade union delegates and made the first official declaration of British war aims. In some particulars—above all, those connected with the territorial settlement—the speech was vague, but it endorsed the idea of a league of nations in general terms. So long as the possibility of disputes between nations continued, said the prime minister, all nations must live under the burden of being compelled to prepare for war. The crushing weight of modern armaments, the increasing evil of compulsory military service, the vast waste of wealth and effort involved in warlike preparations constituted a blot on modern civilization. For these reasons, he declared, a great attempt must be made to establish by some international organization an alternative to war as a means of settling international disputes. Therefore, the creation of such an international body was one of the major aims of British policy.[22]

[21] West, *op. cit.*, pp. 203–204; Wells, *Experiment in Autobiography*, pp. 599–602; *Parliamentary Debates*, Commons, CVII (June 27, 1918), 1223.

[22] *British War Aims. Statement by the Right Honourable David Lloyd George January Fifth, Nineteen Hundred and Eighteen. Authorized Version as Published by the British Government* (New York, 1918), pp. 14–15. Slightly different is the wording in *Documents and Statements relating to Peace Proposals and War Aims*, p. 115. Lloyd George himself, writes F. P. Walters, cared nothing about the idea of a league. Walters, *op. cit.*, I, 19.

The Government's position was further clarified by an official statement made by Lord Curzon on June 26, 1918. During the resumed league debate in the House of Lords, Curzon declared that the Government was in earnest about the matter, that it was exploring the problem, and that it would undoubtedly exchange views on a league with its Allies before long. Three elements, he thought, were necessary for a successful league. They were (1) the institution of a court to which signatories of the league treaty pledged themselves to refer disputes before going to war, (2) delay pending decision, during which no hostilities should be permitted, and (3) sanctions to enforce the decrees of the supreme body.

But when Curzon touched upon some of the concrete aspects of the proposal, he was cold and seemed to repudiate any far-reaching scheme as impracticable. Economic sanctions, he noted, might be in part effective, but the blockade—*i.e.* a form of economic sanction—had not prevented the present war nor curtailed its duration. As for disarmament, he thought that any plan to ration the armaments of members of the league would be impossible. Besides, he asked, how could such restraints be imposed on posterity? It would be unwise to proceed too quickly or too abruptly.

> Once you accept the idea [he said] that before the sword is unsheathed nations shall bring their quarrels to a conference and that the nation declining to do so or breaking loose afterwards commits an offence and becomes a moral outlaw, you have done a great deal. Those are the lines which, I think, are the safe and practicable lines upon which His Majesty's Government is disposed to proceed.

Still more light was thrown on Curzon's approach when he noted that at present there were already two leagues of nations in existence. One was the British Empire, the other the league of Allied nations. Both were being employed now for the prosecution of the war, but could be turned to use in the maintenance of peace. And to make his meaning even more apparent, Curzon declared that until Germany changed her outlook sincerely she could not be made a member of the league. That might mean the continuation of the present alliance system for a short time, but the situation might work itself out, and in any case it was inevitable.[23]

The same theme was repeated by Lloyd George in an address on war aims in September. The British Empire and the Allied nations fighting the battle of "international right" were both leagues of nations. Germany would be welcomed into such a body if after the war she condemned and repudiated the perfidy of her rulers and freed herself from military domination, but the only sure foundation was a complete victory in the battle for justice and international freedom being waged by the Allies. In later statements, Lloyd George continued to insist, in a general way, on his own and his Government's firm intention to see to the formation of a postwar league.[24]

Other members of the Government likewise backed the idea. G. N. Barnes was particularly active, but his view of the league may perhaps best be judged by his statement that "I would include Germany in a League of Nations just as we include the thief and the burglar, as well as the decent law-abiding citizen, in our national affairs." [25] Arthur Balfour, though he also spoke in favor of the limited league advocated by governmental leaders, made it his special business to insist upon a complete victory and an adequate territorial settlement as the basis for successful international organization.[26]

But by far the outstanding governmental supporter of the league was Lord Robert Cecil. He insisted on the need for a league, argued that adequate sanctions were necessary, and

[23] *Parliamentary Debates*, Lords, XXX (June 26, 1918), 394–404.

[24] *The Times*, September 13, November 11, 13, December 10, 1918.

[25] *Handbook for Speakers on a League of Nations*, pp. 76–78; *The Times*, May 17, 1918.

[26] *E.g. The Times*, January 11, October 1, 1918; *Parliamentary Debates*, Commons, CVII (August 1, 1918), 710–714. On the other hand, F. P. Walters argues that Balfour supported the league because he was determined to do everything possible to maintain friendship with the United States. Walters, *op. cit.*, I, 19.

suggested that the Allied governments should take the lead in stimulating public understanding of the scheme.[27] He was disappointed when President Wilson requested that the "Phillimore Report" not be made public,[28] but undertook as a loyal member of the government to put the best face possible on the situation created by that request.

> Our policy, and I believe that of the French Government also, [he said in the House of Commons] has been to submit the Reports of our expert Committees to the Governments of the chief European Allies and of the United States for examination. The next step is to reach such a measure of definite agreement with these Governments as will furnish a basis and terms of reference on which our respective experts may meet and draft a detailed scheme. Such a definite agreement we are now trying to reach and we hope to discuss the matter fully with the United States in the immediate future. Pending this discussion we had reason to believe that the publication of the French and British Reports might be regarded as premature and inopportune.[29]

Actually, no significant discussion with the United States took place until after the war was over. But Cecil himself contributed importantly to public consideration of the league in a speech delivered the day after the signing of the armistice. This address, presented on the occasion of his induction as chancellor of the University of Birmingham, revealed in sharp outline the extent and limitations of the position supported by some members of the Government. It had been submitted by Cecil in written form to a committee of the cabinet, where no objec-

---

[27] *The Times,* February 14, 18, August 16, October 26, 1918; *Parliamentary Debates,* Commons, CVI (May 16, 1918), 623–625, CIX August 1, 1918), 735–736, CX (October 24, 1918), 890–891; Cecil to House, July 22, 1918, in Seymour, *op. cit.,* IV, 39–42; Cecil to Sir William Wiseman, August 19, 1918, in Library of Congress, Woodrow Wilson Papers, file II (copy).

[28] Cecil to Wiseman, August 19, 1918, *loc. cit.*

[29] *Parliamentary Debates,* Commons, CX (October 24, 1918), 890–891.

tion was raised to it, though it was received "respectfully rather than cordially." [30] The Birmingham speech outlined the necessity for international organization in the usual fashion, and pointed to the growing economic interdependence of the world as an augury of hope for its success. Cecil warned that the international body must not be a twentieth-century Holy Alliance, restricted to a certain group of nations. "Our new society of nations," he declared, "must not be a group, however large and important. If it is it will inevitably aim at world domination." Cecil agreed that the league could only be open to nations who could be trusted to accept its principles, yet at the same time suggested that it might perhaps be wise to consider compelling nations who would not enter to do so under economic or other pressure.

When he discussed the concrete nature of a league of nations, Cecil offered nothing beyond cautious suggestions, such as those embodied in the Phillimore plan. He was convinced, he said, that the most important step that could now be taken was to devise machinery which in case of international dispute would at least delay the outbreak of war and secure full and open discussion of the causes of the quarrel. For that purpose no very elaborate international machinery was required. All that would be needed was a treaty binding its signatories not to wage war until a formal conference of nations had been held to consider and if possible to decide the dispute. It was probably true, Lord Robert went on, that decisions would be difficult to obtain, for the decisions of such a conference, like all other international proceedings, would have to be unanimous to be binding. But since the important thing was to secure delay and open discussion, *i.e.*, time for public opinion to act and information to instruct it, this was not a serious objection.

Coercion was to be used, thought Cecil, only to compel recourse to the conference as a first step. For that purpose, economic sanctions seemed to offer the best hope of success. As for the enforcement of the decrees of the conference, he expressed

[30] Cecil, *op. cit.*, p. 62.

his doubts concerning the practicability of any scheme for an international army. The idea implied serious inroads into national sovereignty, and there was grave question whether any sovereign state would agree that its soldiers should be used, and its treasure poured out, to enforce a decree which might be of doubtful justice, or even opposed to its own interests. Consequently, he looked to the force of public opinion as the sanction behind the decisions reached in international conferences.[31]

It is a significant commentary on the views of the British Government that even Cecil, who was by far the outstanding league advocate in the cabinet, should have taken such a limited approach to international organization. In essence, his proposals were those of the Phillimore Committee for an improved Concert of Europe. Cecil expressed his convictions even more clearly in a private conversation with an American acquaintance a few days after the Birmingham speech. As outlined by Oscar T. Crosby in a letter to Colonel Edward House, Cecil's position was the following: (1) He did not believe that a durable peace could be established save through the instrumentality of an international tribunal, backed by an international force. (2) He did not believe that the world was ready for such a body. (3) He believed that some benefit would be derived from the adoption of a compromise method, which would still leave to each nation its sovereign power over its own forces, but which would, theoretically at least, secure some delay in the making of war. (4) He did not believe that a limitation of armaments was possible, since, in the last analysis, each nation would rely on its own forces to implement its own views of its rights and interests. (5) He believed that the general public in all coun-

---

[31] *The Times*, November 12, 1918. The speech was reprinted in full and issued as a pamphlet by the League of Nations Union as *World Opinion and the League of Nations* (LNUP, No. 24) (London, 1918). Also *A League of Nations. An Address Delivered by the Rt. Hon. Lord Robert Cecil, K.C., M.P., in the Town Hall, Birmingham, on the Occasion of his Installation as Chancellor of the University of Birmingham, 12th November, 1918* (Birmingham, [1918]).

tries was expecting (a) the establishment of an effective organism for securing peace; and (b) a drastic reduction of armaments. (6) Since, for the reasons above stated, those expectations were not now to be fulfilled, he believed that the Labor and Socialist parties in all countries would probably demand power, charging the present governing classes with failure and perhaps deception. (7) Having this in mind, Lord Robert was anxious to minimize as rapidly as possible the expectations which the public was now entertaining in these respects, and in his Birmingham speech he had accordingly indicated that he did not expect a limitation of armaments. (8) He was strongly of the opinion that wide discussion now was the most important force available to make clear the kind of organization that was possible. He regretted that such discussion had been limited in the past.[32] It is quite possible that this analysis, which was of course not made public, tended to misrepresent the nature of Cecil's support, and almost certainly it exaggerated his lack of faith in a future international body.[33]

[32] Crosby to House, November 19, 1918, in Library of Congress, Woodrow Wilson Papers (Ray Stannard Baker Collection), series B, box 9 (copy).

[33] Viscount Cecil's view of his own Birmingham speech and of Crosby's report is of some interest. In a letter to the author (June 9, 1948), he states: "I have a very strong opinion that he [Crosby] entirely misunderstood my view. I don't believe I ever said anything about wanting an international tribunal backed by an international force. I have always thought that was unpracticable for a long time. Nor did I suggest that the force proposals in the draft Covenant of the League were a substitute for that arrangement.

"As to the limitation of armaments, what happened was this. In my first draft which I presented to the British Cabinet, I omitted any reference to the limitation of armaments. When that scheme was considered by the War Cabinet, one of the representatives of the Dominions urged strongly that there ought to be a provision for the limitation of armaments, to which I immediately agreed, and in the final scheme that I drafted for the Cabinet I believe there was something to that effect, though I have not been able to find the actual document which contained it.

"I don't think it is right that in my Birmingham speech I said any-

Cecil stepped down from his government post on November 22 over the issue of Welsh disestablishment. A few days later, however, he accepted the leadership of the special league of nations section of the foreign office and in this capacity was destined to attend the peace conference.[34] In the foreign office, meanwhile, a memorandum had been drawn up by Sir Alfred Zimmern, which outlined the bases for international organization. The chief points of interest in the Zimmern memorandum were insistence on arrangements for regular conferences of the members of the league, and provision for an international secretariat, to be held in rotation by the great powers. This foreign office paper argued that the foreign secretaries of the great powers should meet annually for a frank interchange of views, and that the foreign secretaries of all the members should meet at less frequent intervals, possibly every four or five years. Thus, the great powers would be a sort of executive committee of the whole body of sovereign states.[35]

---

thing very definite about the limitation of armaments. What I did say was that I didn't see how any scheme founded on arbitration was practicable at present. Beyond that I certainly indicated in broad lines the scheme that was afterwards embodied in Articles 10 to 17 of the Covenant.

"It is certainly true that I believed that the most important peace weapon for the League was delay and discussion. That was the result of the abortive efforts made by Edward Grey to stop the First World War, when it certainly seemed that if we could have had an International Conference the war need not have taken place. So far as I did change my view at all from the Memorandum of 1918 it was in the direction of making the Covenant more effective but I do not myself believe there was any substantial change from the view which I had taken before that date."

[34] *The Times*, December 6, 1918.

[35] "A Memorandum Prepared for the Consideration of the British Government in Connexion with the Forthcoming Peace Settlement. The League of Nations," Zimmern, *op. cit.*, pp. 196–206. The Zimmern memorandum shows some similarities to the earlier Fabian schemes. Philip Noel Baker (in a letter to the author, June 29, 1948) writes that the Fabian plan and Leonard Woolf's *International Government* "were both considered very carefully in the Foreign Office in the later months of

At the request of Cecil, a "brief conspectus of League of Nations organization" was drawn up. It was based on the Zimmern and Phillimore proposals. The document was submitted to Cecil on December 14, and by him to the War Cabinet on December 17. As the "Cecil draft" it was then taken to Paris, where on January 1 it was shown to David Hunter Miller, President Wilson's legal advisor, together with the proposals of General Smuts. At that point the British and American proposals met, and the league of nations entered another stage of its formation.[36]

The so-called Cecil plan reflected the provisions of the Zimmern memorandum, and thus, while narrowly restricted in its views, was nevertheless more detailed than the earlier Phillimore scheme. It proposed that the general treaty setting up a league of nations should explicitly provide for regular conferences between representatives of the contracting powers. Since the conferences would be made up of statesmen responsible to their own sovereign parliaments, their decisions, as in the case of the various Allied conferences during the war, would have to be unanimous. The conference was to be organized about a system of annual meetings of the prime ministers and foreign secretaries of the British Empire, the United States, France, Italy, Japan, and any other states recognized by them as great powers. Quadrennial meetings of representatives of all the league states were suggested, as well as provision for the summoning of special conferences on the demand of any one of the

that year [1918], and a summary of their argument and conclusions was prepared and circulated to members of the British Cabinet.

"This Memorandum became a standard work of reference for the League of Nations Section of the British delegation to the Peace Conference, and was much used by Lord Cecil, Sir Cecil Hurst, and other members of the Section, who prepared the Covenant. I think it is not too much to say that it thus played a major part in forming the thinking of the authors of the Covenant, and of many men who helped to shape the Secretariat and Council of the League of Nations on questions of international, economic, social and technical co-operation."

[36] Zimmern, *op. cit.*, pp. 194-195.

great powers or, if there were danger of an outbreak of war, of any member of the league. "Untrustworthy and hostile" states, *e.g.*, Bolshevist Russia, were to be excluded.

For the conduct of the work of the conference, the Cecil plan proposed a permanent secretariat, without indicating how it was to be composed other than to note that the general secretary should be appointed by the great powers, and that preference should be given to a national of one of the smaller countries. The secretariat was to be a channel of communication between the conference and all international bodies functioning under treaties guaranteed by the league. The international bodies were listed as falling into three classes:

(a) Judicial; *i.e.* the existing Hague organization with any additions or modifications made by the League.

(b) International administrative bodies. Such as the suggested transit commission. To these would be added bodies already formed under existing treaties (which are very numerous and deal with very important interests, *e.g.* postal union, international labour office, etc.).

(c) International commissions of enquiry: *e.g.* commission on industrial conditions (labour legislation), African commission, armaments commission.

In addition to the above arrangements, the plan indicated that there would probably be a periodic congress of delegates of the parliaments of the states belonging to the league. "A regular staple of discussion for this body," it noted, "would be afforded by the reports of the interstate conference and of the different international bodies. The congress would thus cover the ground that is at present occupied by the periodical Hague Conference and also the ground claimed by the Socialist International." Finally, it was suggested that Geneva, where league officials would have the privileges of extraterritoriality, might be the most suitable meeting place.

The section of the Cecil plan noted above was apparently an effort to reconcile governmental insistence upon sovereignty and great power control with some of the broader ideas suggested during the course of the war. Thus recognition was given to the various instrumentalities of international cooperation, and a rather tenuous connection with the interstate conference was advocated. But the main emphasis was on the prerogatives of the great powers, with an interesting secondary theme of suspicion of the pretensions of the Socialist International.

The second part of the draft went over the question of the prevention of war in virtually the same manner as the Phillimore plan. Delay of hostilities was the essence of the scheme. The only extension of the Phillimore proposals was a provision that the members of the league should bind themselves to make war against non-members if the latter, in the event of a dispute with a member-state, refused to adopt the procedure obligatory for members of the league.[37] In other respects, the Cecil plan paralleled its predecessor very closely.

Of equal importance with this draft was the set of proposals made by General Jan Smuts at about the same time. Perhaps at the suggestion of Lloyd George, he prepared a confidential memorandum on the league of nations, which was published, as has been noted in a previous chapter, on December 16 as *The League of Nations. A Practical Suggestion*. With the circulation of his paper among the members of the cabinet and with subsequent discussion of Cecil's views as well, the league became a fixed part of the policy which the Government directed its delegates to follow at the peace conference. But, it should be emphasized, neither Cecil's nor Smuts' proposal was an official suggestion put forward by the British Government.[38]

A large part of Smuts' plan was devoted to the elaboration of the mandates system which has already been discussed. The *Practical Suggestion* differed from the Cecil draft also in that it

[37] Florence Wilson, *The Origins of the League Covenant. Documentary History of Its Drafting* (London, 1928), appendix F, pp. 181–183.

[38] Lloyd George, *The Truth about the Peace Treaties*, I, 619–620, 628–632; Noel Baker, "The Making of the Covenant," *loc. cit.*, pp. 17–18; Miller, *op. cit.*, I, 39.

proposed a scheme of relative disarmament, the abolition of conscription, and the nationalization of munitions factories. With regard to disarmament, Smuts declared that while limitation in a general sense was impracticable, the council of the league should determine what military equipment and armament was fair and reasonable for the militia or volunteer forces of the respective countries, and that the limits laid down should not be exceeded without permission.

On the other hand, Smuts agreed with Cecil and various other Government officials that the league must not be a superstate. It was necessary, he declared, to abandon all ideas of federation or confederation as not applicable and not likely to be agreed to by any of the existing sovereign states. The conference system, already in vogue in the British Empire, was the inevitable line of approach. Likewise, he made the idea of delay before recourse to war the chief element of his proposals, though he did declare that the league must be more than machinery to prevent hostilities in an emergency. If it were to last, he warned, it must become part and parcel of the common international life of the world. What he had especially in mind were apparently such functions as the supervision of mandates.

In outlining the possible organization of a league, Smuts was a great deal more explicit than either Cecil or the Phillimore Committee. He proposed the hearing of justiciable disputes by courts of arbitration, and the conciliation of non-justiciable ones, under certain circumstances, by the council of the league. The usual economic and military sanctions were outlined to compel the use of this machinery. The council was to be the key organ of the league. It was to include representatives of all the great powers and a slightly smaller number of representatives drawn in rotation from two panels of middle and minor states respectively. Smuts also suggested that a scheme of regional representation might be evolved. In addition to hearing non-justiciable disputes, the council was to act as the executive committee of the league, supervising international arrangements and conventions, controlling property of an international character, formulating for the approval of the governments general measures of international law, and bringing the machinery of international compulsion into operation when required. It was to meet periodically, and in addition hold an annual meeting of prime ministers or foreign secretaries for a general interchange of views and to review the general policies of the league. It would appoint a permanent secretariat and staff, and set up joint committees to study and coordinate the international questions with which it dealt, or questions likely to lead to international disputes. This council represented a frank espousal of great power control in the league, but at any rate it was far less exclusively a great power organ than the conference proposed by Cecil.

As a kind of sop to the susceptibilities of the smaller powers, Smuts advocated the constitution of a general conference, in which all the nations were to be represented and to have equal voting powers. It was to be a body devoted mainly to the public debate of matters of international interest, and its activities were to be severely controlled by the council. General resolutions were to be submitted to it by the council for discussion which, when passed, would have the effect of recommendations to the national parliaments. General measures or codes dealing with questions like disarmament or world peace or rules of international law which had been adopted by the council might be referred to the conference for public discussion before being passed on for approval of the national governments. Similarly, reports of the various international commissions working under the council might be referred for debate.[39] Quite obviously, the conference was to have no real power, except perhaps as a molder of public opinion.

The *Practical Suggestion*, then, went a great deal farther than the Phillimore or Cecil drafts. It provided not only for machinery to prevent the outbreak of war, but for permanent institutions of international cooperation. On the other hand, while it

[39] Smuts, *The League of Nations. A Practical Suggestion*, pp. 6, 27–28, 30–34, 39–40, 53–57.

made concessions to the smaller powers, it was also designed to assure control of the league by the great powers. Smuts himself noted that his aim was to draw in rough outline a "practical, workable" scheme, in contrast to the general or academic proposals current.[40] Yet whatever its practicability, the Smuts plan was not so strikingly original as he implied. Every one of his ideas had appeared in the course of the league discussion during the war, and often in even more detailed form. In any case, the plan made a strong impression on President Wilson and, with the Cecil draft, became the core of the British contribution to the development of the league as it emerged at the Paris Conference.

Thus, while the British Government did not evolve a scheme of its own for a league of nations, by the time of the Paris Conference it had accepted the idea and several of its members had made proposals which were to be important in hammering out the details of the international body. Acceptance had come slowly, however, and at no time did it include acquiescence in any of the more fully-developed projects for international government. A fair estimate of the official British position seems to be that it favored an expansion of the Concert of Europe, with a regular procedure designed to delay the outbreak of war, and with international machinery firmly in the hands of the sovereign great powers.[41] Even Lord Cecil and General Jan Smuts, despite the latter's mandates scheme, did not in any essentials diverge from this general viewpoint. Cecil and Smuts were the foremost British delegates in the league commission at Paris and their proposals, as has been demonstrated in discussion

[40] *Ibid.*, pp. 3–4. F. P. Walters, writing in glowing terms of Smuts' contribution, comments that "he marked out the line of advance, showing forth the League, not as a set of dry legal obligations, nor as a Utopian dream of peace, but as the natural and necessary development of the political institutions of civilized life." See Walters, *op. cit.*, I, 29–30.

[41] Walters, *op. cit.*, I, 16 puts it more strongly. "This was the deep and grave weakness of the League of Nations. The experts did not want it." He is writing of experts of all countries, but, with the obvious qualifications indicated, the description fits the British experts fairly accurately.

after discussion of the Paris Conference, were in large measure embodied in the final draft of the League of Nations Covenant. That Covenant, therefore, with its acceptance of the doctrine of the limited league, can safely be said to have reflected the official British position in many of its most important aspects.

X

Conclusion

THE PLANS FOR A LEAGUE of nations developed from 1914 to 1919 bore eloquent testimony that many Englishmen were determined to find new means by which to avoid the catastrophe of war in the future. The most striking feature of the entire league discussion was the fact that by the end of the conflict outspoken support for the idea of a permanent international organization was to be found in virtually every area of public life. In the confused and emotion-charged atmosphere of the first war years, it is true, there was little disposition to consider dispassionately projects for the prevention of future international struggles. Gradually, however, the thinking of many individuals and groups began to crystallize about the concept of a league of nations. The idea became a symbol of the hope that somehow men might devise institutions to banish the threat of war and establish a genuine community of peaceful nations. This was the real significance of the great debate that came into focus in war-torn Britain. It would be a mistake to exaggerate the importance of any particular plans that evolved, for in the final analysis the concrete character of the League was determined, not by the projects of the war years, but by the decisions of the League of Nations Commission at the Peace Conference in Paris. Nevertheless, it is clear that the key British members of the Commission, Viscount Cecil and General Smuts, were fully aware of the suggestions outlined in such great profusion in the period discussed in this volume. The specific proposals have, therefore, a fundamental bearing on any understanding of the League which did eventually come into existence. And it is on this level of specific proposals that the diversity of ideas offered as solutions to the problem of war becomes clear and requires comment. For while there was fairly widespread agreement on the general conception of a league of nations, the detailed nature of the desired international machinery was defined differently by the various proponents.

It is clear that the project most widely favored was that which conceived of a league as a body whose major function was to serve as an instrument for the peaceful settlement of international disputes. Outlined by the Fabian Society and the Bryce Group comparatively early in the war, this scheme was taken up by numerous individuals, and was essentially the basis upon which the League of Nations Society conducted its propaganda. The League of Free Nations Association differed sharply from the Society in that it proposed to restrict league membership to the "free nations," that is, the Allies. While the parallel with the period after the Second World War is by no means exact, it is incidentally of interest to note that the conception of a league limited to the democratic nations has had a substantial revival in recent years. Like their predecessors, the contemporary advocates of this notion have based their program on the argument that only such democratic nations can be expected faithfully to carry out the international obligations required by an organization such as a league to maintain peace. It is apparent that the question is one upon which there can be a wide range of disagreement among men of unquestioned good will. The problem, certainly, is not one that has had as yet any definitive solution, even in our own day. In any event, to return to our major consideration, whatever their differences respecting membership, the League of Free Nations Association was in substantial agreement with the earlier organization on the matter of the function of a league.

Most of the supporters of a "limited league" made sharp distinctions between justiciable and non-justiciable disputes. With regard to the latter, it was assumed that because they were concerned with "vital interests" or "national honor" no international organization could hope to impose a settlement against the wishes of the nation states involved. Usually the best that was hoped for was the requirement of a period of delay to allow tempers to cool and to promote negotiations that might avert open war. With few exceptions, no real attempt was made to cope with the possible causes of war itself.

A few men, such as J. A. Hobson and H. N. Brailsford, opposed this narrow view with a much more ambitious conception of world organization. They proceeded from the premise that in order to eliminate war it was necessary to strike at its roots. They argued that the struggle for markets and sources of raw materials, contests for opportunities to invest capital, and the general scramble for colonial dependencies were the major causes of war. Consequently, they proposed, in one way or another, that the future league of nations must be empowered to supervise a wide field of economic matters. They supported the idea of a genuine international government, whose main function would be to ensure the legitimate requirements of the various nations and minimize the tensions caused by competitive and antagonistic policies. These advocates of a league with wide powers did not deny the necessity of machinery to settle disputes, but they pictured it as only a part of the working organization of a league.

It is tempting to try to equate these proposals with contemporary schemes for world government, but such an equation would be only partly accurate. None of these earlier British advocates of international government, for example, ever worked out such a detailed program of organization as appears in the proposals of present-day world federalists or committees to form a world government. In essence, they proposed that on certain basic matters the area of competence of an international body be enlarged. For the most part, they thought in terms of *international*, not *world*, government. It is true that in some of his suggestions H. N. Brailsford came close to some of the more recent conceptions of organization, but on the whole "genuine" international government was to them a more limited idea than to their mid-century successors. On the other hand, despite their lack of success in 1919, it seems possible to say that they helped clarify the issue and to see something of a thread of their ideas continuing into the present discussion of the central problem faced in both periods.

For the most part, both the proponents of a limited league and the advocates of international government agreed that economic and military force would have to be at the disposal of the new international organization. Only a minority of pacifists believed that it would be possible to obtain complete acceptance of its decisions and policies by the use of moral suasion alone.

Among the political parties, the Conservatives were the least enthusiastic about international organization. The more intransigent Conservative newspapers and periodicals, as well as individuals, either ignored the league project completely or damned it as a scheme to enslave the British people and liquidate the British Empire. The less violent tended to point out the difficulties in the way of establishing a league, or to be content with an endorsement of the cautious approach taken by the government. The few prominent Conservative supporters of the project, notably Lord Robert Cecil and Lord Lansdowne, stood out as exceptions to the general tendency of their party.

Liberal advocacy of a league was much more widespread. Herbert Asquith and Viscount Grey took the lead in their party's campaign to foster the idea of international organization. They were followed by the organs of public opinion which supported the official Liberal party and by most of the leaders of that party as well. For the most part, the Liberal reading of the nature of the league was in terms of the more narrow of the general approaches sketched. The leaders of the party, its press and its periodicals, with a few notable exceptions among the latter, seemed content to support a league in general terms. Such specific proposals as were made usually assumed that the league's task was to ward off war when it threatened rather than to reduce the causes of war by regularized international co-operation.

Among the political groups in England, the various sections of the Labor party were, by the end of the war, the most whole-hearted supporters of the drive for world organization. The majority of the Labor party, in contrast to the less cautious Independent Labor party, was not really won over to the idea of a powerful league until 1917. But then it accepted such a body as the central pivot of international relations. To the rep-resentatives of Labor, the league became an organization whose primary task was to supervise the normal peacetime activities of the world. The idea of colonial trusteeship under such a league, for example, was more fully developed and more vigorously fostered in the labor movement than anywhere else in England. Unlike the Liberals, who tended to support a narrow league in vague terms, British labor on the whole was willing to outline concrete plans for a very comprehensive league.

Part of the reason for labor's attitude is of course to be found in the ideological (if not always the functional) international-ism which was still taken for granted by most of its leaders. But it is equally clear that many of the most far-reaching of the proposals made by labor came late in the game, after the lead-ing representatives of the Labor party had withdrawn from the coalition government. In 1918, when its projects for a league of nations came to a head, the labor movement was not really burdened by the limitations of official responsibility. Its leaders no longer had to make binding decisions from day to day, nor to face the constant necessity of reaching accommodations with Allied and Associated governments, to say nothing of the impor-tant neutrals. As a result, labor was in an excellent position to serve as a goad and a challenge, making demands which were usually not accepted, but which influenced the responsible British leaders to concern themselves with the question as a serious matter of future policy. Labor's lack of responsibility, however, should not be exaggerated into an easy, monistic explanation of the comprehensiveness of its plans for maintaining the peace. It is worth noting, for example, that the Asquith Liberals were out of power throughout 1917 and 1918, but while the leaders of this group supported the idea of a league loyally and effectively, their conception of it, as we have seen, was a much more limited one. It may perhaps be argued that these opposition Liberals anticipated that they would in the course of time again be in office and hence felt unwilling to commit themselves in too concrete a fashion. But British labor, too, looked forward to the responsibilities of office, if not in the immediate postwar years, then at least in the foreseeable future. Its proposals for a league, therefore, were a great deal more than the irresponsible dreams of a permanent and pessimistic minority party. They stemmed from a vision of the future in which Labor believed that it had a very real part to play. In any case, whatever the motivation, the labor movement was unquestionably the organized political group most fully behind the idea of international organization.

Finally, it is necessary to point out that even the more cautious schemes of the war period went considerably beyond the limits acceptable to the British Government. Propaganda for a league of nations did not become a potent force until 1917. In that year, the activities of its advocates in England were aided enormously by the entrance of the United States, whose President was looked upon as the leader of the campaign for a league, into the war. By that time the coalition of Lloyd George Liberals and Conservatives was in power. While certain individuals in the Government such as Lord Robert Cecil and General Jan Smuts were prominent in advocating an international organization, none of them was willing to permit any effective check upon the control exercised by the great powers.

Officially, the Government gave its public support to the league of nations, and set up a committee to study the project. The recommendations of the Phillimore Committee went no further than the suggestion of a kind of strengthened Concert of Europe designed to consider international crises as they developed. The Cabinet considered the proposals for a league of nations but only reiterated its acceptance of the idea in principle. It did not at any time evolve a specific scheme to be promoted by the British government. Once again, however, the point must be made that the Government, unlike its critics, was compelled to think in terms of immediate responsibilities. It should be recalled that Woodrow Wilson himself, the very symbol of support for a league of nations, was loath for a long time to consider specific details of organization while the war was still being waged. He feared particularly that if such questions became a matter of premature discussion among the governments opposing the Central Powers, the differences that would appear might help prolong the war and jeopardize the possibility of establishing any international organization. Seen in this light, the failure of the British Government to devise a detailed blueprint for a league of nations cannot be regarded simply as a reluctance to implement an idea already accepted in principle. It is evident that one of the reasons for caution was the desire to preserve a measure of freedom of action when binding decisions had to be made in conjunction with other governments. Nevertheless, the plans worked out by Lord Robert Cecil and General Smuts became in a certain sense the policy of the Government, for these men were the leading British delegates in the League Commission at the Paris Conference. Their proposals helped shape the final League of Nations Covenant, which bore, therefore, the imprint of many British ideas and attitudes.

That the British Government was willing to go even as far as it did in accepting the league was of course in part the result of the necessity to cooperate with President Wilson, the leading advocate of such an organization. But it would seem from this study that the Government was also prodded by the demand built up in Great Britain for international machinery to prevent war. By 1919 that demand had achieved impressive proportions and had been met by the writing of the League of Nations Covenant. It remained to be seen whether the League would fulfill the task which all groups agreed was its main purpose. In a brief span of years, the answer was to be given.

The factors contributing to the failure of the League are hardly a matter for analysis here. Yet in a period one of whose major tragedies remains the weakness of international organization in the face of the implications of atomic and bacteriological warfare, it may be useful to emphasize certain aspects of the British campaign for world organization which throw some light, however dim, on present problems. The most striking feature of that campaign was the extreme tenderness displayed for the dogma of national sovereignty. That the Government was unwilling to countenance any effective limitation of national freedom of action is understandable enough, but it is a significant commentary on the state of informed opinion in Great Britain that most of those who saw the need for international organization insisted, nevertheless, that it must be developed substantially within the framework of a state system that had already demonstrated its inability to keep the peace. Observers who are convinced that international peace requires more than a nice balance of national power or a system of defensive alliances and arrangements will perhaps see in the inherent conservatism of the league campaign a clue to the failure of the organization that came into being. Others may conclude that the plans were ambitious enough, perhaps too ambitious, arguing that in the final reckoning schemes for international organization could not possibly go beyond existing institutions which had grown up slowly and were firmly established. Our own generation which, despite the hopes of advocates of world government, has witnessed serious challenges even to the limited competence of the United Nations, can perhaps assess the nature of the problem and recognize why the league was generally considered in such limited terms. At any rate, most of the major plans of organization revealed this limitation. Their proposals were echoed by the bulk of the press, the periodicals, the politicians, and the most active of the societies engaged in propaganda for a league.

Only a handful of individuals considered that prevention of international war required the application of genuinely international—perhaps it would be better to say supranational—methods. The work of these individuals pointed, if only vaguely, to the emergence of a genuine world government as the solution to the problem of recurrent conflict. The leadership of Labor was the only important sector in public life partly to accept, however slowly and hesitantly, the need for some kind of world government and to give its support to the idea.

Labor was not in political power, however, while those who had a more limited view of international organization were. The result, when added to similar currents in other countries, was a League of Nations not fully equipped to cope with its major reason for existence. It may be that there are no lessons to be learned from the past, but it is at least clear that in terms of fundamentals of organization the United Nations bears a remarkably close resemblance to the deceased League. Some critics would say that the same errors of structure have been made, the same limitations placed upon effective cooperation and action. The implication would seem to be that the same failures may perhaps be anticipated. At the same time, it is clear that the institutional pattern of an international body may be only one factor in determining whether it will or will not function adequately. If the will to cooperate is generally present, even the most limited of structures can be used successfully. If there is no such will, Leagues of Nations, United Nations, even world governments have little chance of keeping the peace. Nevertheless, the organizational arrangements, if only because they are the concrete criteria of a genuine will to international cooperation, are important and require close study. Their failure from 1919 to 1939 meant the most devastating war in modern history. Failure now may mean the end of modern society. Here then lies some of the significance of an analysis of the alternatives and choices of thirty years ago. Here also is the imperative challenge of the present.

Bibliography

Primary Sources

MANUSCRIPT AND DOCUMENT COLLECTIONS

Carnegie Endowment for International Peace. Division of International Law (no. 31). *Official Statements of War Aims and Peace Proposals, December 1916 to November 1918.* New York, 1921.

Documents and Statements Relating to Peace Proposals and War Aims (December 1916–November 1918), with an Introduction by G. Lowes Dickinson. London, 1919.

Latané, John H. (ed.). *Development of the League of Nations Idea: Documents and Correspondence of Theodore Marburg.* 2 vols. New York, 1932.

Library of Congress, Woodrow Wilson Papers.

PARLIAMENTARY DEBATES

Great Britain. *Parliamentary Debates,* Commons (fifth series), 1914–1919.

Great Britain. *Parliamentary Debates,* Lords, 1914–1919.

REPORTS

Fabian Society. *Thirty-Second Annual Report.* London, 1915.

———. *Thirty-Third Annual Report.* London, 1916.

———. *Thirty-Fourth Annual Report.* London, 1917.

———. *Thirty-Fifth Annual Report.* London, 1918.

———. *Thirty-Sixth Annual Report.* London, 1919.

Independent Labour Party. *Report of the Annual Conference Held at Leeds, April, 1917.* London, 1917.

———. *Report of the Annual Conference Held at Leicester, April, 1918.* London, 1918.

———. *Report of the Annual Conference Held at Newcastle-on-Tyne, April, 1916.* London, 1916.

———. *Report of the Annual Conference Held at Norwich, April, 1915.* London, 1915.

League of Nations Society. *Monthly Report for Members,* IX–X (1918).

———. *Second Annual Report, March 1917–March 1918, As Approved at the Annual Meeting, June 14th, 1918.* ("League of Nations Society Publications," No. 38) London, 1918.

Report of the Fifteenth Annual Conference of the Labour Party, Bristol, 1916. London, 1916.

Report of the Independent Labour Party to the Executive of the International Socialist Bureau in response to the Manifesto Issued on May 1st, 1916. London, 1916.

Report of the Proceedings at the Forty-Ninth Annual Trade Union Congress Held in the Palace Hotel, Blackpool, on September 3rd to 8th, 1917. London, 1917.

Report of the Proceedings at the Forty-Seventh Annual Trade Union Congress Held in Association Hall, Bristol, on September 6th to 11th, 1915. London, 1915.

Report of the Seventeenth Annual Conference of the Labour Party, Nottingham and London, 1918. London, 1918.

Report of the Sixteenth Annual Conference of the Labour Party, Manchester, 1917. London, 1917.

NEWSPAPERS

Bradford Pioneer. 1914–1919.
British Citizen and Empire Worker. 1916–1919.
Call. 1914–1919.
Clarion. 1914–1919.
Daily Chronicle. 1914–1919.
Daily Mail. 1914–1919.
Daily News and Leader. 1914–1919.
Daily Telegraph. 1914–1919.
Glasgow *Forward.* 1914–1919.
The Herald. 1914–1919.
Labour Leader. 1914–1919.
Manchester Guardian. 1914–1919.
Morning Post. 1914–1919.
The Times. 1914–1919.
Westminster Gazette. 1914–1919.

BOOKS AND PAMPHLETS

An Address Delivered by the Right Honourable Lord Shaw of Dunfermline at a General Meeting of the Society, 15th December, 1916. ("League of Nations Society Publications," No. 7) London, 1917.

Alexander, William Menzies. *Leagues of Nations in History.* ("League of Nations Union Publications," Ser. 2., No. 14) London, [1918].

Angell, Norman. *America and the New World State.* New York, 1915.

———. *The Prussian in Our Midst.* ("Union of Democratic Control Publications," No. 13) London, n.d.

———. *Shall This War End German Militarism?* ("Union of Democratic Control Publications," No. 2) London, [1914].

Angell, Norman. *War Aims: the Need for a Parliament of the Allies.* London, [1917].

Ashbee, C. R. *The American League to Enforce Peace: An English Interpretation.* London, 1917.

Asquith, Herbert H. *"Eyes Open, Hands Free." Liberal Watchwords for the General Election. A Speech Delivered at the Caxton Hall, London, on November 18th, 1918.* London, 1918.

———. *The League of Nations. The True Crusade. A Speech Delivered at a Dinner to American Officers, at the National Liberal Club, on July 10th, 1918.* London, 1918.

———. *The Liberal Programme. A Speech Delivered at the Free Trade Hall, Manchester, on September 27th, 1918.* London, 1918.

Astor, Waldorf. *Co-operative Basis for a League of Nations (Some Problems of Reconstruction).* London, [1919].

Barker, Ernest. *A Confederation of the Nations: Its Powers and Constitution.* London, 1918.

Bennett, Arnold. *The Embargo v. the Gun.* ("League of Nations Union Publications," Ser. 2, No. 1) London, 1918.

———. Independence and Sovereignty. ("League of Nations Union Publications," Ser. 2, No. 12) London, [1918].

Berry, Trevor T. *The Hope of the World. An Appreciation of the League of Nations Scheme.* London, 1919.

Brailsford, H. N. *The Covenant of Peace: An Essay on the League of Nations.* New York, 1919.

———. *A League of Nations.* London, 1917.

———. *The Origins of the Great War.* ("Union of Democratic Control Publications," No. 4) London, [1914].

———. *The War of Steel and Gold.* 3d ed. London, 1915.

British War Aims. Statement by the Right Honourable David Lloyd George January Fifth, Nineteen Hundred and Eighteen. Authorized Version as Published by the British Government. New York, 1918.

Bryce, Viscount James. *Essays and Addresses in War Time.* New York, 1918.

Bryce, Viscount James and others. *Proposals for the Prevention of Future Wars.* London, 1917.

Bull, Father Paul B. *Sermon on the "League of Nations" Preached at Holy Trinity, Sloane Street, on July 7th, 1918.* ("League of Nations Society Publications," No. 41) London, 1918.

Buxton, C. R. (ed.) *Towards a Lasting Settlement.* New York, 1916.

Cecil, Lord Robert. *World Opinion and the League of Nations.* ("League of Nations Union Publications," Ser. 2, No. 24) London, 1918.

Clifford, John. *The League of Free Nations: Facing the Facts.* ("League of Nations Union Publications," Ser. 2, No. 18) London, 1918.

Corbett, Sir Julian. *The League of Nations and Freedom of the Seas.* London, 1918.

———. *The League of Peace and a Free Sea.* London, 1917.

Davies, Major David. *The Church and the League of Nations.* ("League of Nations Union Publications," Ser. 2, No. 17) London, [1918].

———. *Some Problems of International Reconstruction and a League of Nations.* ("League of Nations Society Publications," No. 31) London, 1918.

———. *Some Problems of International Reconstruction and a League of Nations.* ("League of Nations Union Publications," Ser. 2, No. 23) London, [1918].

———. *Why An Association Is Necessary* ("League of Free Nations Association Publications," Ser. 2, No. 6) London, [1918].

———. *Why Not Form the League Now?* ("League of Free Nations Association Publications," Ser. 2, No. 2) London, [1918].

Dawson, William Harbutt. *Problems of the Peace.* London, 1918.

The Demand of Labour for a League of Nations. ("League of Nations Society Publications," No. 25) London, 1918.

The Demand of the Churches for a League of Nations. ("League of Nations Society Publications," No. 33) London, 1918.

Dickinson, G. Lowes. *After the War.* London, 1915.

———. *The Choice before Us.* New York, 1917.

———. *The European Anarchy.* London, 1916.

———. *The War and the Way Out.* London, n.d.

Dickinson, W. H. *Disarmament and a League of Nations.* ("League of Nations Society Publications," No. 28) London, 1918.

———. *A League of Nations and Its Critics.* ("League of Nations Society Publications," No. 14) London, 1917.

Ebor, Cosmo, Archbishop of York. *The Need and the Hope of a League of Nations* ("League of Nations Union Publications," Ser. 2, No. 28) London, 1919.

Fayle, C. Ernest. *The Fourteenth Point. A Study of the League of Nations.* London, 1919.

———. *The Great Settlement.* New York, 1915.

Garvin, J. L. *The Economic Foundations of Peace.* London, 1919.

General Smuts and a League of Nations. Includes also Speeches by Lord Bryce, the Archbishop of Canterbury, Lord Buckmaster, Lord Hugh Cecil, M. P., and Others. ("League of Nations Society Publications," No. 11) 2d ed. London, 1917.

Gore, Charles, Bishop of Oxford. *The League of Nations. The Opportunity of the Church.* London, 1919.

Grant, A. J. and others. *An Introduction to the Study of International Relations*. London, 1916.

A Great French Statesman Explains Why We Must Form the League of Free Nations Now. ("League of Free Nations Association Publications," Ser. 2, No. 9) London, [1918].

Grey, Viscount Edward. *The League of Nations*. London, 1918.

Gribble, James. *Your Case, Mr. Workman. An Appeal to Labour.* ("League of Nations Union Publications," Ser. 2, No. 20) London, [1918].

"A Group of Women." *Woman's Part in the League of Nations* ("League of Nations Union Publications," Ser. 2, No. 29) London, 1919.

Hart, Heber L. *The Bulwarks of Peace*. London, 1918.

Hawkin, R. C. *Central Africa and the League of Nations. Fabian Tract No. 186*. London, 1918.

Henderson, Arthur. *The Aims of Labour*. London, 1918.

———. *The League of Nations and Labour*. London, 1918.

The Herald. *Why Labour Left the Coalition*. London, 1918.

Hobson, John A. *Towards International Government*. London, 1915.

Hocking, Silas K. *The Moral Aspect of the League of Nations.* ("League of Free Nations Association Publications," Ser. 2, No. 8) London, [1918].

How to Prevent War. ("League of Nations Society Publications," No. 10) London, [1917].

Hyde, H. E. *The International Solution*. London, 1918.

———. *The League of Nations and the Peace Conference.* ("League of Nations Union Publications," Ser. 2, No. 27) London, [1918].

———. *The Two Roads: International Government or Militarism.* London, [1915].

Inter-Allied Labour and Socialist Conference, *Memorandum on War Aims Agreed Upon at the Central Hall, Westminster, London, S.W., on February 20th to 24th, 1918*. London, [1918].

Jacobs, A. J. *Neutrality versus Justice*. London, 1917.

Jones, Sir Henry. *Form the League of Peace Now: An Appeal to My Fellow-Citizens* ("League of Nations Union Publications," Ser. 2, No. 5) London, [1918].

Keen, Frank Noel. *Hammering Out the Details*. London, 1917.

———. *Towards International Justice*. London, 1923.

———. *The World in Alliance. A Plan for Preventing Future Wars.* London, 1915.

Kiek, Rev. Edward S. *Brotherhood and World Peace.* ("League of Nations Union Publications," Ser. 2, No. 22) London, [1918].

Knight, Joseph. *Leaguing the Nations. How? What For?* ("League of Nations Union Publications," Ser. 2, No. 30) London, [1919].

The Labour Party (unnumbered Labor Party Leaflet). London, 1918.

Labour Party. *Labour and the New Social Order: A Report on Reconstruction.* London, 1918.

———. *Labour and the Peace Treaty.* London, [1919].

———. *Memoranda on International Labour Legislation: The Economic Structure of the League of Nations.* London, 1919.

Lamont, Rev. Daniel. *The Church and International Peace. Substance of Presidential Address Delivered to the Glasgow College Union by the Rev. Daniel Lamont, B.D. of Hillhead United Free Church, Glasgow.* ("League of Nations Union Publications," Ser. 2, No. 25) London, [1918].

Lawrence, T. J. *The Society of Nations. Its Past, Present, and Possible Future.* New York, 1919.

A League of Nations. An Address Delivered by the Rt. Hon. Lord Robert Cecil, K.C., M.P., in the Town Hall, Birmingham, on the Occasion of His Installation as Chancellor of the University of Birmingham, 12th November, 1918. Birmingham, [1918].

A League of Nations. A Scheme of Study. ("League of Nations Society Publications," No. 20) London, 1917.

League of Nations: Scheme of Organization Prepared by a Sub-Committee of the League of Nations Society. 1918. With a Foreword by the Rt. Hon. W. H. Dickinson, M.P. ("League of Nations Publications," No. 42) London, 1918.

League of Nations Society. *A Handbook for Speakers on a League of Nations.* London, 1918.

The League of Nations Society ("League of Nations Society Publications," No. 26) London, 1918.

The League of Nations Society. Explanation of the Objects of the Society ("League of Nations Society Publications," No. 2. Printed for Private Circulation) London, 1916.

The League of Nations. Speech by the Right Hon. Lord Shaw of Dunfermline. House of Lords, June 26th, 1918. ("League of Nations Society Publications," No. 39) London, 1918.

The League of Nations Union. ("League of Nations Union Publications," Ser. 2, No. 10) London, 1918.

Liberal Policy in the Task of Political and Social Reconstruction. London, 1918.

Lodge, Sir Oliver. *The Functions of a League of Nations.* ("League of Nations Union Publications," Ser. 2, No. 15) London, [1918].

MacDonald, J. Ramsay. *Labour and International Relations.* Burton-on-Trent, 1917.

MacDonald, J. Ramsay. *National Defence. A Study in Militarism.* London, 1917.

———. *War and the Workers. A Plea for Democratic Control.* ("Union of Democratic Control Publications," No. 8) London, n.d.

Maclagen, O. F. *International Prohibition of War.* London, 1915.

———. *Mutual Defence of Nations.* London, 1915.

Marriott, J. A. R. *The European Commonwealth.* Oxford, 1918.

Mathews, Basil (ed.). *The League of Nations.* London, 1919.

McArthur, Irene. *Women and the League of Nations.* ("League of Free Nations Association Publications," Ser. 2, No. 4) London, [1918].

McCurdy, Charles A. *A Clean Peace. The War Aims of British Labour. Complete Text of the Official War Aims Memorandum of the Inter-Allied Labour and Socialist Conference, Held in London, February 23, 1918.* New York, [1918].

———. *The League of Free Nations.* ("League of Free Nations Association Publications," Ser. 2, No. 3) London, 1918.

Morel, E. D. *Africa and the Peace of Europe.* London, 1917.

———. *The African Problem and the Peace Settlement.* ("Union of Democratic Control Publications," No. 22a) London, 1917.

The Morrow of the War ("Union of Democratic Control Publications," No. 1) London, [1914].

Muir, Ramsay. *Nationalism and Internationalism.* London, 1916.

Murray, Gilbert. *The League of Nations and the Democratic Idea.* London, 1918.

———. *The Way Forward: Three Articles on Liberal Policy.* London, 1917.

National Liberal Federation. *Proceedings in connection with the Meeting of the General Committee of the National Liberal Federation, Held at Manchester, September 26th and 27th, 1918, with the Resolutions and Speeches Including That Delivered by the Right Hon. H. H. Asquith, K.C., M.P., in the Free Trade Hall.* London, 1918.

The National Policy As Set Forth by Mr. Asquith, Sir Edward Grey, Mr. Churchill, Mr. Lloyd George, Mr. Austen Chamberlain, Mr. Balfour, Mr. Bonar Law, Mr. Arthur Henderson, and Others. ("Union of Democratic Control Publications," No. 6) London, n.d.

National War Aims Committee. *Grey's Message. The League of Nations.* London, [1918].

Olivier, Sir Sidney. *The League of Nations and Primitive Peoples.* London, 1918.

Oppenheim, Lassa. *The League of Nations and Its Problems: Three Lectures.* London, 1919.

Paish, Sir George. *The Economic Interdependence of Nations.* ("League of Nations Society Publications," No. 27) London, 1918.

———. *A Permanent League of Nations.* London, 1918.

Pamphlets and Leaflets for 1915–1918, Being the Publications for Four Years of the Liberal Publication Department. London, 1919.

Pares, Sir Bernard. *The League of Nations and Other Questions of Peace.* London, 1919.

Parrott, Sir Edward. *The Aims of Liberalism.* London, [1918].

The Peace Settlement—and After. London, [1919].

A People's Peace. ("I.L.P. Women's Peace Crusade Leaflet," No. 6) London, 1916.

Pethick Lawrence, F. W. *U.D.C. Memoranda on a Democratic Peace. II. Making Germany Pay.* ("Union of Democratic Control Publications," No. 30a) London, 1919.

Phillimore, Baron Walter G. F. *Schemes for Maintaining General Peace* ("Handbooks Prepared under the Direction of the Historical Section of the Foreign Office," No. 160) London, 1920.

———. *Three Centuries of Treaties of Peace and Their Teaching.* London, 1917.

Pollard, A. F. *The League of Nations. An Historical Argument.* London, 1918.

———. *The League of Nations in History.* London, 1918.

Pollock, Sir Frederick. *The League of Nations and the Coming Rule of Law.* London, 1918.

Ponsonby, Arthur. *The Control of Foreign Policy* ("Union of Democratic Control Publications," No. 5a) London, 1918.

———. *Democracy and Diplomacy. A Plea for Popular Control of Foreign Policy.* London, 1915.

———. *Parliament and Foreign Policy.* ("Union of Democratic Control Publications," No. 5) London, [1914].

Problems of the International Settlement. London, 1918.

Proceedings of the First Annual Meeting Held at the Caxton Hall, July 20th, 1917. ("League of Nations Society Publications," No. 16) London, 1917.

The Project of a League of Nations. ("League of Nations Society Publications," No. 15) London, 1917.

Reichel, Harry R. *Why a League of Free Nations?* ("League of Nations Union Publications," Ser. 2, No. 21) London, [1918].

Report of a Conference of the Legal Profession (Convened by the League of Nations Special Conference Committee) to Discuss: "The Possibility of a Durable Settlement by means of a League of

Nations." ("League of Nations Society Publications," No. 17) London, 1917.

Report of Meeting, May 14th, 1917. Speeches Delivered by Viscount Bryce, O.M., General Smuts, the Archbishop of Canterbury, Lord Buckmaster, Lord Hugh Cecil, M.P., and Others. ("League of Nations Society Publications," No. 11) London, 1917.

Research Committee of the League of Nations Union. *The Idea of a League of Nations: Prolegomena to the Study of World Organization.* London, [1919].

————. *The Way to the League of Nations.* London, 1919.

Russell, Bertrand. *War—the Offspring of Fear.* ("Union of Democratic Control Publications," No. 3) London, [1914].

Scheme for the World League. Speech Delivered by the Late Lord Parker in the House of Commons on March 19th, 1918. ("League of Nations Union Publications," Ser. 2, No. 16) London, [1918].

Shaw, George Bernard. *Peace Conference Hints.* London, 1919.

Smuts, J. C. *The League of Nations: A Practical Suggestion.* London, 1918.

————. *War-Time Speeches: A Compilation of Public Utterances in Great Britain.* New York, 1917.

Spalding, H. N. *What a League of Nations Means.* ("League of Nations Society Publications," No. 22) London, 1918.

Stallybrass, W. F. S. *A Society of States.* London, 1918.

Stead, F. Herbert. *The Case for an International Police Force.* ("League of Nations Union Publications," Ser. 2, No. 7) London, [1918].

Tawney, Lieut. R. L. *The War to End War. A Plea to Soldiers by a Soldier.* ("Union of Democratic Control Publications," No. 21a) London, 1918.

Tentative Draft by an American Committee. Scheme of International Organization No. III ("League of Nations Society Publications," No. 30) London, 1918.

The Treaty between the Argentine Republic, the United States of Brazil, and Chile. ("League of Nations Society Publications," No. 5) London, 1917.

Treaty between the United Kingdom and the United States of America with regard to the Establishment of a Peace Commission. ("League of Nations Society Publications," No. 4) London, 1917.

Unwin, Raymond. *Functions of a League of Nations. Schemes of International Organization No. II.* ("League of Nations Society Publications," No. 19) London, 1917.

Viscount Grey Explains Why a League Is Necessary and What It Will Do. ("League of Nations Union Publications," Ser. 2, No. 19) London, 1918.

Viscount Grey On a League of Nations at a Meeting Held at Central Hall, Westminster, October 10th, 1918. ("League of Nations Society Publications," No. 44) London, 1918.

Walsh, Walter. *The World Rebuilt.* London, 1917.

Walston, Sir Charles. *The English Speaking Brotherhood and the League of Nations.* Cambridge, 1919.

————. *The Next War, Wilsonism and Anti-Wilsonism, with an Open Letter to Col. Theodore Roosevelt.* Cambridge, 1918.

————. *Patriotism, National and International.* London, 1917.

War after War. The Inaugural Meeting of the League of Free Nations Association Held in the Town Hall, at Northampton, on September 13th, 1918. Speech by Viscount Bryce. ("League of Nations Union Publications," Ser. 2, No. 13) London, 1918.

Wells, H. G. *British Nationalism and the League of Nations.* London, 1918.

————. *In the Fourth Year: Anticipations of a World Peace.* New York, 1918.

————. *The War That Will End War.* London, 1914.

————. *What Is Coming? A European Forecast.* New York, 1916.

Wells, H. G. and others. *The Idea of a League of Nations.* Boston, 1919.

Why Women Should Join the Labour Party and Vote for the Labour Candidates. (Labour Party Leaflet, No. 3, new series) London, 1918.

Why Labour Supports a League of Nations. (Labour Party Leaflet, No. 17, new series) London, 1918.

Why I Shall Vote Labour. (Labour Party Leaflet, No. 26, new series) London, 1918.

Williams, Aneurin. *A League of Nations: How to Begin It.* ("League of Nations Society Publications," No. 8) London, 1917.

————. *The Minimum of Machinery. Schemes of International Organization No. I* ("League of Nations Society Publications," No. 18) London, 1917.

Winton, Edward, Bishop of Winchester. *The Spiritual Sanctions of a League of Nations.* London, 1919.

Withers, Hartley. *The Financial Aspect of a League of Nations.* ("League of Nations Union Publications," Ser. 2, No. 11) London, [1918].

————. *The League of Nations. Its Economic Aspects.* London, 1918.

Woolf, Leonard S. *A Durable Settlement after the War by means of a*

League of Nations. ("League of Nations Society Publications," No. 21) London, 1917.

Woolf, Leonard S. *The Framewirk of a Lasting Peace.* London, 1917.

———. *International Government: Two Reports Prepared for the Fabian Research Department, Together with a Project by a Fabian Committee for a Supernational Authority That Will Prevent War.* New York, 1916.

World-Wide Support for a League of Nations. ("League of Nations Society Publications," No. 34) London, 1918.

Younghusband, Sir Francis. *The Sense of a Community of Nations. An Address by Sir Francis Younghusband.* ("League of Nations Society Publications," No. 13) London, 1917.

ARTICLES

Aitken, George. "A League of Nations," *English Review,* XXVII (1918), 167–183.

"America and a League of Nations," *War and Peace,* IV (1917), 101–106.

"Anglo-Saxons and a League of Nations," *War and Peace,* V (1917), 29–32.

Archer, William. "The Obstacles to a League of Nations," *Fortnightly Review,* CXIV (1918), 567–573.

"Bargaining by Threat and the Alternative. Section III: The First Principles of International Government," *War and Peace,* IV (1917), 77–81.

Brailsford, H. N. "The League of Nations. Prize Essay. Foundations of Internationalism," *English Review,* XXVII (1918), 87–101.

———. "On Preventing Wars," *War and Peace,* II (1915), 71–72.

"British Labor's War Aims," *International Conciliation,* CXXII (1918), 45–56.

Buckmaster, Lord. "A Policy for Liberals," *Nation,* XXII (1917), 296–297.

Burns, C. Delisle. "The Balance of Power," *War and Peace,* V (1917), 147–149.

Burns, Emile. "Problems of Disarmament," *War and Peace,* V (1918), 228–229.

———. "Problems of Disarmament. II," *War and Peace,* V (1918), 255–258.

Buxton, Noel. "The International Factor in the African Settlement," *Contemporary Review,* CXIV (1918), 513–520.

Caird, Mona. "The Greater Community," *Fortnightly Review,* CX (1918), 742–755.

Dawson, William Harbutt. "The Future of the German Colonies. II. The Case for Conditional Return," *Contemporary Review,* CXII (1918), 256–263.

Dickinson, G. Lowes. "The American 'League to Enforce Peace,'" *War and Peace,* III (1916), 134–135.

Dickinson, Sir Willoughby H. "A League of Nations and Its Critics," *Contemporary Review,* CXI (1917), 665–673.

Dillon, E. J. "The Empire and the World League," *Fortnightly Review,* CX (1918), 489–501.

———. "The World in Flux," *Fortnightly Review,* CXI (1919), 11–25.

"The Economic Task of a League of Nations," *War and Peace,* V (1917), 128–130.

Fabian News, vol. XXV–XXX (1914–1919).

"Faint-Hearted Leaguers," *Nation,* XXIII (1918), 615–616.

Fayle, C. Ernest. "Some Factors of the Settlement: II," *War and Peace,* II (1915), 55–56.

Firth, J. B. "The Government and the League of Nations," *Fortnightly Review,* CX (1918), 367–375.

———. "An Illusory League of Nations," *Fortnightly Review,* CX (1918), 39–51.

———. "President Wilson and the League of Nations," *Fortnightly Review,* CXI (1919), 553–565.

"The Foundation of the League," *New Statesman,* XII (1919), 436–437.

"The Framework of Peace," *War and Peace,* IV (1917), 85–100.

"The German Colonies," *Spectator,* CXXI (1918), 476–477.

"The German Colonies in the Pacific," *Round Table,* VIII (1918), 650–660.

"Germany and the African Native," *Spectator,* CXXI (1918), 295–296.

Hall, John. "Leagues to Enforce Peace. (I) The Failure of the Holy Alliance," *Nineteenth Century and After,* LXXXI (1917), 689–699.

Harris, John H. "Colonial Dependencies: 'Possession' or 'Trusteeship'?" *Contemporary Review,* CXIII (1918), 207–212.

———. "Germany's Colonial Empire: Seven Reasons against Restoration," *Nineteenth Century and After,* LXXXI (1917), 1157–1163.

———. "Self-determination and the British Commonwealth. V Equatorial Africa," *New Europe,* VI (1918), 173–179.

———. "Tropical Colonies—'International Government,'" *Fortnightly Review,* CVIII (1917), 742–747.

Harrison, Austin. "America, the 'Center-Board' of Europe," *English Review,* XXVII (1918), 229–238.

Harrison, Austin. " 'For the Duration'–" *English Review,* XXVI (1918), 368–379.

———. "Ides of March," *English Review,* XXVI (1918), 275–284.

———. "A League of Nations Again," *English Review,* XXVII (1918), 297–306.

———. "Lord Lansdowne's Interrogation," *English Review,* XXVI (1918), 76–92.

———. "Peace or War?" *English Review,* XXVIII (1919), 72–79.

———. "Towards the New Europe," *English Review,* XXVII (1918), 448–457.

———. "A World Declaration of Rights," *English Review,* XXVII (1918), 369–378.

Harrison, Frederic. "Obiter Scripta," *Fortnightly Review,* CIX (1918), 642–651; CX (1918) 161–169, 321–329.

Henderson, Arthur. "The Outlook for Labour," *Contemporary Review,* CXIII (1918), 121–130.

Hewlett, Maurice. "The Flaw in the Metal," *War and Peace,* V (1918), 328–329.

"How to Form a League of Nations," *Nation,* XXIII (1918), 272–274.

"How to Make the League," *New Statesman,* XI (1918), 365–366.

"The International Control of Supplies after the War," *War and Peace,* V (1917), 107–111.

Johnston, H. H. "Africa and the Peace of Europe: A Review of Mr. E. D. Morel's Latest Book," *War and Peace,* V (1917), 48–49.

———. "The Disposal of the German Colonies," *New Statesman,* V (1915), 368–369.

———. "The Future of the German Colonies. I. The Case for Retention," *Contemporary Review,* CXII (1917), 250–255.

"Labor's Suspicions of a League of Nations," *War and Peace,* V (1918), 226–227.

"Labour's Terms of Peace," *New Statesman,* IX (1917), 436–437.

"A Lasting Peace," *New Statesman,* X (1917), 91–92.

"The League and the German Colonies," *New Statesman,* XII (1919), 363–364.

"The League and Revolutions," *New Statesman,* XII (1918), 174–175.

"The League and the Peace," *New Statesman,* XII (1919), 388–389.

"The League of Nations," *New Statesman,* XII (1918), 125–128.

"The League of Nations," *Spectator,* CXXI (1918), 444–445.

"A League of Nations. I.—Introductory," *New Statesman,* IX (1917), 342–344.

"A League of Nations. II.—Economic Rights of Way," *New Statesman,* IX (1917), 368–369.

"A League of Nations. III.—Economic Rights of Way (continued),"
   New Statesman, IX (1917), 392–393.

"A League of Nations. IV.—Overseas Possessions," *New Statesman,* IX
   (1917), 416–418.

"A League of Nations. V.—The Need for International Co-operation,"
   New Statesman, IX (1917), 440–441.

"A League of Nations. VI.—Objections to a League," *New Statesman,*
   IX (1917), 464–466.

"A League of Nations.—II," *Spectator,* CXXI (1918), 37–39.

"A League of Nations Now? A Symposium," *War and Peace,* V (1918),
   305–309, 326–328.

"A League of Nations—When and How?" *Nation,* XXII (1918), 643–
   644.

"The League to Enforce Peace," *Spectator,* CXVII (1916), 433–435.

"Leagues to Enforce Peace," *Spectator,* CXVIII (1917), 60–62.

Liberal Magazine, XXII–XXVII (1914–1919).

Lilly, W. S. "Vengeance," *Nineteenth Century and After,* LXXXIV
   (1918), 401–414.

Low, Sidney. "The Conference of Nations," *Fortnightly Review,* CX
   (1918), 865–873.

MacDonald, J. Ramsay. "Peace Guarantees," *Socialist Review,* XIV
   (1917), 17–32.

Macdonell, John. "Armed Pacifism," *Contemporary Review,* CXI
   (1917), 290–300.

———. "Beyond the Battlefield," *Contemporary Review,* CXIII
   (1918), 14–21.

———. "The League of Nations in Jeopardy," *Contemporary Review,*
   CXIV (1918), 126–133.

———. "Super-Nationalism," *Contemporary Review,* CXIII (1918),
   250–256.

MacNeill, J. Swift. "Is a League of Nations Illusory?" *Fortnightly Review,* CX (1918), 294–305.

Malleson, J. P. "A League of Nations and a Change of Heart," *Contemporary Review,* CXV (1919), 83–88.

"The March of an Idea," *Nation,* XXII (1917), 112–113.

Marriott, J. A. R. "The Supreme Issue," *Nineteenth Century and After,*
   LXXXI (1917), 709–725.

McCurdy, C. A. "A League of Nations Now," *War and Peace,* V
   (1918), 288–289.

Muir, Ramsay. "The Difficulties of a League of Peace," *New Europe,*
   II (1917), 65–77.

———. "Europe and the Non-European World. III—The Backward
   Peoples," *New Europe,* III (1917), 403–408.

"Musings without Method," *Blackwood's Magazine*, CCIII (1918), 413–424; CCIV (1918), 266–273, 687–696, 832–842.

New Statesman, X (1918), 437–441; XI (1918), 281–283.

"News of the Week," *Spectator*, CXX (1918), 25–27, 49–51.

"No Peace Conference," *Spectator*, CXXI (1918), 221–222.

Olivier, Sir Sidney. "The Repartition of Africa," *Contemporary Review*, CXV (1919), 15–22.

"Once More: the International Magna Charta," *English Review*, XXVI (1918), 66–75.

"Opposition to the League of Nations," *War and Peace*, V (1917), 11–12.

"Our War Aims," *Spectator*, CXX (1918), 28–29.

"The Organization of Africa," *War and Peace*, V (1917), 64–65.

"A Paris Conference for a League of Nations or Failure of the War," *War and Peace*, IV (1916), 33–52.

Parmoor, Lord. "The League of Nations (An Address Delivered by Lord Parmoor in Gray's Inn Hall on April 10th, 1918)," *Transactions of the Grotius Society*, IV (Problems of the War: Papers Read before the Society in the Year 1918), XVII–XXIII.

———. "Lord Lansdowne and the League of Nations," *Contemporary Review*, CXIII (1918), 8–13.

———. "President Wilson and the Peace Settlement," CXV (1919), 10–14.

Pethick Lawrence, F. W. "Towards a Federated World," *Socialist Review*, XII (1915), 738–746.

Phelps, Edith M. (compiled by). *Selected Articles on a League of Nations*. New York, 1919.

Phillimore, Lord. "A League of Nations," *Quarterly Review*, CCXXXI (1919), 206–227.

Phillips, W. Alison. "The Balance of Power," *New Europe*, V (1917), 65–75.

———. "National Federations and World Federation," *Edinburgh Review*, CCXXVI (1917), 1–27.

———. "President Wilson's Peace Program and the British Empire," *Edinburgh Review*, CCXXV (1917), 227–248.

———. "The Price of the 'Society of Nations,'" *New Europe*, IX (1918), 173–176.

Pigou, A. C. "The Conditions of a Permanent Peace," *War and Peace*, III (1916), 54–55.

"The Political Initiative," *Nation*, XXIII (1918), 516–517.

Pollock, Sir Frederick. " 'The Difficulties of a League of Peace,' " *New Europe*, II (1917), 112–114.

Pollock, Sir Frederick. "Sovereignty and the League of Nations," *Fortnightly Review*, CX (1918), 813–818.

———. "What of the Law of Nations?" *Fortnightly Review*, C (1916), 895–904.

Ponsonby, Arthur. "The Sanction Behind a League of Nations," *War and Peace*, V (1918), 329–330.

"President Wilson's Address to the Senate," *Spectator*, CXVIII (1917), 93.

"President Wilson's Visit and Its Sequels," *Spectator*, CXXI (1918), 684–685.

"The Prevention of War," *New Statesman*, V (1915), 317–318.

Runciman, Walter. "The Radical Outlook," *Contemporary Review*, CXIII (1918), 1–7.

"The Sanctity of International Contracts," *Spectator*, CXX (1918), 308–309.

Sardonyx. "Observations," *New Statesman*, X (1918), 449–450.

"Schemes of International Organization," *War and Peace*, V (1918), 216–218.

Shadwell, Arthur. "Is Peace Possible?" *Nineteenth Century and After*, LXXXIV (1918), 1–23.

———. "A Swiss Jurist on the League of Nations," *Nineteenth Century and After*, LXXXIV (1918), 485–506.

"Shall the Nations Enforce Peace?" *War and Peace*, IV (1917), 53–68.

"Some Principles and Problems of the Settlement," *Round Table*, IX (1918), 88–120.

Spender, Harold. "The League of Nations: A Voice from the Past," *Contemporary Review*, CXIV (1918), 407–414.

Steed, Henry Wickham. "A Program for Peace—Revised," *Edinburgh Review*, CCXXVIII (1918), 209–229.

Stephen, Herbert. "The American Dream of Peace," *Nineteenth Century and After*, LXXXI (1917), 799–810.

———. "The League of Dreams," *Nineteenth Century and After*, LXXXV (1919) 11–24.

Stone, F. G. "Leagues to Enforce Peace. (II) An Illusion of To-day," *Nineteenth Century and After*, LXXXI (1917), 700–708.

"Suggestions for the Constitution of a League of Nations," *Spectator*, CXXI (1918), 445.

Sydenham, Lord. "The Greatest 'League of Nations,'" *Nineteenth Century and After*, LXXXIV (1918), 251–259.

"The Two Paths," *Nation*, XXIII (1918), 106–107.

"The Two Policies," *Nation*, XXIII (1918), 188–189.

"A Treaty of Mutual Defence," *War and Peace*, V (1918), 293–294.

"War on the League of Nations," *Nation*, XXIII (1918), 465–466.

Wells, H. G. "The Liberal Fear of Russia," *Nation*, XV (1914), 755–757.

"What Is Clear and What Is Not Clear," *New Statesman*, X (1918), 344–345.

Whelpley, James D. "America's Weapon for Peace," *Fortnightly Review*, CIX (1918), 116–123.

"Why Not a League Now?" *War and Peace*, V (1918), 167–168.

Whyte, A. F. " 'The Freedom of the Seas,' " *New Europe*, IV (1917), 360–366.

"Will a League of Nations Be a Tool of Capitalism?" *War and Peace*, V (1918), 186–187.

"Windows of Freedom," *Round Table*, IX (1918), 0–47.

Winton, Edward, Bishop of Winchester. "The End of the War and After," *Contemporary Review*, CXIV (1918), 597–603.

Wood, T. McKinnon. "A Necessary Guarantee of the Peace," *Contemporary Review*, CXIV (1918), 477–483.

"Wrecking the League," *Nation*, XXIII (1918), 302–303.

" 'A Year's Notice,' " *Spectator*, CXXI (1918), 752–753.

Young, George. "The League of Nations. (I) As a Progressive Principle," *New Europe*, V (1917), 289–295.

———. "The League of Nations. (II) As a Practical Procedure," *New Europe*, V (1917), 330–336.

Secondary Works

Angell, Norman, *After All. The Autobiography of Norman Angell*. New York, 1951.

Asquith, Earl of Oxford and. *Memories and Reflections, 1852–1927*. 2 vols. Boston, 1928.

Baker, Ray Stannard. *Woodrow Wilson and World Settlement*. 3 vols. New York, 1922.

———. (ed.) *Woodrow Wilson Life and Letters*. 8 vols. New York, 1927–1939.

Balch, Emily Greene. *Approaches to the Great Settlement*. New York, 1918.

Barnes, George N. *From Workshop to War Cabinet*. New York, 1924.

Bartlett, Ruhl J. *The League to Enforce Peace*. Chapel Hill, 1944.

Brailsford, H. N. *If We Want Peace*. London, 1932.

Brand, Carl F. *British Labour's Rise to Power*. Stanford University, California, 1941.

Cecil, Viscount. *A Great Experiment*. London, 1941.

Charvet, J. F. *L'Influence Britannique Dans la S.D.N., des Origines de la S.D.N. Jusqu'à Nos Jours*. Paris, 1938.

Cole, G. D. H. *A Short History of the British Working Class Movement, 1789–1927.* 3 vols. London, 1927.

Ensor, R. C. K. *England: 1870–1914.* Oxford, 1936.

Fisher, H. A. L. *James Bryce (Viscount Bryce of Dechmont, O. M.).* 2 vols. New York, 1927.

Forster, E. M. *Goldsworthy Lowes Dickinson.* New York, 1934.

Gretton, R. H. *Modern History of the English People, 1880–1922.*

Hamilton, Mary Agnes. *Arthur Henderson. A Biography.* London, 1938.

————. *Remembering My Good Friends.* London, 1944.

Hemleben, Sylvester John. *Plans for World Peace through Six Centuries.* Chicago, 1943.

Hendrick, Burton J. *The Life and Letters of Walter H. Page.* 2 vols. New York, 1923.

Kellogg, Paul and Arthur Gleason. *British Labour and the War.* New York, 1919.

Lloyd George, David. *The Truth about the Peace Treaties.* 2 vols. London, 1938.

————. *War Memoirs.* 6 vols. Boston, 1933–1937.

Lord Riddell's War Diary. London, 1933.

Maanen-Hellmer, Elizabeth Van. *The Mandates System in relation to Africa and the Pacific Islands.* London, 1929.

Maurice, Sir Frederick. *Haldane, 1915–1928.* London, 1939.

Miller, David Hunter. *The Drafting of the Covenant.* 2 vols. New York, 1928.

Millin, Sarah Gertrude. *General Smuts.* 2 vols. London, 1936.

Morley, Felix. *A Society of Nations.* Washington, 1932.

Munch, P. (ed.). *Les Origines et L'Oeuvre de la Société des Nations.* 2 vols. Copenhagen, 1923–1924.

Newton, Lord. *Lord Lansdowne. A Biography.* London, 1929.

Parmoor, Lord. *A Retrospect: Looking over a Life of More Than Eighty Years.* London, 1936.

Playne, Caroline E. *Britain Hold On, 1917, 1918.* London, 1933.

Pollock, Sir John, *The Everlasting Bonfire.* London, 1940.

Potter, Pitram B. "Origin of the System of Mandates under a League of Nations," *American Political Science Review,* XVI (1922), 563–583.

Reynolds, E. E. *The League Experiment.* London, 1939.

Seymour, Charles (ed.). *The Intimate Papers of Colonel House.* 4 vols. Boston, 1926–1928.

Snowden, Philip. *An Autobiography.* 2 vols. London, 1934.

Spender, J. A. *Great Britain: Empire and Commonwealth, 1886–1935.* London, 1936.

Spender, J. A. and Cyril Asquith. *Life of Herbert Henry Asquith, Lord Oxford and Asquith.* 2 vols. London, 1932.

Swanwick, H. M. *Builders of Peace.* London, 1924.

Tchernoff, J. *Les Nations et la S.D.N. Dans la Politique Moderne.* Paris, 1919.

Temperley, H. W. V. (ed.). *A History of the Peace Conference of Paris.* 6 vols. London, 1920–1924.

Trevelyan, Charles. *The Union of Democratic Control (an Organization Created to Secure the Control over Their Foreign Policy by the British People, and for the Promotion of International Understanding), Founded in November, 1914, Its History and Its Policy.* 3d and rev. ed. London, 1921.

Trevelyan, G. M. *Grey of Fallodon.* London, 1937.

Waugh, Arthur. *A Hundred Years of Publishing. Being the Story of Chapman and Hall, Ltd.* London, 1930.

Walters, F. P. *A History of the League of Nations.* 2 vols.; London and New York, 1952.

Wells, H. G. *Experiment in Autobiography. Discoveries and Conclusions of a Very Ordinary Brain (Since 1866).* New York, 1934.

West, Geoffrey. *H. G. Wells.* New York, 1930.

Willis, Irene Cooper. *England's Holy War. A Study of English Liberalism during the Great War.* New York, 1928.

Wilson, Florence. *The Origins of the League Covenant. Documentary History of Its Drafting.* London, 1928.

Wright, Quincy. *Mandates under the League of Nations.* Chicago, 1930.

Zimmern, Alfred E. *The League of Nations and the Rule of Law 1918–1935.* London, 1936.

Index